'VERP is a dynamic "complex and creative dance" in Kennedy, Landor and Todd's hands. They tell how videos create challenging "retrospective mirrors", bringing practitioners face to face with themselves and previously unperceived elements, including unfounded assumptions. Hard questions are asked, helping practitioners develop greater understanding, trust in, and respect for, themselves and their clients.'

— Gillie Bolton, PhD, author of Reflective Practice Writing and Professional Development, 4th Edition (Sage, 2014)

'What will strike any reader of this book is the diversity of contexts in which VERP has been developed. Instead of pigeon-holing the practice to a specific sector or desired outcomes, the case studies illustrate both its core qualities and its dynamic flexibility. Unlike many new interventions, VERP has a genuine and authentic history of sustained development meaning that practices have become theorised and nuanced. VERP allows users to make change visible and thus persuades them that it is possible.'

— Rachel Lofthouse, Head of Teacher Development and Learning, School of Education, Communication and Language Sciences, Newcastle University, UK

'I wish that this book had been around when we started to implement the VIG model in the area of helping professions. Reading the book brought back to me all the excitement I experienced when confronted with these ideas for the very first time. This same excitement was always present when I witnessed individuals change through using VERP. I hope the reader will find, in the breadth and depths of the projects described and in the enthusiasm of the participants, encouragement to start the VERP journey and inspiration for those readers already on it.'

— Kateřina Šilhánová, Founder and Director, National Training Institute for VIG, Czech Republic

'*Video Enhanced Reflective Practice* applies a new idea concerning how respectful responses to an individual's expressions of their purposes and concerns sustain thriving relationships; from infants and parents in families, through to the successful management of roles in a school, corporation or city. This path-finding book reports and explains the successes of VERP for many relationships across many countries.'

— Colwyn Trevarthen, PhD, FRSE, Professor (Emeritus) of Child Psychology and Psychobiology, The University of Edinburgh, UK

GW00775589

by the same editors

Video Interaction Guidance
A Relationship-based Intervention to Promote
Attunement, Empathy and Wellbeing
Edited by Hilary Kennedy, Miriam Landor and Liz Todd
ISBN 978 1 84905 180 4
eISBN 978 0 85700 414 7

of related interest

Creative Supervision Across Modalities
Theory and Applications for Therapists,
Counsellors and Other Helping Professionals
Edited by Anna Chesner and Lia Zografou
ISBN 978 1 84905 316 7
eISBN 978 0 85700 696 7

Supervision as Transformation
A Passion for Learning
Edited by Robin Shohet
ISBN 978 1 84905 200 9
eISBN 978 0 85700 509 0

Best Practice in Professional Supervision
A Guide for the Helping Professions
Allyson Davys and Liz Beddoe
ISBN 978 1 84310 995 2
eISBN 978 0 85700 384 3

Video Enhanced Reflective Practice

PROFESSIONAL DEVELOPMENT THROUGH ATTUNED INTERACTIONS

Edited by Hilary Kennedy,
Miriam Landor and Liz Todd

Jessica Kingsley *Publishers*
London and Philadelphia

Figures 3.1 and 3.2 on pp51–2 are reproduced from Simpson and Henderson (1995) with kind permission.

First published in 2015
by Jessica Kingsley Publishers
73 Collier Street
London N1 9BE, UK
and
400 Market Street, Suite 400
Philadelphia, PA 19106, USA

www.jkp.com

Library of Congress Cataloging in Publication Data
Video enhanced reflective practice : professional development through attuned interaction / edited by
Hilary Kennedy, Miriam Landor and Liz Todd.
    pages cm
 Includes bibliographical references and index.
 ISBN 978-1-84905-410-2 (alk. paper)
 1. Career development. 2. Interpersonal relations. 3. Video recording. I. Kennedy, Hilary, editor. II.
Landor, Miriam, editor. III. Todd, Liz, editor.
 HF5381.V53 2015
 658.3'124--dc23
                          2014037496

British Library Cataloguing in Publication Data
A CIP catalogue record for this book is available from the British Library

ISBN 978 1 84905 410 2
eISBN 978 0 85700 787 2

Printed and bound in Great Britain

Dedicated to Jenny Cross and Ruth Cave
Their wisdom and companionship are missed

CONTENTS

PREFACE

Miriam Landor

This is the book I wish I had had on many occasions in the past. Video Enhanced Reflective Practice (VERP) is a model of professional development that has been in use for over 20 years. It involves a particular kind of shared reflection on very short video clips of one's own work that show attuned interaction. Numerous journal articles and book chapters have been written about it over the years, but there was no one place for those interested to find out about the research and theory base, the history and present applications, the potential for future development – the what, the how, the why and the where next of VERP.

The solution was to invite Hilary Kennedy and Liz Todd, co-editors of our previous book on Video Interaction Guidance (VIG) (Kennedy, Landor and Todd 2011), to fill the gap by producing this book with me. We started by organizing the first international research conference on VERP, which took place at Newcastle University in June 2013. Innovative VERP projects were presented that came from all sectors (education, health, social work, voluntary, private and commercial) and from around the world – the Americas, Australia and many European countries. Conference delegates' responses to the presentations were gathered and thematically analysed; workgroups based around these themes explored issues relating to VERP in research, in management, in the early years, in group processes and, most importantly, in the future. Collaborations between authors for the proposed book, *Video Enhanced Reflective Practice (VERP): Professional Development through Attuned Interactions*, were then planned around similar themes. This book is made up of chapters written by these presenters, and by invited specialists in VERP-like methods in other countries, such as

Marte Meo, which was developed by Maria Aarts in parallel with VIG (Aarts 2008).

Video Enhanced Reflective Practice: Professional Development through Attuned Interactions can stand alone as an innovative addition to the literature on reflective practice. It can also be read as a companion volume to our earlier *Video Interaction Guidance: A Relationship-based Intervention to Promote Attunement, Empathy and Wellbeing* (2011), edited by Hilary Kennedy, Miriam Landor and Liz Todd.

VERP is derived from Video Interaction Guidance (VIG), as we describe in the Introduction that follows, where VERP is fully described and explained. An exemplary application, its history and the underpinning theory are explored in the chapters that follow in order to show what it is, where it came from, and why and how it works. Some people will choose to read all the way through the book in the intended order, but we also recognize that others may want to dip into sections of particular interest to them; we recommend that they read Chapters 1 and 2 for an understanding of VERP before doing so. It should be noted that all clients' names in the pages that follow are pseudonyms.

Descriptions of a diverse range of VERP applications form Part 2 of the book. For example, one chapter describes how VERP helps practitioners become more effective in their interactions with carers of infants. Another looks at the development of mind-mindedness (that is, the ability to think about children's possible thoughts and feelings) by teachers in nurture groups. VERP training for teaching assistants in schools may counter concerns over their effectiveness. 'Connect, reflect and grow' provides a useful framework for VERP programmes in the early years. A case study about VERP for leadership skills in the French banking sector follows.

Three innovative VERP or VERP-like projects are next described in Part 3 on profound and multiple learning disabilities, helping whole staff teams improve their interaction skills when their clients' skills are few or deteriorating, or when their clients have complex communication needs, or dementia. These chapters come from Australia, Finland and Sweden.

The increasing use of video in the initial training of professionals is underlined in Part 4 on the role VERP plays in higher education.

Interesting projects are discussed for social work students, medical students and trainee educational psychologists in England and Scotland.

Organizational change at the systems level through meticulously planned VERP programmes has exciting potential, and chapters in Part 5 describe projects in an English infant school, Glasgow's children's services, the Scotland-wide post-school careers service and management, a Mexican non-governmental organization (NGO) for street children and their families, and a US therapeutic foster family project.

A meta-analysis of video feedback methods comes next, in Part 6, followed by two research-based projects that apply VERP to a Scottish early literacy project and to a secure adolescent unit in England.

Finally, in Part 7, the conclusion looks at VERP as an agentic (that is, proactive and self-organizing) approach to professional development and reflection.

Hilary Kennedy is an educational psychologist and a leading developer of VIG and VERP within the Association of Video Interaction Guidance UK (AVIGuk). Her lifetime achievement in bringing VIG to many agencies and many countries has been recognized by The British Psychological Society's award for outstanding contribution to educational and child psychology. Liz Todd is an AVIGuk supervisor and trainer in VIG and VERP, and is Professor of Educational Inclusion at Newcastle University. She has published widely on inclusive education. I am a freelance AVIGuk National Supervisor and trainer in VIG, VERP and Video Feedforward, and a former preschool home visiting teacher, educational psychologist and university lecturer. I am a member of the AVIGuk Board of Directors, with a special interest in training and publication.

All the chapters went through a rigorous process of academic and professional peer review, being read by up to six other people as well as ourselves. Whilst I acted as 'project manager' we worked collaboratively and each of us took 'lead' editorial responsibility for a number of chapters. We found the principles of attuned interactions to be invaluable as we negotiated meaning, content and differences of opinion. As in our previous book *Video Interaction Guidance*, the alphabetical order of our names reflects our equal and complementary knowledge and skills, which have helped us to achieve this ambitious project.

We hope that you, the reader, will find inspiration and information in equal measure in the pages that follow, and that the book stimulates further exploration of the benefits of Video Enhanced Reflective Practice.

ACKNOWLEDGEMENTS

We would like to thank the many people who have helped bring this book into being. Most important of all, the chapter authors have shared their knowledge so generously, and it has been a pleasure to work with them, through many meetings, phone calls and emails. Katerina Šilhánová and Christo Bjalovski from the Czech Republic generously added their graphic design skills to the figures and diagrams used in Chapter 1. We are indebted to the vast team of external readers who are listed below; they have taken pains to give detailed comments on every aspect of the chapters they read. The staff at Jessica Kingsley Publishers have been ever available and supportive, and we were delighted when Lisa Clark, Senior Commissioning Editor, addressed the Newcastle-upon-Tyne VERP Conference 2013. Finally, we would like to thank our families and friends for their love and support while we worked.

List of external readers

Vicky Alexander, Shonagh Anderson, Clare Atherton Gilfillan, Jeremy Baster, Mary Bendermacher, Jacqueline Bristow, Sharon L. Brown, Anne Bruce, Sara Bryson, Cathy Byron, Monika Celebi, Sylvia Copley, Chris Cuthbert, Kath Davies, Vanessa Easton, Sheridan Forster, Penny Forsyth, Victoria Franklin, Liz Gajjar, David Gavine, Nancy Gillespie, Louise Goodall, Maureen Granger, Pam Green Lister, Charmian Hobbs, Sarah Hulme, Divya Jindal-Snape, Polly Jones, Yvonne Jungnitz, James Kennedy, Claire Kerr, Rene Koglbauer, Karen Laing, Reni Landor, Rachel Lofthouse, Åse Ljungquist-Svantesson, Nevine Mahmoud, Eddie McGee, Elizabeth Meins, Emma Miller, Trisha Murray, Brahm Norwich, Rose Pipes, Rhiannon Quinn, Penny

Rackett, Angela Roger, Giselle Rothenberger, Jill Sandeman, Stephanie Satariano, Astrid Schepers, Felicity Shenton, Gillian Shotton, Heather Sked, Alison Smith, Stavros Stavrou, Mary Taylor, Ulrike Thomas, Denise Thorn, Kathy Wesolowski, Ingegerd Wirtberg.

Part One

VIDEO ENHANCED REFLECTIVE PRACTICE (VERP)

CHAPTER 1

Introduction

Hilary Kennedy and Miriam Landor

By far the most helpful elements of the VERP process were the use of real video footage of me actively engaged in the process that I wanted to change, [and] the sessions with the VIG guider. These were very powerful in enabling self-reflection and consideration of strategies for improvement. The setting of individual objectives at the start of the process was another helpful element in that it created clarity around the purpose of the process and allowed for reflection on progress.

These [VERP] sessions were extremely helpful in allowing me to see aspects of my communication of which I was not fully aware. The sessions really made me think about what I was doing in the interactions and have influenced my interactions since, in a number of contexts.

These quotations come from two members of a staff team who received training in VERP from author Miriam Landor. Their comments show how the microanalysis and reflective review of video of their working practice, which are at the heart of VERP, enhanced their professional development.

What is VERP?

Video Enhanced Reflective Practice™ (VERP) is a method of professional development that focuses on enhancing attuned interactions through a specific way of using video reflection. VERP is the review, often in groups, of short video clips of one's own professional practice. The focus is on the practitioner's goal for change. Usually the practitioner will take the video and select the clips. Repeated sessions over two to four months supports sustained reflection on practice. Through 'reflective practice', people can take ownership of their own development in their work environment by reviewing and reflecting on their professional action. The term 'attuned interactions' describes a communication where two or more people have an effect on each other by being mutually receptive and sensitively responsive. The term comes directly from Colwyn Trevarthen's view of intersubjectivity (Trevarthen and Aitken 2001), with the proposition that in any conversation there are two equally important people where the emotional dialogue is of central importance.

VERP supports individuals or groups to reflect on and develop their communication skills with their clients, through reviewing short video clips of their day-to-day practice. With the guidance of an accredited facilitator (VERP guider), trainees identify clips that demonstrate moments where their attuned interaction helps them towards achieving their self-set goal. VERP programmes of two to five sessions support sustained development. VERP has developed from Video Interaction Guidance™ (VIG) (Kennedy, Landor and Todd 2011), and uses the same key values, theory and principles. It gives individuals a chance to explore and reflect on their interactions, drawing attention to elements that are successful, and supporting them to make changes where desired. VERP is delivered by VIG practitioners, or those in VIG training under supervision. For clarity, the term 'VERP guider' is used for the person who is delivering the VERP training.

The aim of VERP is to support active, enthusiastic learners who experience exciting changes in their professional interactions. They discover how important they are in any interaction, and that as they change, their client also changes. For example, it is powerful to hear the volume of children's voices go down when they, the teacher, lowers their voice.

There are many methods for reflective practice that are enhanced by the use of video. VERP is unique because it is linked to VIG.

This means that the values and beliefs underpinning the method, the way the trainee sets learning goals, the framework used to microanalyse the video, the way the video clips are reviewed and the way the VERP guider reflects on their contribution to the process are all in line with VIG.

Values and beliefs

The Association for Video Interaction Guidance (AVIGuk) 'values and beliefs' (see Box 1.1) are of central importance to the way VERP training is negotiated and delivered. By appreciating both the trainees' existing skills and also their wish to develop further, the foundations for a trusting, respectful, learning relationship are set.

Box 1.1: AVIGuk values and beliefs
Our Values[1]
Respect   Trust   Hope Compassion   Co-operation   Appreciation Connections   Empathy
Our beliefs[2]
• Everybody is doing the best they can at the time • All people, even in adverse situations, have the capacity to change • People have an innate desire to connect with others • People must be actively involved in their own change process • Affirmation and appreciation of strengths is the key to supporting change • Recognition and empathetic regard for what people are managing builds trust

Setting learning goals

The trainees set their own goals or 'helping questions', for instance 'How can I help Emma (who has not yet spoken or looked at any adults in nursery) start to communicate with me?' When the trainee makes their first video of themselves with a client, they already have an understanding (from prior knowledge and the initial VERP course) of what makes a good interaction, and so they will, in a sense, be 'acting for the camera'. This first video is likely to be more attuned than normal, as they already have knowledge of the principles that make good interaction. They may already have discussed their goal and possible strategies to try in the first video, in line with the attunement principles (Table 1.1). These may, for instance, be using ideas from the 'encouraging initiatives' section, especially naming what you and they are doing, instead of asking questions when with Emma.

Framework for selecting video clips

The trainee, once the video is taken, selects short 'attuned' clips with two dimensions in mind: the VIG principles of attuned interactions and guidance, sometimes shortened to 'attunement principles' (see Table 1.1), and 'better than usual' moments relating to the trainee's goals. VERP, like VIG, is a microanalytic approach where the 'attuned interactions' are looked at moment by moment, exploring the effect on the other of each person's communication (non-verbal, verbal and the emotional message). As Landor has written in Bolton's new edition of *Reflective Practice* (Landor 2014, p.56), these video clips are chosen to show the best possible example of interaction between two people, the exceptional – the model for future development and change. The point is that the model is provided from the person's own repertoire of behaviours, so it is within their capacity and experience.

---

1   The size of the words in rows 'Values and Beliefs…, Respect… Trust… Hope' signifies the ranking of 52 AVIGuk Supervisors with respect to their views of the importance of short-listed VIG-VERP values in January 2014.

2   The beliefs statements have been adapted from SPIN (the Netherlands) 1990 originals. They were debated by AVIGuk Supervisors in meetings and by discussion forum over the Autumn of 2013.

Table 1.1 AVIGuk principles of attuned interactions and guidance (for professional reflection on their own communication)		
Are you?	**By**	**In order to develop**
Being attentive	• Looking interested • Turning towards • Friendly intonation and posture • Giving time and space for other • Wondering about what they are doing, thinking or feeling	The foundations for intersubjectivity
Encouraging initiatives	• Waiting • Listening actively • Showing emotional warmth through intonation • Naming positively what you see, hear, think or feel • Naming what you are doing, hearing, thinking or feeling • Looking for initiatives	
Receiving initiatives	• Showing you have heard, noticed the other's initiative • Receiving initiative with friendly body language • Returning eye contact, smiling, nodding in response • Receiving what the other is saying or doing with words • Repeating/using the other's words or phrases	Intersubjectivity

Developing attuned interactions	• Receiving and then responding • Checking the other is understanding you • Waiting attentively for your turn • Giving a second (and further) turn on same topic • Giving and taking short turns • *Interrupting long turns by checking for reception* • *Supporting turn-taking round a group (if in a group)* • Contributing to interaction/activity equally • Co-operating – helping each other (Italics show new interactions added for professional reflection)	Intersubjectivity
Guiding	• Extending, building on the other's response • Scaffolding – judging the amount of support required and adjusting • Giving information when needed • Providing help when required • Offering choices that they can understand • Making suggestions that they can follow	Mediated learning
Deepening discussion	• Supporting goal-setting • Sharing viewpoints • Discussing collaboratively and problem-solving • Naming differences of opinion • Investigating the intentions behind words • Naming contradictions/conflicts (real or potential) • Reaching new shared understandings • Managing conflict (back to being attentive and receiving initiatives with the aim of restoring attuned interactions)	

Shared review

Trainees bring these clips to a 'shared review' session when they reflect with the VERP guider on what they were doing that was making the interaction successful. They can be prompted to remember what they were thinking and feeling at the time, and what they feel on watching it in the present. They *see* the effect of their action on their interaction partner – whether child, pupil, colleague or employee – and *reflect* on what this tells them. The video acts as a retrospective mirror.

Again, the success of the method depends on the way the guider embodies the attunement principles (Table 1.1) and on the active open learning style of the trainee. There are two equally important people in this interaction and the energy between them will be enhanced when they are both active, learning from each other, and open to new possibilities as they work together.

The atmosphere needs to be encouraging, enjoyable and safe, where compliments are only used with matching video evidence and are often better elicited from the trainee themselves (for example, 'What did you do just there that helped Emma look towards you?'). Although VERP looks at strengths, the use of praise for talents or behaviours is much less effective than noticing and naming specific behaviours that have changed through 'effort'. The intersubjective relationship, where both guider and trainee are equally important, may be lost if the guider praises too much, as the power balance is disturbed and the guider becomes the judge of 'effective' communication.

The process of the VERP 'shared review' follows the VIG 'seven steps' (see Figure 1.1), which have at their core the balance between activating the trainee and providing help when needed, perhaps by returning to the video clip (the centre of Figure 1.1). It is most important that the VERP guider gives space to the trainee and fully receives their initiatives or responses before coming in with their ideas (Steps 3 and 4), followed by the guider checking for reception from the learner of their viewpoint (Step 5). Once the pattern of lively short turns is established, reflecting together on micro-moments of video, understanding deepens and new meanings can emerge (Steps 6 and 7).

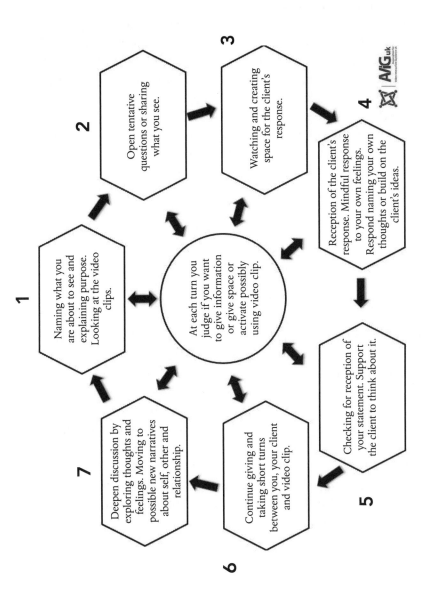

1 Naming what you are about to see and explaining purpose. Looking at the video clips.

2 Open tentative questions or sharing what you see.

3 Watching and creating space for the client's response.

4 Reception of the client's response. Mindful response to your own feelings. Respond naming your own thoughts or build on the client's ideas.

5 Checking for reception of your statement. Support the client to think about it.

6 Continue giving and taking short turns between you, your client and video clip.

7 Deepen discussion by exploring thoughts and feelings. Moving to possible new narratives about self, other and relationship.

At each turn you judge if you want to give information or give space or activate possibly using video clip.

Figure 1.1 Seven steps towards effective shared review

Source: K. Šilhánová and H. Kennedy, from Kennedy, Landor and Todd (2011)

It is important to make clear that the 'seven steps' are a map to help reflective practice in the shared review, not a formula for the guider to master and follow. Delivering a VERP intervention is a complex, creative 'dance', and cannot be learnt by following instructions.

The VERP guider leads the trainee through the process, guided themselves by the values of respect, hope and appreciation and their beliefs (see Box 1.1), which combine to build a safe, lively conversation. Considerable skill is required to provide an optimal learning environment for each trainee in a group, especially as looking at themselves on video may initially be a challenging process. The trainees' observed communication skills may be at very different levels and not in line with professional hierarchies. For instance, a manager may find it hard to show they have heard what is said, whereas others may be naturally good listeners. The guider's role is to support the trainees to discover their own unique, effective style.

When author Miriam Landor led a small VERP group, a nursery worker (Jane) brought clips of herself and a 'difficult, unresponsive' (her description) four year old (Jimmy). During this group shared review, Jane commented several times that, contrary to her memory, Jimmy was sometimes paying attention to her, and did seem to be enjoying the time they were spending together. Jane saw video 'evidence' that reinforced a new and different narrative about their relationship. The VERP guider, Miriam, received and amplified this new narrative by repeating it back to her, so she could reflect on this new possibility, and then most importantly pointed out her agency in the interaction: 'So what did you do to get him to pay attention to you, to enjoy being with you?' By going back to the video clips again and again, Jane could see that what had made the difference was when she followed Jimmy's lead, when she read and followed his cues and responded sensitively to his needs, whether expressed verbally or non-verbally. She then reflected on times when things had gone better than usual and also when they had gone badly, and began to see that improving their relationship was in her own locus of control. Jane already had the skills she needed to bring about positive change.

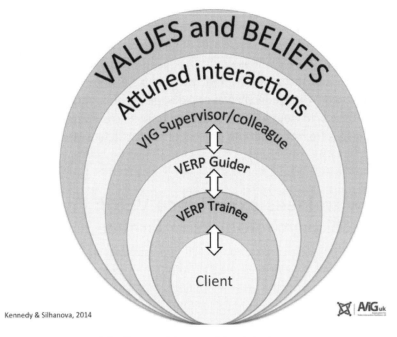

Kennedy & Silhanova, 2014

Figure 1.2 Model of Nested 'Intersubjectivity'

Source: H. Kennedy and K. Šilhánová 2014

Nested intersubjectivity

VERP guiders will often video themselves delivering the VERP programme, and reflect with a VIG supervisor/colleague on the clips where the trainees are active in the learning process. Supervisors might also take a video of themselves to intervision (peer supervision) for reflection. This 'nested' process, where the same values and principles are the framework for all interactions, is strongly experienced by those in VIG training. Figure 1.2 shows how VERP and VIG are based on a model of nested 'intersubjectivity' where the arrows between the people involved are two-way – client and VERP trainee, VERP trainee and VERP guider, VERP guider and VIG supervisor/colleague – within the overarching values that underpin the attunement principles of AVIGuk. It is very important to understand that the attunement principles are not a set of behaviours to learn to use. Nearly always, the first step is to support the trainee to create a space for the other before they respond. They are only 'attuned' if they are responding to (or encouraging) an initiative of the other, with the 'respectful, appreciative' values that lead to beliefs such as 'everyone is doing the best they can at the time'. The emotions and intentions behind the guider's actions are of central importance. When judgemental and derogatory thoughts are around, even if the behaviour looks friendly the learner senses this, and either disengages from the learning process or takes a defensive stance.

How trainees experience VERP: Five clinical psychologists in Greece

In many chapters of this book there are examples of the ways that trainees have experienced VERP. Another example is given here. VERP was used for the first time in Greece by Kornilia Hatzinikolaou with a group of five clinical psychologists working for a non-governmental organization (NGO) that provides mental health services to a community of migrant families. VERP was facilitated by Kornilia as a VIG trainee guider in her third stage of training, supervised through Skype by an accredited VIG supervisor in Scotland (the author, Miriam Landor). None of the group members had used video before in research or clinical practice. A preparatory session on VERP was organized, during which theoretical and practical training was given. The professionals had the opportunity to analyse video-recorded interactions and to discuss the principles of attuned interactions based on these clips.

It was then decided to begin the VERP course with the professionals making video recordings of their own team communicating on work issues such as case management. This activity was evaluated as being extremely helpful for understanding group dynamics, realizing ways of communicating with each other, and building group confidence and closeness. In particular, empowering comments on communication and other professional skills made by one colleague to another resulted in a boost to professional confidence, which enhanced the will to share with the group the doubts and difficulties concerning the management of particular cases.

For example, while watching the video a group member said, 'I would like to have a more friendly posture and be more relaxed when we work as a group'. Another group member, responded:

> I find you friendly and relaxed! Last year, when we started working together I could see you were not so relaxed, but I have noticed such a great change during this past year! Let me show you here in the video, how you show a friendly interest in what P. was saying.

And she pointed out some active receiving, accompanied by a smile.

Concerning the group management of cases, another group member admitted:

> I was feeling angry towards my client. Gradually, my anger was transformed into guilt because I was thinking that I am not good; I am bad, principally because of feeling angry towards my client. When I discussed this case in our group, and after I received feedback from you [pointing towards the other members of the group], I started feeling more empowered and able to deal constructively with the case. I knew it was important I had recognized my feelings and I was ready to re-evaluate my work with this particular client.

Each psychologist then brought video recordings from individual psychotherapeutic sessions they had held with their clients. The variance in clients' characteristics (for example, age, cultural background, initial request, etc.) and VERP group members' communicative styles enriched the group's conversation. Working points for each group member came up smoothly due to the containing environment that had been created between them.

Throughout the five-session VERP course, discussion increasingly made reference to the principles of attuned interactions. Professionals were more able to focus on their strengths and think how they would be able to use these for attaining their working points. They were also able to identify their colleagues' strengths, and found innovative and interesting ways to provide positive feedback on their colleagues' improvement following VERP and VIG attunement principles.

How VIG trainees experience VERP

VIG and VERP are, of course, intertwined. VIG is an intervention through which a practitioner aims to enhance communication within the relationships of others (Kennedy *et al.* 2011). When professionals use the same method to reflect on their own communication with service users, it is referred to as Video Enhanced Reflective Practice (VERP). In both versions, the aim is to give individuals a chance to reflect on their interactions, drawing attention to elements that are successful, and supporting clients to make changes where desired. Furthermore, the training for VIG also enables trainees to work on their own communication skills. Therefore, VERP guiders have first-hand experience of their own personal VERP throughout their VIG training. They reflect in supervision sessions on the way that they use the VIG attunement principles when selecting video clips and delivering the shared reviews. In order to become an accredited practitioner, they must demonstrate on video that they can engage with clients and activate them on their own change journey by developing fluency in the 'seven steps' (see Figure 1.1). In the final reflections written by VIG trainees, the theme of enhancement of their own communication patterns is dominant in both their professional and personal lives.

How VIG supervisors experience VERP

It is not only the trainees who develop practice through VERP. Everyone is learning all the time: supervisors, guiders and trainees. The next chapter in this book, by Jenny Jarvis and Susan Lyon, gives some insight into supervisor reflections and actions. Author Miriam Landor reflects here on her own skills as a supervisor:

> [As I reflect on the questions I ask trainees when I am facilitating VERP shared reviews] I am aware that I am reflecting on my own skills as a supervisor; when I am helping my trainees reflect successfully, I realize I am following their initiatives, responding sensitively to their needs, and asking myself what I can do more of to improve things further. Using video to enhance reflection within the

VIG/VERP approach is therefore a nested construction, with the reflection deepening at every level. I remember one of my trainees describing at a conference her learning through VERP and saying that even when she wasn't being videoed, it felt as if she was. The audience groaned in sympathy, but she said, 'No, it was like…while I was doing things I could watch myself doing them and think how to do better.' That sounded to me like a reflective practitioner experiencing reflection in action (Schön), following her VERP work!

What does VERP look like in practice?

The following model is typical of many group VERP programmes, and was developed by author Miriam Landor. It is delivered by a team of VERP guiders for up to 20 adults who wish to improve their interaction skills, usually in their work situation. The trainees are often from the same workplace or organization, but need not be from the same agency or possess the same level of experience or status. VERP may also be used in a one-to-one context or with parents, when the following programme will be modified accordingly.

The programme begins with a one-day training session when trainees are introduced to the attunement principles, and to the theory and values underpinning the VIG approach. The VERP guider demonstrates the microanalysis of video to find brief clips exemplifying the attunement principles, and trainees are given the opportunity to try this themselves. It is helpful to include some ice-breaking activities throughout the programme, so that all the trainees become accustomed to expressing personal but not private information in a safe space. The session finishes with trainees recording a personal 'helping question', or some aspect they want to work on. In some cases, supplementary training may be required on the use of the video equipment. Issues of permission, confidentiality, video ownership and secure storage should be negotiated with the trainees' management. Trainees are asked to bring a brief video of themselves and their interaction partner(s) (for example, pupil, client or patient) to the next session, and to have noted the timings of a few clips when things went better than usual related to their working points and which exemplified the attunement principles.

This initial training is followed by two to four half-day sessions. Trainees work in small groups of up to five, with each group being facilitated by a VERP guider. The time available for each trainee is shared out equally at the start, and is usually about half an hour. Trainees take turns to discuss their video clips with the VERP guider, and are prompted to reflect on what is happening, what they did to make it happen, what the impact was on the other person and on their next step. The video is explored through microanalysis, often pausing and then going back to unpick the tiny moments that contribute to this particular attuned interaction. The other trainees observe this VERP 'shared review', and at the end are asked for appreciative attuned comments. Finally, the trainees review their helping questions, record what they were pleased with and set their goals for the following session, deciding what situation to video next.

In the final session the trainees are asked to select clips that show where a helping question is turned into a 'pleased with' moment. Together, the group members reflect on their learning journey and celebrate their achievements.

The reflective process in this model can be deepened by a brief additional presentation before or after the shared review sessions. These may cover a range of topics appropriate to the requirements of the specific group, for example, contingent mirroring, difficult conversations and so on.

The following is an example of a leaflet produced by Miriam for her VERP trainees:

VERP – Trainee tasks

- Choose a typical professional activity where you're working with other(s), which relates to your strengths and working point as noted in your logbook.

- Video yourself in this activity for about 5–10 minutes; make sure:
  - you have the other people's/parents' permission first
  - your camera position includes all the relevant people in the video – it's most important to include all of yourself and all of whoever you're talking to/working with

- ◦ you're not videoing into strong light (e.g. any window should be behind the camera!)

- Review the video, writing down exact timings for 2–3 brief clips (can be a few seconds, but definitely well under 1 minute) which show a couple of moments you're 'pleased with' and your 'next step' in your professional development, to share in a group at the next session.

- At each group session, each person in turn will have about 30 minutes to show their chosen video clips and to discuss why they chose them. This may sound nerve-wracking but it is actually a wholly positive and confidence-building experience, people always find. VIG and VERP are strengths-based. We use the 'reflective team' approach (more on this later).

- After each group session, record your new 'strengths' and working points in your logbook. In this way you work on your own professional development goals, building on your strengths and setting yourself the next challenge.

The reflective team

The reflective team approach is a way of deepening the discussion by structuring the reflective process:

Step 1: The trainee and VERP guider review and discuss the video clips identified by the trainee (making a triangle of video, trainee, guider). *(The reflective team makes a back row and observes in silence.)* The guider asks the trainee to look for examples of strengths, and of principles of attuned interactions, in the light of their helping question:

- 'What did you see? What happened here?'

- 'What did YOU do to bring that about?'

- 'What was the impact on the other?'

- 'What will you do next time?'

Step 2: The trainee and guider are silent and listen while the reflective team discuss together what they saw and what they thought, using similar questions:

- What happened?
- What did the trainee do to bring that about?
- What principles of attuned interactions were seen?
- What was the impact on the other?

Step 3: The reflective team are silent while the trainee and guider discuss what they have just heard, the trainee's reaction and what deeper insights they may now have. They round off with the trainee identifying their 'pleased with' and working points, to record in their logbook.

Conclusion

As this book is written, there are over 1000 AVIGuk trainees in the UK, Greece, France, Ecuador, Mexico, Australia and Malta, and there are over 1000 AVIGuk trainees making the VIG training journey and discovering deep-level changes in their communication styles. Many of them will be delivering VERP interventions as part of their training.

This introductory part continues with a chapter where the impact of a VERP intervention is explored, followed by a chapter about the origins of VERP in the Netherlands and the systemic journey of VERP to the present day in Eindhoven, ending with a theory chapter where the reasons why VERP works are unpacked.

At the end of this introductory section we hope that you have a good idea about what VERP is, its origins, potential and its strong link to theory.

CHAPTER 2

What Makes Video Enhanced Reflective Practice (VERP) Successful for System Change?

Views of Participants from a Primary School

Jenny Jarvis and Susan Lyon

Introduction

Described here is the experience and impact of using Video Enhanced Reflective Practice (VERP) in a primary school to change the quality of interaction between staff and children. Medium and small-scale research studies into Video Interaction Guidance (VIG) and VERP in schools (see Gavine and Forsyth 2011) have suggested that these interventions lead to cognitive and emotional gains for children and young people, as well as improvements in partnerships between staff members and teachers and parents. Author Susan Lyon, a paediatric speech and language therapist (SLT), was using Elklan training materials for staff supporting children with speech, language and communication needs (SLCN) (Elklan 2009) with a group of primary school professionals. As a VIG guider, she thought it likely that the model of training she was using could be enhanced by encouraging greater reflection on communication styles through the use of video, and so introduced VERP alongside her usual practice. The authors were interested in whether this would bring about any changes in the interaction between staff and children, and whether this would make a difference at the level of the school system.

In this particular school the number of pupils who had special educational needs or disabilities (SEND), or both, was almost twice the national average for primary schools. I CAN, the children's communication charity, claims that over one million children in the UK – that is, two or three in every primary school classroom – have some kind of SLCN that requires specialist intervention (I CAN, no date). In areas of high deprivation this percentage can rise to 50 per cent. Worryingly, some experts comment on the high proportion of adult talk there is in the majority of classrooms, compared to observable child-initiated talk, both to adults and to other children. For example, Lin (2007) observes that direct adult questions and inequality in turn-taking are inherent in classroom discourse. The most effective way of developing children's talking is by 'recasting', that is, the adult listening to the child talk, and then remodelling what the child has said, adding more complex grammatical structures or vocabulary. This can only be done if the adult talks less, allowing the child the space to contribute.

Research questions

The research questions centred on two areas:

- What factors of the VERP intervention were seen to be significant or effective by participants? In particular, what was the value of the VERP practitioner's role and manner of relating?

- Did VERP make a difference within the school system and, if so, what were these changes?

The authors also wanted to provide insight into the content of the shared review sessions.

VERP process

Five members of staff, including the manager in the Early Years Foundation Stage (EYFS) of the school, took part in the VERP project. An initial training day gave an outline of the VIG principles of attuned interactions and guidance (Kennedy, Landor and Todd 2011; see also Chapter 1, this volume), along with information on the development of communication skills. Subsequently, each member of staff brought edited clips of themselves taking part in an activity with a child or small group of children once a month for three months. Staff edited their videos to highlight where they had met a personal aim such as 'giving space' or 'following an initiative'. Each month the SLT (hereafter known as 'the VERP guider') met the staff for the shared review of each video in groups of two or three.

Participant perceptions of VERP

In order to elicit participant perceptions of whether VERP was seen to be effective within this project, the first author, Jenny Jarvis, reviewed the videos taken of the shared review group sessions. She edited these to highlight moments that seemed to indicate a process of change, and sections where the group process was particularly striking. Three months after the VERP project had finished, she showed these edited clips to each of the five professionals on an individual basis, and they discussed significant moments together. These interviews took approximately 50 minutes. The content of these interviews was transcribed and analysed loosely within the grounded theory method of data analysis (Glaser and Strauss 1967). Specific themes were identified, which are reviewed below.

Theme 1: Initial concerns about using video

Each of the five participants admitted to feelings of anxiety or concern before the VERP project began. Some of the fears expressed were of criticism, being watched, feeling self-conscious in front of colleagues or about a physical aspect of themselves that they felt would be highlighted on video. Other anxieties focused on whether they had recorded the 'right' aspects of their teaching during classroom activities, and on using the technology (iPads).

Theme 2: How VERP differs from other models of professional development

Participants identified initial expectations that VERP would be similar to their usual professional development sessions, which were perceived quite negatively as target-driven and critical, as described by one participant below:

> Even when we review our performance we say 'What are you going to do to make it better?', it's never what did you do well…the focus is more on how you're going to do it better so 'Okay you're a good teacher now but how are you going to be outstanding…so you're an outstanding teacher, how are you going to maintain that?'

However, in this project the use of strength-based language helped them to understand what they would be looking for in the videos of their teaching practice, and the participatory role of the manager made them feel more comfortable about taking part in the project.

Theme 3: The important role of the manager

The manager of the pre-school unit had initiated the VERP project, participated in it, and was also one of the interviewees for this evaluation. She had clear aims and expectations for the VERP project, not only for herself in improving her communications in the classroom situation, but also for the whole team's development. There were a number of goals the staff had identified (for example, talking less, listening and waiting more, commenting to show listening instead of asking questions) that she felt would be addressed through this approach, and she recognized that it was imperative that she allowed herself to undertake something that she was asking her team to do.

Theme 4: Impact of VERP guider modelling strengths-based language

Although participants had brought clips demonstrating their successful use of the principles of attunement, they nevertheless initially had difficulty expressing their strengths within the group setting. Very early in the supervision session the VERP practitioner played a role in guiding participants to see the effect of their successful moments of attunement, and this subsequently set the tone for finding strengths. This was felt by participants to be an important factor in helping them feel relaxed in front of their colleagues and manager. Questions such as 'What do you see yourself doing well?' and 'How are you showing (the child) that you're listening?' were extremely important to the participants:

> She's asking me to say good things about myself, this is weird for someone to come in and not criticize...helping you look for the good things is a massive turnaround.

Participants spoke of their enjoyment of celebrating with colleagues, alongside embarrassment and a need to refer to other group members for reassurance that it was okay to be doing something well.

Theme 5: How aims and goals developed

Goals at the end of the first supervision were generally more detailed than they had been at the start of the session, and involved using specific non-verbal elements of communication more thoughtfully. During their interview three months later, participants not only remembered the goals they had set for themselves, but also talked about how they had expanded and developed these goals into other areas of their teaching practice.

Theme 6: The process of change in individual teaching practice when using VERP

All the participants commented on personal changes over the time of the project, with a preponderance of comments indicating that their focus had shifted from target-focused approaches to interactional-focused awareness.

> Not something you really think about day to day, you only think about what observations you can write on them or how you can progress their learning…but by making him feel more positive about himself I probably got more out of him educationally than I would have otherwise…well, because I was interested in everything he said, he was so enthusiastic and just carrying on…all I had to do was just smiling and nodding and asking him about what he was doing – not masses of technical stuff.

> Because you are taking the time to 'look at children, stand back, not bulldoze in'…giving yourself time and space enables you to give them time and space.

All staff members mentioned an increase in both listening and following child initiatives, identifying changes such as a decrease in asking questions and an increase in commentary.

> I think I used to talk too much, and just get 'yes' and 'no' answers so when I saw C…and saw that when I stepped back and gave him space to think rather than jump in too quickly…it made him expand on what he said.

> I've definitely got my confidence back and that's important to me. I am more conscious to let children have a go at getting the answers, not assuming they won't have an answer.

Theme 7: Impact on staff confidence

What appeared to be central to these changes in teaching practice identified above was an increase in confidence, which led directly to an improvement in perceived competence. Staff reported less reliance on colleagues and more self-reliance after the project than before.

> I used to judge myself that I am not up to everyone else's level…I thought they handled that better than I could… now I have seen my good moments of interaction I think I am doing it okay… I don't compare myself with others

much, and I am gaining confidence in situations I am not used to.

[Improved confidence]…makes us better at our jobs… you can make your own judgement call, and not have to be running and checking all the time…you don't have to involve another person you can just get on and do your job.

Theme 8: Benefits of group supervision

This VERP project relied on looking at videos in a group, as opposed to on an individual basis. Equality is inherent within the expectation that all group members bring a video to the supervision and each takes an equal turn. The advantages of this group approach are numerous, and were acknowledged by the staff within the interviews. These included: the benefits of learning from each other; incorporating strengths from another's practice into their own; and realizing that the supportive nature of this method allowed them to comment favourably on each other's interactions in a respectful manner. Because the VERP method allows all group members to see the clear observable detail of attuned interactions, comments during the shared reviews were more specific than general praise, and included questions which allowed a group member to observe more closely the effect of a moment of interaction on the child.

[This]…now enables us to know *what* is different about our interactions instead of saying 'something was different, but I don't know what it was'.

In addition, the VERP practitioner's skilful use of systemic circular questions, for instance, asking one person what another person has done well, was a useful tool in sharing turns equally within the group, bringing in quieter group members and allowing a group experience of 'shared expertise'.

Now I realize I wasn't giving the quieter ones time to speak, so now I feel like I can say to the confident speakers, 'hang on…so and so has something to say, let's listen to that person'.

Theme 9: Systemic change

Several participants mentioned that their relationships within the team had strengthened as a result of this intervention, enabling them to be more open to each other. This was particularly pertinent for the team manager, who felt that not only had the team given more time for reflection since the project, but that they had become 'closer', and that there was a now a shared vision for the whole school.

> Now at lunchtime we all sit together and reflect, how did the lessons go…or can you look out for a particular child… we've given ourselves time for reflection as a team… I can see lots of my staff's strengths, they've been reinforced… before I thought 'I've got a feeling you can do that, or I expect you will be able to do that', now I know that they can do that, and I can tell you that you can do that because you've seen it and I've seen it.

Role and impact of the VERP guider

In this section the authors focus their analysis specifically on the role and impact of the VERP guider, first from their own direct observation of the content of the shared reviews, and second from the participants' views of what the VERP guider contributed to the process.

Authors' views on what the guider did that helped

Use of clear structure: The structures that seemed to be highly significant were the clear guiding principles of attuned interactions and guidance (Kennedy *et al.* 2011; see also Chapter 1, this volume), which were used from the beginning to name the expectations and to link these to the aims of the individual or group:

> Do you remember, we are looking for your being attentive.

All participants were encouraged to use the chart of attunement principles, and were helped to find examples of their own attunement by microanalysing the video footage, demonstrating these and the effect of this on the child:

> So if we look at the first part of the ladder [on the chart], which one are we looking at for you?

> Let's concentrate on those few seconds, what can you see there?

Flexibility: Realistic expectations were required to fit around very difficult time constraints, staff shortages and classroom demands. Shared reviews took place during assembly time, when the most staff could be available. If only one member of staff turned up initially, the VERP practitioner began the session, allowing other team members to arrive when and if they could.

Activating: Asking participants to pause the video at a specific point and waiting for their response inevitably prompted an immediate response, but often the participant would notice the child, rather than themselves. Questions such as 'Can you find the child's initiative, and see what you did as a result?' activated participants to see more interaction.

Complex questions referring not only to what was happening but also to what was in the mind of the child or adult involved in the interaction helped keep the focus on *inter*action, rather than action:

> How do you think that makes him feel…with all that going on, (when you are looking at him and smiling)?

> And why was she able to say that about wanting to make a star, what had you done?

Guiding and mediated learning: Within other VIG or VERP projects it has often been observed that during an initial shared review the participants are able to name the actions observed such as eye contact, waiting and head nods, but have fewer ideas about the meaning or significance of these principles. The principles of scaffolding and learning with the help of a mediator (Wood, Bruner and Ross 1976) are thought to play a large part in increasing the effectiveness of learning, where in this case the VERP practitioner notices whether a learner is lost and provides just enough information to allow a mutual understanding, as in the example below:

What had you done before that helped? [blank look from participant] You named it, didn't you, so that shows her that you listened again.

Participants' views on what the guider did that helped

The relationship: All participants mentioned the quality of the relationship they felt with the VERP guider, naming in particular warmth, reassurance, positive feedback, a relaxed attitude, humour and joint exploration as key factors. There were also comments that the guider's help with microanalysis and looking again at the video was a highly relevant factor in improving future practice:

> Since I've been working with [guider] I do feel very relaxed around her…we've got that little bond where I know if I've got it right she is going to tell me I've got it right, whereas if I need that reassurance, I know she's going to give it to me.

Time for structured reflection with a skilled facilitator: Time for reflection alongside a clear structure was seen to be highly significant by participants, and allowed them to develop ideas within the receptive space provided:

> She's definitely helped me think about it more…it's easy to just sit and look at the video, but she's made me really look at it, see the different points and really break it down…if I'd been looking at it on my own, I'd have just seen myself listening because I'm looking at her…the questions have really made me think.

Developing action points for the future: This was seen by all participants as a quality they had before the VERP project; however, the project allowed this to occur in a gentle way without shame or embarrassment, and was helped by the VERP practitioner giving choices on what areas each individual would like to develop:

> [Guider] made it so unthreatening, and just so nice, because she focused on the positive…if there were areas for improvement, she would say 'it would be really lovely if

next time…' rather than 'gosh, you weren't doing that very well…' We wanted to be better.

Discussion

Chapter 16 in this publication, by Hayes, Brown and Todd, describes several theories of systemic change (Checkland and Scholes 1990; Dalin 1993; Schein 1999) within schools, and which factors are perceived to be most predominant for systemic change. They summarize how the conditions of change are met through the use of VERP. The reports cited above also demonstrate this, and exemplify the theories described. At the heart of VERP lies the belief that the key to change lies within the individual or group itself, and that change is best achieved through a strengths-based, self-modelling structure in which there is dialogue between all members of the group in order for new meanings and future plans to be owned by all individuals in that group.

The most striking observation from all members of staff, including the manager, was that before the VERP project, it was evident that they were all used to a governmentally constructed educational target-driven culture. Staff were all familiar with educational goals for children and targets for themselves to help children, but this had the effect of making staff feel insecure, preoccupied and overwhelmed with issues of development. All staff showed themselves to be extremely diligent in trying to do their best, and all had the children's achievements at heart. Before the project this had resulted in frequent requests for help, with staff feeling under-confident in their own ability to help children learn interactively.

The VERP project demonstrated to the participants through first-hand experience that the quality of the relationship with an adult is hugely significant in the development and refinement of language and in furthering a child's learning potential. Post-VERP, all staff reported that the emphasis of their teaching practice had shifted, with much more awareness of their own interactions and the effect of these on children.

The importance of both the visual and guided discovery aspect of VERP is hypothesized to promote more effective learning over and above a purely verbal teaching style. The empowerment and self-modelling structure within VERP enables individuals to take charge of their own learning, and this makes it more likely that individuals and groups will generalize this knowledge across different areas of their working practice.

Conclusion

To sum up our findings, the factors that were reported by participants to be particularly important were the strengths-based language, the positive support and the reflective structure provided by the VERP guider, the participation of their manager and the supportive group process.

The authors were surprised by the extent of the systemic changes reported by the school staff, and were particularly pleased that participants' targets had been met in such a short time. In addition to personal goals, the self-reported increase in confidence and competence appears to have made an enormous difference to many aspects of teaching practice, and to have improved staff relationships. The scope and extent of these changes were not an anticipated consequence of the VERP project, but are seen as indicative of the model of empowerment.

CHAPTER 3

From the Beginnings of Video Enhanced Reflective Practice (VERP) to Today

A Collaborative Journey between Eindhoven and Tayside

Lia van Rosmalen and Hilary Kennedy

Introducing the authors

Hilary Kennedy is an educational psychologist and a key developer of Video Interaction Guidance (VIG) in the UK. Lia van Rosmalen is a social worker in Eindhoven, the Netherlands, currently Head of HRM (Human Resource Management) and Development at de Combinatie Jeugdzorg (Combined Organization for Youth Care).

Hilary invited Lia to write this chapter as her work in Eindhoven using VIG principles with groups of professionals and parents was the inspiration for the early development of VERP in Scotland, which has, in turn, influenced the format of many effective VERP courses forming chapters in this book. Lia adds that Hilary has also been influential in the development of VERP within de Combinatie Jeugdzorg, as her visiting lectures have given inspiration and provided new visual materials and ideas.

This chapter is the story of a synergy and creative development between two people and the organizations where they have worked for over 20 years, with a strong focus on Lia and de Combinatie Jeugdzorg, since the rest of this book concerns development outside the Netherlands. The first half was written jointly from dialogue between Lia and Hilary, and the second half was written by Lia as the sole author.

Lia started work in 1982 as a care worker in child protection. As a (family) guardian she accompanied difficult, complex families where parental authority was wholly or partially restricted by the judiciary, and only too often children were placed outside their families. She often felt powerless to break this seemingly inevitable downward spiral, even when she knew in her heart that, despite everything that had happened between them, they ultimately wanted only one thing: to be a happy family.

In 1987 Lia was fortunate because, just when she was despairing about the plight of troubled families, the organization she worked for was chosen to test VIG in child protection, and she was one of the first three employees to be trained. From the very first moment she started working with VIG she entered a learning process that has had a huge influence on how she now functions as a professional. When using video with families, searching together for what was still intact, she realized that they gained tremendous strength to take charge of their own lives once more, to enjoy contact with their children and to believe in their own abilities again.

In parallel, she noticed changes emerging in *her* abilities to attune to families in a way that had seemed blocked before, despite her best intentions. In supervision, when she reflected on the video recordings of herself working with the families, she saw how she could make attuned empathetic contact with families. With this affirmation, she began to reflect on how she could build on her strengths (for example, interrupting in an affirming way long turns from families, rather than sitting passively as they rambled on, exploring solutions that parents wanted rather than giving advice that was not received). Her reflections in supervision gave her the energy and confidence to see that parents became active when she asked them to speak, how they stopped repeating their story when she acknowledged them, and that they came up with new ideas when she supported and built on their initiatives.

She thinks it no exaggeration to say that in a few months she was transformed from a care worker who talked *about* families to a care worker who mostly talked *with* families. For the first time she really felt able to help families improve their interactions with each other, even those entrenched in child protection situations. She strongly felt that she had benefited from the power of reflecting on her practice using video, and so the seeds of using video to reflect on professional practice (VERP) were sown.

In 1990 she started work at de Combinatie Jeugdzorg, which was then the Medical Day Care Centre, Tomteboe, employed to introduce, implement and deploy VIG and VERP.

Beginnings of VERP in the UK

Hilary and Lia first met in Manchester Town Hall in 1993 at a conference of an international initiative to bring together professionals developing methods of intervention that empowered parents to be central to their own change process. In a group discussion, Hilary made the comment that 'some parents may not be ready for groups', to which Lia quickly responded: 'it depends *how* the group is run'. This disagreement was the beginning of a long friendship and many lively debates. Lia was focused on the process of engaging families in change that Hilary was inspired to explore. This journey continued on a ten-day study tour to Israel in 1994, when 40 helping professionals from ten countries presented video-based empowering methods. As their discussions deepened, Lia and Hilary found partners in each other for future exchange and development.

At this time Hilary and Raymond Simpson were training in VIG in the Netherlands (see the Preface to Kennedy, Landor and Todd 2011), and visited Lia at Tomteboe. They were excited to see a group course designed for parents and professionals working with young children with developmental delay based on the VIG contact (now known as attunement) principles. They immediately set about finding Marianne Henderson, who agreed to translate the booklets for them into English.

Penny Forsyth first piloted these booklets with parents and professionals at the Frances Wright Pre-School Centre in Dundee.

This was the very first course in VERP in the UK, and was called 'Communicating with Children'. Following positive feedback from the first few courses, the model was refined and rolled out to the early years professionals in education and social work in Dundee City as part of ongoing staff development. These courses were then developed at the University of Dundee as part of the VERoC (Video Enhanced Reflection on Communication) Centre, and became undergraduate and postgraduate modules in education and social work.

The spread of VERP in the UK to 2011 is summarized in the chapter on VERP in the 2011 book on VIG (Strathie, Strathie and Kennedy 2011), and this chapter now continues the story, focusing on the development of VERP in Eindhoven.

Early research evidence from the Netherlands

In 1993 Hilary met Ben van Bruxvoort, Director of Tomteboe, and was very interested in his and Lia's plans to involve parents and care workers in supporting the quality of interactions experienced by youngsters with special needs at Tomteboe.

Ben made it his mission to focus on strengths and solutions, rather than the impossibilities of problems, in the collaboration between parents and group leaders, and on activating instead of compensating. Naturally there was some scepticism and resistance at Tomteboe, where the group leaders had been highly trained in diagnosis and categorization of youngsters with difficulties. These group leaders, who were sincerely motivated to help these children, were sometimes baffled by what they saw in the recordings. The first step was to support the group leaders and parents to observe and reflect on the (sometimes inept) initiatives of the children, and to respond to them sensitively and contingently.

The focus group for this project was those children who did not seem to be able to have reciprocal contact, whether or not as a result of autism. In this project, 12 children were video recorded in the group and at home, and the group leaders discussed these recordings with and without the parents. Prior to the intervention, both parents and group leaders received group-oriented training in VIG principles. This training course provided experiential experiences of the VIG principles (for example, feeling the difference between being received and not received in conversation), and were illustrated by line drawings and videos. The two illustrations below, from the English translation of the Tomteboe course, contrast trying or not trying to receive a young child's initiative, and were used as a basis for discussion on the course.

Figure 3.1 Receiving and exploring the child's initiative

Simpson and Henderson (1995)

In this example the mother tries her best to understand Johnny
Johnny does his best to tell his mother what he has drawn.
Through his mothers questions Johnny knows that he has not
been able to make his mother understand.
He loses the incentive to continue telling his story.
His mother is none the wiser concerning his drawing.

Figure 3.2 Not receiving or exploring the child's initiative

Simpson and Herderson (1995)

The first VERP course at Tomteboe was fully evaluated by Kees van
der Sande, and the research findings were presented at conferences
in the Netherlands and Edinburgh (van der Sande 1995). The VERP
intervention was undertaken with parents and group leaders in
separate groups for theory input and sharing video clips, coming
together to share ideas before the next video session, as shown in
Figure 3.3.

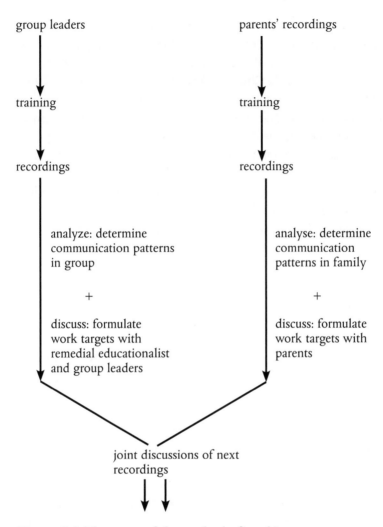

Figure 3.3 The route of the method of working

Van der Sande (1995)

Before and after the intervention, the group leaders and parents completed questionnaires (AUTI-R: Aiming to create a picture of the social interaction skills of the children, van Berckelaer-Onnes and Hoekman 1991; CBCL: Child Behavior Checklist, Achenbach 1992; NCSQ: Nijmegen Child Rearing Situation Questionnaire, Wels and Robbroeckx 1996). The group training was also video recorded, focusing on the changes in the focus of discussions through the different sessions through the videos, with an extensive questionnaire to explore the process of the intervention.

The results from the AUTI-R showed that, at the start, six children (out of twelve) were considered to be autistic by the parents, and four by the group leaders. At the end of the project, only two children were indicated as autistic by the parents, and none by the group leaders.

The results of the CBCL showed that both parents and group leaders observed a reduction in withdrawn behaviour (significant for mothers, $p<0.01$) and that aggressive behaviour had diminished.

The NCSQ was used to investigate the subjective burden of the child on the adults. All scores showed improvement, and there was a significant change in both parents feeling more able to cope with the situation ($p<0.01$), having fewer problems ($p<0.05$ mothers, $p<0.01$ fathers) and the mothers seeing the child as less of a burden ($p<0.05$).

The VIG guiders' contributions during the group video feedback (now known as shared review) were examined to identify possible mechanisms of change. Their 'advice' statements during group video feedback sessions were charted over the three months of the intervention. In general, the groups were more active in later sessions with less advice being given by the guiders. The advice relating to the foundational attunement principles of being attentive, encouraging and receiving initiatives that was introduced in the initial sessions were barely present by the end. However, advice on developing attunement interactions and guiding the children to relate to other children continued to play an important role right to the close.

Hilary was impressed with the innovative quality of this course, where parents and group leaders worked together to enhance their interactions with the children in their care. The results of this research on the first VERP group process were impressive. They showed it was possible to influence radically how parents and group leaders experienced the possibilities/diagnosis of a child with autism, and to reduce the stress on the adults when caring for the children. The parents and group workers together discovered interaction strategies that actually reduced the behaviour that was causing them concern.

How VERP is currently embedded at de Combanatie Jeugdzorg[1]
VERP as connecting link

After the early promising and profound experiences with VIG and VERP, further supported by the research results, VERP developed quickly into 'the water that flows through all the methods'. After all, no matter which method or intervention is chosen, it all depends on *how* it is employed. This has everything to do with how form and content is given to the alliance between care worker and client, because communication and interaction are the ultimate means of transfer.

De Combinatie Jeugdzorg VERP was, and is, a byword for 'the art of the normal': the ability to continue to communicate normally or even to enhance one's communication in highly complex and challenging circumstances. This involves attunement principles such as making contact with, listening to, being interested in and acknowledging the other, rather than becoming 'diverted' by the complexity of problems.

As part of a complex merger with an organization for day and night care, Lia had extensive opportunities to use VERP as core training. For example, the day and night care was primarily focused on behaviour regulation, which in practice (too) often meant use of a reward system. By combining VERP with a focus on behaviour, a dynamic whole was created that reinforced itself. When care workers watched video recordings of themselves in contact with teenagers, many of them discovered that they were more occupied with the behavioural programme than the teenager. On the other hand, using only VERP regularly yielded inadequate results in achieving real behavioural changes in the teenagers. In this case, the task skills programme represented the 'what' and VERP the 'how'.

---

1   This section is by Lia van Rosmalen, as sole author.

VERP in the centre of professional development

With Ben's strong support, Lia has embedded VERP as a staff development tool at de Combanatie Jeugdzorg (now with 600 employees) in induction, ongoing reflection and troubleshooting.

VERP used as an induction tool for all employees

All new employees are actively involved in a VERP course when they are given information about the Dutch VIG principles for attuned interactions and guidance (Biemans 1990). They then reflect on their own communication style in work situations during group video feedback sessions. However, it is recognized that every employee will start work at a different level depending on experience, education and communication skills. This means that the VERP courses are differentiated, both in terms of information given and the way the VERP guider interacts in group feedback. VERP guiders can work out how to position themselves by using the Dreyfus model of *From Novice to Expert* (Benner 1984).

A beginner, it is recognized, may be searching for security and support. At this stage the use of checklists, protocols, rules and regulations, and plans can be highly beneficial. The VERP training is designed with this in mind. An introduction to VERP is part of the training programme, and includes trainees making and discussing three video recordings of themselves during client contact. Potential practitioners are informed about this during the selection procedure.

When new practitioners are *absolute beginners* in the field, we adapt for reasons of security and support. The focus of the video recording is on basic communication between the care worker and client. We ask the employee to prepare carefully by:

- specifically focusing on those moments the trainee is satisfied with

- using a checklist of basic communication.

In addition, VERP delivery is carefully scaffolded by the work experience and with the specific strengths of the practitioner in mind.

We have a protocol for video use that beginners use as a crucial tool. They often follow the protocol strictly when working with clients, and adhere closely to the steps described.

The advanced beginner is strongly focused on the quality of the task. How can they perform this task better, faster and more effectively? In the VERP training we use the 'what and how' model to teach this. Practitioners record a video of themselves with a client while carrying out a pre-set task. Afterwards, the practitioners analyse:

- WHAT they intended to achieve and whether they succeeded. Which aspects worked, and which aspects can be improved?

- HOW they carried out the task (using the interaction diagram as a framework).

The danger is that advanced beginners are so focused on the task that they overlook the 'human being', neglecting to identify with the client and to give and ask for acknowledgement. By focusing on the interaction, both the content and the process are discussed simultaneously, and staff members understand what they see in the recording.

From the above examples, the reader can see how VERP may be adapted for less experienced practitioners, who will be given the opportunity to take a strong lead in the direction of their professional development in a much more open-ended and creative process.

VERP as a method of ongoing reflection

All employees attend an intervision meeting at least twice a year, during which they submit a video of themselves in contact with a client. This is a different approach from the usual progress meeting, when the focus is the strengths and limitations within the family. In VERP intervision meetings, the focus is on the development of the care worker's communication skills.

VERP when communication breaks down

We work with complex families where the care worker coaches the family. Sometimes the coaching comes to a halt, for example because the client stops progressing, or because the care worker is involved in the conflict or is no longer able to guide the process. Our experience is that these matters often lead to long, complicated and unproductive talks that are not always helpful. Especially for skilled professionals, it is helpful if they observe themselves and their behaviour when experiencing communication breakdown. They have an overview of the process and are able to 'zoom in' from this external perspective, precisely because they understand that small adaptations can subtly change the interaction. When care workers are in a tense care-giving relationship, natural communication is lost. Often, negative interaction patterns may become visible, and they are shocked to realize they interrupt clients, do not acknowledge or ask for acknowledgement, give monologues and allow the client to give monologues. From their earlier VERP training, they know how to adopt an attuned pattern so are quickly working back in the 'yes cycle' with the family.

VERP as a building block for the carrying out of methodologies

In the Netherlands, the clients' strengths receive much attention. Giving back control of their lives to clients and, consequently, the care-giving process, is prioritized by using solutions that are proposed by themselves. These 'social network strategies', developed in Australia with Native Australians, are based on the premise that problems can and should be solved within a client's network. The role of the care worker is especially aimed at tracking down the existing network to strengthen or to extend it, or both.

This method asks for a different mindset from that of care workers. They, and their expertise, are no longer central in the process, but instead the clients and their networks. The implementation is slow going as clients point out that they have no or only a very limited network, that they do not want to ask their network for help, that the network has already been exhausted, that the clients specifically want the expertise of the care worker, and so on. However, some practitioners effectively manage to promote an active network for almost every family with whom they work. Unsurprisingly, these practitioners are usually the ones most active in the application of VERP principles. Broad terms such as 'giving control', connecting to the solution's direction and the use of strengths are given a concrete image within the VERP. Care workers who recognize the client's initiatives and who are able to receive and extend these initiatives give back control to the client. By using clients' solutions, their strengths are activated.

Complex and sometimes hard-to-grasp notions are explained with VERP. This means VERP may be used to access a deeper layer: translating our care work vision into something concrete. Also, to our own surprise, it again shows that VERP is a powerful and practical tool to develop a new methodology.

Future national registration plans for youth care workers

At this moment the professionalization of the youth care worker is very much underway. Important in this process is the law, only recently passed, enforcing the registration of youth care workers on a professional register from 1 January 2014; before this there was no register of youth care workers. One of the requirements is that there should be systematic reflection on the basis of intervision or supervision, according to an accredited method. There are currently only three accredited methods available, and we are working hard to establish the same recognition for VIG principles.

According to the professional register, the essence of reflection is to improve insight into, and the quality of, their own functioning as a professional, in particular the handling of interactions. VERP meets all requirements: there is a pre-determined methodological framework and, specifically, the handling and positive influencing of interactions is centralized. The intervision description in VERP and the accompanying argumentation are currently being assessed for the national professional register. Achieving this would be an enormous breakthrough in the Dutch youth care system, because organizations will be stimulated to cultivate VERP further as a feedback instrument for professionals to enable them to reflect powerfully on their professional attitudes and skills.

CHAPTER 4

How and Why Video Enhanced Reflective Practice (VERP) Works

The Theory Underpinning the Practice

Miriam Landor

Introduction

Video Enhanced Reflective Practice (VERP) is a method to support individuals or groups to develop their interaction skills in their work, through guided reflection on their chosen video clips of day-to-day practice. This is a strengths-based approach where participants are helped to identify and build on their present skills and to set themselves their next goal or challenge. It was developed from the therapeutic intervention of Video Interaction Guidance (VIG), and shares the same methodology, values and 'principles of attuned interactions and guidance' (Kennedy, Landor and Todd 2011, p.28; see also Chapter 1, this volume). VERP is usually delivered by a VIG-trained guider in a short course format of an initial training session followed by three or more 'shared review' (supervision) sessions. Trainees film themselves in their usual work context, and select two or three brief clips showing their target-related attuned interactions for reflective discussion with the VERP guider.

Looking at the theory behind VERP can explain how and why the method works, and on what principles it was developed. I write this chapter with a range of readers in mind. Some will be familiar with VIG, and their focus will be on how VERP has developed from VIG as a method of helping professionals improve their practice. Others, from a range of backgrounds, will be interested in exploring another way of looking at reflective practice for professionals.

What is the aim of VERP?

The aim of VERP is *change* – change in a person's attuned interaction skills in their work context that will enable them better to serve their client (who may be a child, a patient, a care-seeker, a prisoner, a member of staff, a member of the general public, and so on). This can be achieved through improving the individual's skills and knowledge or through organizational change, or both. VERP can be used along a continuum from individual professional development to systemic change at all levels of an organization. There are many models of change that guide planning and evaluation of change. Target monitoring evaluation (TME) (Dunsmuir *et al.* 2009) provides a simple way for VERP trainees to set their own targets and to monitor their achievement. At the other end of the continuum is the theory of change (Taplin and Clarke 2012), where all involved in planning the change map out their long-term goals, or outcomes, the conditions required to meet them, underlying assumptions and preconditions, interventions and indicators of success. Another model that resonates with the strengths-based approach of VERP is appreciative inquiry (Cooperrider and Whitney 2005), a social constructionist approach to organizational development and change management, which starts with a focus on all involved 'discovering' what already works in an organization, 'dreaming' the extrapolated end goals, 'designing' the necessary strategies and then 'deploying' them.

Reflective practice enhanced by video
Reflective practice

VERP is one of many reflective practice methods. Reflective practice is a way of helping people *learn* so that they can improve what they do in their work – their practice. Indeed, it is a common requirement for professionals to undertake some form of regular learning through continuing professional development (CPD), with a 'focus on lifelong learning and work-based learning strategies' (Harrison and Kessels 2004, p.5), to ensure that quality and standards are upheld in a rapidly changing knowledge economy. Knowles' theory of andragogy (adult learning) proposes that previous experience, intrinsic motivation, practical relevance and self-direction in a trusting, respectful collaboration are the most important features (quoted in Earley and Bubb 2004). VERP starts with individual trainees and their work practice, regardless of their current status and level of understanding; each brings to the training their previous experience, their self-set targets and their personal commitment to improving their practice through their own agency. Transformative learning, or changes in one's self-understanding, convictions and actions, can result from self-confrontation through the video, which may act as a 'disorientating dilemma' (Mezirow et al. 2009) or a 'learning edge' (Wlodkowski 1999).

Learning takes place through the mediation of a more experienced 'other' (Feuerstein and Feuerstein 1991) in areas that are in the learner's capacity: within their 'zone of proximal development' (Vygotsky 1978). VERP guidance resembles a 'learning conversation', which has been described variously as a 'planned systematic approach to professional dialogue' (Zwozdiak-Myers 2012, p.98) and a 'safe professional environment where true reflection can take place' (Tarrant 2013, pp.43–44). Within the safe relationship created by the VERP guider, difficult conversations may also be held, where a battle of messages is transformed into a learning conversation (Stone, Patton and Heen 1999). The VERP guider 'scaffolds' (sensitively supports; see Bruner 1977) the trainee's learning by judging what would help at that moment – returning to the video, prompting with a question, giving information, and so on.

Reflection is a vital part of the learning cycle. Practitioners reflect on their past action (reflection-on-action) or during their current action (reflection-in-action) (Schön 1983), learn from this and alter their next action accordingly (reflection-for-action) (Thompson and Thompson 2008). This simple model of learning ('single-loop learning') can be self-limiting and self-protective; Argyris and

Schön (1978) used the term 'double-loop learning' to describe deeper reflection on the values and assumptions that underlie the action–reaction pattern in order to challenge them with new thinking (Bolton 2014). The guider in VERP aims to 'deepen the discussion' with the trainee, both by exploring and by modelling the principles of attuned interactions and guidance (Kennedy *et al.* 2011; see also Chapter 1, this volume).

Reflective practice covers a variety of methods in social contexts where there is no obvious solution, involving complex and 'messy' human situations; it entails being open, curious, patient, honest and rigorous (Bager-Charleson 2010; Ghaye 2011; Howatson-Jones and Standing 2013; Moon 2005). Hargreaves and Page (2013) suggest that the focus of reflective practice varies according to professional agencies, from its use in medicine and dentistry as a tool to help complex decision-making, to being a cognitive tool for learning in education, to health and social work where deeper personal, critical and sociopolitical aspects are to the fore. Its personalized learning can develop 'soft' skills, such as working in a team or independently, and becoming creative, resilient and responsible for one's own learning (Pollard 2008). VERP can be employed across any work context and, because the trainee sets the targets, it can serve in any paradigm.

In VERP, the medium for reflection is the video of trainees in their own work situation. By starting with reflection from life, rather than theory, pedagogical reflection (on positive impact) can lead to pedagogical thoughtfulness (change and development of self) and then to pedagogical tact (greater sensitivity to one's client) (van Manen 1991). The process of reflective practice may lead a person to become more reflexively aware and questioning of their social, political and psychological position, and more mindful of their own influence on the situation (Bolton 2014; Fook 2012).

Video enhanced

In VERP, short video clips of themselves in their work situation are selected by the trainees that relate to the trainees' self-set targets, and that show 'better than usual' moments of attunement and vitality. It is important to realize that the video is therefore used as a constructed artifice, rather than an objective measure. Using video in this specific way to enhance the reflective process is one of the main differences between VERP and other methods for professional development. There are two underlying theoretical aspects to the use of video: self-modelling and self-confrontation.

Self-modelling is a development from social learning theory (Bandura 1977a), which proposed that novices learn by observing and imitating more experienced others. Further proposals, that the closer the model was to oneself the better the learning, led to the use of self-images that were skilfully constructed to demonstrate the target behaviour (Dowrick and Biggs 1983). Dowrick, the main proponent of this field, proposes that self-modelling is the most fundamental form of observational learning (Dowrick 2011). The term 'self-modelling' describes a positive change in behaviour and confidence after viewing oneself performing exemplary behaviours (Murray and Noland 2013; Nikopoulos and Keenan 2006) or, in other words, imitating one's own best performance. The fact that VERP trainees actively seek out video images of their own best practice taps into the efficacy of self-modelling.

Self-confrontation through seeing oneself on video is 'a unique opportunity to gain greater insight into one's behaviour...' 'Seeing yourself as others generally see you...' (Wels 2002, p.52) often causes anxiety in advance, as one may expect to be judged. There can also be cognitive dissonance (stress caused by conflicting beliefs and evidence) caused by the real image not living up to one's ideal image. However, and just as frequently, cognitive dissonance can be evoked by the video clips not matching the person's negative self-image. Those who have sought VIG or VERP often see themselves as having some sort of relationship problem, personal or professional, that they want help with. It takes the skill of a trained VIG guider to reframe critical self-doubt into positive exceptions in an authentic way. Dweck's work on self-theory (2000) showed that the manner of giving positive feedback or praise is critical to a person's self-image and to their subsequent performance; praise for innate attributes leads to a mindset where people believe their ability is fixed, and then they become unwilling to expose their limitations to another. In VERP the guider encourages the person to see for themselves their action and effort evidenced in the video clip, leading to Dweck's growth mindset, where a belief in the capacity to improve and change through one's own efforts leads to better future performance.

The use of video, which gives the method its power, adds to the ethical responsibility of the guider. Self-modelling from the video can work negatively, as well as positively. Christine Brons (1999) points out that the camera position chosen by the guider can give different subliminal messages: for example, looking upwards gives the impression of a powerful subject, whilst looking downwards can make the subject seem vulnerable, perhaps evoking the viewer's care-giving response. The camera can be focused close up on a single interaction, or from further away to give the context of the situation, depending on the main issue. In VIG, guiders skilfully select positive clips for their clients that have been minutely edited to show interactions that are better than usual because these exemplify the attunement principles and relate to their 'helping question' or goal. In VERP, the trainees analyse their own film to find those significant learning moments; they have to be both trained and supported by their guider to focus on their successful attuned moments, a difficult task for most people. As Goldman (2007, p.34) says, we face an ethical challenge to 'use digital video…to create the kinds of stories, cases, and examples of learning…for the purpose of building convivial learning communities, as Ivan Illich (1973) would propose.'

Why is VERP unique amongst video reflective practice methods?

As we saw at the start of this chapter, VERP was developed from VIG, as supervisors and trainees alike saw the potential of VIG for improving their own interactions in their professional practice. There are two stages that differentiate VERP from other reflective practice methods, however.

Selection of clips

One of the chief factors for the success of both VIG and VERP is that they are *strengths-based* approaches. In practical terms, this means that video is microanalysed to find moments showing successful attuned interactions, even if these are exceptions to normal behaviours. These clips are the focus of the reflective dialogue that the guider facilitates with the client (VIG) or trainee (VERP). It is initially difficult for people to speak about what they are doing well, as Western culture appears to be predominantly problem-focused, and our tendency is towards self-criticism. However, the belief behind solution-focused psychology is that whatever we focus on grows. Studying what is happening when things are going well, and relating this to the 'preferred future' (the trainee's self-set target), will enable us to learn how to maximize our potential, whereas pathologizing problems will not (de Shazer 1988; Maslow 1954).

The selection of video clips by the trainee is based on both the 'principles of attuned interactions and guidance' (Kennedy *et al.* 2011; see also Chapter 1, this volume) and their self-set targets. These attunement principles were developed by Biemans (1990) following discussions with Colwyn Trevarthen about his work on parent–baby interactions (Trevarthen 1980). The principles are arranged hierarchically, and range from the basic skills of primary intersubjectivity (being attentive, encouraging and receiving initiatives, and turn-taking) to the complex communication skills of guiding and deepening discussion. The VERP guider follows the same attunement principles, aiming to be attentive, to encourage and receive initiatives from the trainee, to take short turns and so on.

The concepts of primary and secondary intersubjectivity underpin the attunement principles. The term 'intersubjectivity' refers to the interactions between two people as they negotiate meaning and intent. It is an innate human capacity, preverbal, dyadic and dialogic in nature: 'Infants, it appears, are born with motives and emotions for actions that sustain human intersubjectivity' (Trevarthen 2011a, p.121); its 'pre-linguistic forms of communicative competence' (Beebe and Lachman 2014, p.29) are also the basis for adult psychodynamic therapy.

Primary intersubjectivity refers to the mutual embodied expression and perception of emotion and intention between two people, in a sensitive and contingent communicative exchange (Crittenden 2009; Murray 1998; Nagy and Molnar 2004; Papousek and Papousek 1997; Trevarthen 2004; Zeedyk 2006, all cited in

Cross and Kennedy 2011). In other words, it can be seen in the non-verbal communication between two people when their body language, hand movements, eyes, voice tones and facial expressions all combine in a synchronized communicative 'dance'. It is evident in VERP interactions at the level of trainee and interaction partner, trainee and guider, and, in a group VERP context, trainee and peer (see Figure 1.2 in Chapter 1, this volume).

In secondary intersubjectivity, a later stage in infant development, the capacity to interrelate whilst sharing attention with other contextual aspects emerges. Again, this is harnessed at all levels of VERP, as the trainee, guider and in many cases colleagues explore the video clips, whilst reflecting together on meaning and intention, and on present skills and future potential.

The trainee's selection of video clips is also guided by the notion of 'vitality'. Trevarthen (2014, pp.10–11) reminds us that 'zest for learning' occurs through our bodily movements and emotional response, through non-verbal communication and affective behaviours, even before language is involved. Stern (2010) describes dynamic vitality (including movement, aliveness, time and intensity) as the medium for evaluating the state of others and for implicit relational knowing, and explains that it is an additional element to emotion and cognition. In a VERP session, the skilled guider will be aware of all these aspects in the trainee's video, and will facilitate reflection on the tiny moments that led to a successful outcome, in line with the trainee's self-set targets for their own professional development.

Shared review

The second stage in the VERP framework that distinguishes it from other reflective practice methods is the 'shared review'. The clips that the trainee selected are the focus of a reflective discussion, a shared review meeting with a VIG-trained guider, either one-to-one or in a small group. The guider models the attunement principles and follows the 'seven steps' model (Kennedy *et al.* 2011; see also Chapter 1, this volume), sensitively judging when to activate the trainee's reflective processes and when to intervene by reframing or by reviewing the video.

Lia van Rosmalen (Chapter 3) writes about video as an instrument of feedback:

> In my daily work I was constantly supported with [work] supervision, intervision, collegial consultation, and so on, which were all of great value to my professional development. However, and I only fully realized this when I saw the first recordings of myself, all these forms of support were based on my own perception of reality: my memories, my selection of priorities and my perception of the client. With the video recordings my reality was extended and became more nuanced, and was sometimes even turned topsy-turvy, which was an extremely profound experience. (Personal communication)

Hattie and Timperley (2007) define feedback in general as 'information provided by an agent…regarding aspects of one's performance or understanding' (p.81). They point out that whilst it is a major factor in learning, its impact can be either positive or negative, and that it can be accepted or rejected. Hattie's previous synthesis of meta-analyses found that the most effective forms of feedback take the form of reinforcement to learners (such as video-assisted); relate to goals; provide information on correct rather than incorrect responses; build on changes from previous attempts; and pose a low, as opposed to high, threat to self-esteem. The VERP shared review is a form of feedback but it goes further; it builds on trainees' strengths, focuses on video showing their better than usual performance and tracks the improvements in their self-set targets over several sessions.

There are an increasing number of studies and meta-analyses that show that one of the critical success factors in an intervention is that it works through building relationships (Murphy 2008). For example, Lakey and Orehek (2011) hold that sharing activities and ordinary conversations, which are the stuff of relationship-building, have more impact on stress than problem-based talk: 'RRT [relational regulation theory] predicts that social support and psychotherapeutic interventions will be more successful if designed to reflect relational influences' (p.490). The relationship between guider and trainee in the VERP context is as important as between guider and client in VIG. Adults, just as much as children, need to feel secure before they can explore difficult issues, and the skill of the guider in a VERP context is to build that safe relationship with the trainee (Landor 2014). Attachment relational behaviours of care-seeking, whether of an adult or child, depend on sensitive attunement, repair and empathic responsiveness from the caregiver (McCluskey 2005), as is modelled in the VERP trainee–guider relationship.

Mentalization, or metacognition – 'thinking about thinking' (Fonagy 1991) – is an important component in the development of self-regulation and securely attached relationships (Fonagy *et al*. 2004). Mindfulness (attunement to one's own mental state; see Kabat-Zinn 1990/2013) and mind-mindedness (attunement to the other's mental state; see Meins *et al*. 2011) are part of mentalization; together they enable a person to interpret the behaviour of others and to regulate one's own behaviour within interactions in a relationship. It is this high level of metacognition, brought about by VERP trainees microanalysing video of their own work practice and reflecting on their development of attuned interaction that is one of the main distinguishing features of VERP.

The role of the VIG-trained guider in a VERP shared review is thus fundamental to the method. Guiders model the principles of attuned interactions and guidance whilst focusing on the interactions of the trainee with their client or interaction partner (Šilhánová and Sancho 2011). VERP guiders may be from the same or from a different agency as their trainees, and their job status need not be higher; their skill is in the facilitation of reflective practice. The VIG practice of sensitive naming of thoughts, feelings and contradictions can avoid the potential difficulties of supervising across professions and paradigms (Callicott and Leadbetter 2013). Looking at one's work practice in minute detail can make any trainee feel exposed and vulnerable. It is the responsibility of the guider to build a safe relationship to contain this (Hawkins and Shohet 2012; Scaife 2010), whilst upholding as the prime concern the needs of the trainee's client, who is virtually present in the shared review through the video.

VERP can also harness the power of the group in learning, through peer coaching (reciprocal relationships with peers and colleagues) or mentoring (by a more experienced colleague) (Hawkins and Smith 2013): 'Potentially the group *is* the supervisor…[containing] not only the resources of supervisor and each group member, but…the rich creativity of a complex living group system' (Proctor 2008, p.12). The constructivist 'reflecting team' method, whereby the rest of the group observe during the shared review of the guider and trainee and then discuss together their reflections, can add structure and metacognition to the group process (Prest, Darden and Keller 1990).

In the VERP model there is a further step, as guiders also reflect on and develop their own professional skills through analysing their interaction with the trainee. As part of their AVIGuk accreditation, VERP guiders are expected to engage in regular intervision (peer supervision) where they share and reflect on video of their own practice as guiders. Guiders have relational agency that is central to their ability to work with trainees. Relational agency is the 'capacity to engage with the dispositions of others in order to interpret and act on the object of our actions in enhanced ways' (Edwards and D'Arcy 2004, p.147). It is a capacity to offer support, 'not dependency, but a capacity to both seek and give help when engaging with the world' (Edwards and Mackenzie 2005, p.294).

Conclusion

VERP is a complex construct, applying the core principles and methodology of VIG to professional development. There are therefore many interweaving theoretical models that can explain 'how and why it works'. In this chapter I have focused on some that I hold significant, but this is inevitably a subjective selection. It is one of the aims of this book to trigger further research on VERP, which will doubtless bring to light many other theories and models.

Part Two

APPLICATIONS OF VERP

CHAPTER 5

Perinatal and Infant Mental Health

Using Video Enhanced Reflective Practice (VERP)

Angela Underdown

Introduction

Infants are born socially interactive, and the way in which their psychological, emotional and social development unfolds is largely dependent on the nature of the relationships in which they participate. They have an innate desire to connect with others and, while many will develop within the context of loving attuned relationships, others may experience insensitivity that impacts on the way the brain wires and emotion and behaviour is regulated. Increasing recognition of the importance of early sensitive care as a foundation for optimal development has driven the search for interventions that can enable relational changes to take place. Relating to infants in a sensitive, reflective way can be challenging, especially for individuals who themselves have never experienced such care, or who have little 'space in their minds' because of life pressures or mental health difficulties, or both. Observing interaction on film is a powerful medium to enable parents to create space where their own positive communication patterns can be explored, reflected on and developed. In parallel, practitioners who aim to help parents and infants develop loving, attuned interaction patterns also need time to reflect on their own communication with families. Video Enhanced Reflective Practice (VERP) encourages deep reflection about the Video Interaction Guidance (VIG) principles of attuned interactions and guidance (Kennedy, Landor and Todd 2011) as they become consciously embedded within practice. Observing parent–infant interactions provides 'a systematic view of the origins of the processes of relatedness itself' (Beebe and Lachmann 2002, p.xv), and an exciting realization that effective adult-to-adult patterns are mirrored in optimal parent–infant communication.

VERP enables exploration of the micro-moments of interaction, and it focuses specifically on developing the communication skills of the practitioner, whereas VIG focuses on guiding parents to reflect on their own successful interactions with their infant. Infant mental health practitioners who undertake VERP become increasingly aware of the parallel process of optimal interaction played out in healthy parent–infant relationships. Thus VERP will support practitioners to consciously model attuned interactions when supporting families and, if using a VIG intervention, practitioners can reflect on the parallel processes on film.

The chapter begins by outlining how pioneers in the Netherlands have developed the use of VERP to enhance practitioners' skills in supporting parental bonds with their infants. This is followed by a summary of the crucial nature of early interaction and the impact on infants' development, now and in the future. Two examples follow to show how VERP is being developed to support infant mental health practitioners' skills. The first illustrates how VERP enabled a health visitor to reflect on her skills when working with a mother and baby, and the second describes practitioners reflecting on their group facilitation skills.

Background to using VERP in early infancy

Parenting is the most sensitive of activities, often fraught with feelings of not being good enough in a culture that sometimes criticizes and blames parents. Bruschwelier-Stern (2004) highlights the perinatal period as time when women and men are psychologically vulnerable, needing acceptance and validation in their new roles. Practitioners' communication with parents therefore seeks to validate their roles and ensure nothing undermines delicate emotional bonds. Psychologists Harrie Biemans and Saskia van Rees in the Netherlands understood the sensitivity of early parental bonding and pioneered the medium of video to scaffold (support) parents to themselves discover positive interactions with their infants. Over the past quarter of a century in the Netherlands, the use of video to support early relationships has spread rapidly, and Marij Eliens developed a training programme for pedagogic workers and nurses in maternity units to ensure that high-quality guidance is offered consistently. VIG methodology focusing on professional–patient communication (in the UK now called VERP) developed as a powerful method for highlighting and developing practitioners' interpersonal communication skills. As child protection refocuses towards early preventative practice, there is an increasing imperative to skill practitioners so that they can scaffold parents to be sensitive, reflective interactional partners for their children. The next section outlines the crucial early development of interaction within relationships, and offers a rationale for the importance of using VERP to support infant mental health practitioners' skills.

Infants are socially interactive

Infants' optimal development depends on being nurtured within loving relationships. Infants' brains develop rapidly in response to early interaction, and the evidence from neuroscience, physiology, psychology, biology and psychoanalysis indicates that early care-giving relationships have long-term influences on the way individuals regulate their emotions and behaviour, and how they make relationships (Fonagy et al. 2004; Panksepp 1998; Schore 1994).

Babies are born to relate, and from mid-pregnancy the unborn child begins to recognize familiar sounds (Underdown and Barlow 2012). Newborns innately prefer to look at faces and can discriminate amongst surprise, fear and sad expressions in caregivers, and produce corresponding facial expressions of their own. Babies show preference for their parents' voice, face, smell and touch. Infants are able to detect contingencies between what they do and what the environmental response is to their actions, thereby facilitating an early sense of agency; they also develop schemas about what to expect from social interactions based on earlier experiences (Beebe and Lachmann 2002). Interactions not only stimulate the way neurons in the baby's brain connect, but also the way in which chemicals such as hormones and neurotransmitters work. Loving interactions are likely to stimulate 'feel-good' hormones such as serotonin, dopamine and oxytocin, which are particularly linked with close, loving touch (Music 2011; Uvnas Moberg 2013). This is a two-way process; Strathearn *et al.* (2008) used magnetic resonance imaging (MRI) scans to investigate first-time mothers' chemical responses to their own infants' expressions, and reported activation of extensive dopamine-associated reward-processing brain networks in response to their infant's happy face. Unpleasant or frightening interactions result in different and complex chemical responses, with the release of cortisol and adrenalin.

Early experiences of seriously suboptimal parenting, such as persistent neglect and trauma, have been shown to result in overdevelopment of the neurophysiology of the brainstem and midbrain (leading to anxiety, impulsivity, poor affect regulation and hyperactivity), and deficits in cortical function (leading to difficulties with problem-solving) and limbic function (leading to a reduced capacity for empathy) (Gerhardt 2004). Research shows that early disturbances in parent–child interactions are implicated in a range of longer-term adverse child cognitive and emotional outcomes, including behavioural problems (Kobak and Madsen 2008). These findings have major implications for furthering understanding of the neuro-scientific processes that underlie attachment and for the possible impact of interventions, such as VIG (Kennedy *et al.* 2011).

Which aspects of parenting are important for infants?

Sensitivity and warmth, conveyed through eye contact, voice tone, pitch, rhythm, facial expression and touch, have long been identified as crucial elements in healthy interactions. When two people are attuned (Stern 1985), an empathetic understanding of shared emotions is experienced. However, infant and adults are not attuned all the time, and it is through frequent healthy 'ruptures and repairs' of attunement that much learning about interaction and the regulation of emotions and behaviour happens. 'Serve and return' is a concept used by the Center on the Developing Child at Harvard University in the US to describe the reciprocal interaction between a baby and parent.

Reciprocity involves turn-taking, and occurs when infants and carers are involved in initiating, sustaining and terminating interactions. Infants learn about their emotions by seeing them mirrored in the face of their caregiver, for example when a parent shows a contingent response to an infant such as looking sad when the baby is crying. It is important that mirroring is 'contingent', to show the infant that their emotion is understood, but also that it is 'marked' or sufficiently different to demonstrate that the parent is not overwhelmed and that the emotion can be managed (Beebe 2004; Gergely and Watson 1996). When parents soothe their baby, they are helping the baby to regulate emotions, both now and in the future. Increasing understanding about the sensitivity of interaction has extended the focus to the importance of parents treating their infants as 'agents' in their own right, with their own individual temperaments and underlying feeling states. This understanding enables parents to closely connect with their infants because they can reflect on their unique characteristics. The capacity to mentalize (think about their infant's behaviour and their environment from the infant's point of view) relies on parents adopting a reflective stance so they can wonder about the meaning of their infant's behaviour. Parents who can mentalize will approach a confusing situation with curiosity and interest as they try to make connections between their child's feelings and behaviour (Underdown 2013).

Creating a reflective space

Helping parents to take a reflective stance is highly skilled and sensitive work where a practitioner creates enough stimuli for the parent to discover what is happening in the moment of communication

(Underdown 2013). The word 'enough' is important, because this is not about directing or telling parents what they should be doing; it is about creating a reflective space where individuals can draw on resources to work things out for themselves. For example, a practitioner showed a short video clip to a parent who was concerned about his relationship with his baby, who had been nursed in the neonatal unit for several weeks. The clip showed the baby reaching out and smiling as he touched his father's finger and looked up towards his face. The father acknowledged the baby's smile, and the practitioner simply said that she was wondering what had happened to make the baby smile. The father reflected on how he had taken time to respond attentively to his baby's initiative. He was pleased to make this discovery for himself, and remarked on how these micro-moments of interaction are usually missed.

Perhaps this example makes creating an exploratory reflective space seem simple, whereas in reality it takes much thought and skill. Clients may have been previously disaffected from services, so building an initial trusting, attuned relationship for strengths-based work can involve considerable effort. It can also be challenging for practitioners to shift from an advice-giving, educative or assessment role to facilitating reflection and exploration. Although cognitively the differences between didactic and facilitative approaches are easily understandable, it can be hard to change one's style, and practitioners often benefit from using VERP when considering what works best within their own communication patterns.

Practitioners reflecting on their own practice with parents and infants

Many practitioners conduct sensitive work within the confines of home visits or a busy clinic environment. If practitioners are to support early parent–infant relationships effectively in practice, they need opportunities to reflect on their own communication style. Creating a reflective space, focusing on film of selected communications, can enable practitioners to become mindful of how they can best guide parent–infant interaction and promote parents' confidence without adopting an advice-giving stance. VERP offers a structured framework where practitioners select video clips of themselves in a work situation to bring to supervision. The VERP guider and practitioner together microanalyse what is going well, replaying to watch for details for discussion. As part of a postgraduate module, practitioners were asked to bring a short film of themselves working with a client. The following case vignette outlines a first VERP supervision session with a health visitor (HV) who had videotaped herself working with a new mother who was stressed with a fractious infant.

The HV had watched the video by herself prior to supervision and felt things were a 'bit slow' in the film, and she wondered whether this was because she had been anxious not to appear as 'the expert who could calm the baby'. After watching the first short clip together, the VERP supervisor asked the HV what she saw herself doing, and she responded:

> You see, as we are discussing it now, I think I have a calm manner. When I was looking back at the video it surprised me how quiet I was actually and the whole thing seemed a bit slow but now I feel quite pleased at how I was talking to the baby.

The HV had stepped back to watch the mother and the infant on her lap. Her stance was showing friendly concern and she gently addressed the baby, repeating 'What is it then, what's happening?' Her eye contact and gentle voice tones gradually helped the baby calm and regulate his emotions. The HV included the mother by moving her gaze and warm questioning facial expression towards her. After watching the film the HV thought the mother found it helpful to be calm, especially with a baby who was fractious. The HV explained that she could see on the film how she and the mother were together trying to understand the baby:

> Because he is spending a lot of time in that fractious state and certainly taking a little bit of time to say this is him, this is what he does... I can see now that me modelling chatting to him is very helpful.

The HV was asked how she felt the mother was feeling as her baby calmed, and the film was rewound so that the mother's responses could be observed. The HV studied the mother's facial expression and broke into a broad smile as she observed how pleased the mother looked.

In a few minutes of film, the HV was able to see for herself that there was a great deal happening. The calming aura she created was necessary for the work to begin, and it seems likely that directing her 'wondering' aloud about what was wrong directly to the baby, took pressure and possibly guilt feelings away from the mother, who noticeably relaxed. The baby also calmed and relaxed, perhaps feeling understood because his sadness was mirrored in the HV's facial expression and contained by her soft tones. The HV had been initially mindful about not disempowering the mother, and she identified from watching the film that she had achieved this by being calm, listening, wondering and talking directly to the baby. By relaxing the atmosphere and wondering aloud to the baby about his distress, she had created a reflective space where the mother might become free to mentalize about her baby's feelings and experiences. The unspoken and spoken message portrayed by the HV in the film was about accepting and getting to know the baby, and puzzling and wondering together with the mother. Without the film evidence, processes such as this can be difficult to articulate in our fast-moving, solution-focused culture. After the session the HV commented:

> Before my [VERP] session, I was a bit negative about the video clips, and very critical of how I looked on film! However, I was surprised at how quickly I forgot about that. [VERP guider] was very skilled at enabling us to look closely at the details of my interaction…and encouraged me to look positively at my skills. I wasn't sure what to expect from the session, and was surprised at how much it encouraged me to really think about what I was seeing in front of me… It felt like a really rich learning experience, and very affirming of the skills that I was rather reluctant to acknowledge.

VERP uses a strengths-based approach, building on microanalysis of what is going well and, in this example, the HV could clearly identify benefits of her actions for both mother and baby. The relationship between the VERP guider and practitioner is based in theories of intersubjectivity (Trevarthen and Aitken 2001) and focuses on strengths while jointly identifying working points. This creates an accepting, respectful relationship, fostering confidence to discuss different approaches and development points. In the next example, VERP is used in a group setting.

Using VERP to support group facilitation

This example describes a perinatal group programme and the part that VERP can play in enhancing group leaders' facilitation skills. The Baby Steps Programme, consisting of nine interactive group sessions, aims to prepare expectant parents for the emotional and social transition to parenthood. Each group is led by two facilitators who seek to establish trusting attuned relationships to encourage parents to fully engage with the programme. The programme encourages and guides parents to reflect on and respond to their babies' feelings and needs, and aims to support strong relationships between partners and wider support networks. Baby Steps facilitators aim to create a reflective space where parents can feel received and affirmed so that they can hear others and develop their own thinking. During the training to lead the programme, a number of activities aim to enable facilitators to take a reflective stance. For example, facilitators are encouraged to keep a journal and record reflections about their own communications patterns. Peer reflections are also encouraged, so when an effective interaction is noted, any member of the group might record it on a Post-it note and place it in a personal envelope for the colleague to reflect on later. For example:

> I liked the way you affirmed Mary's comment by smiling, pausing for a moment and then saying that was such an interesting point and one you had not previously thought about, before smiling and asking the rest of the group. Mary's face lit up because you made her feel so valued.

The aim of this observational activity is to heighten awareness and focus on how facilitators:

- create and maintain the group atmosphere

- activate parents and infants to participate

- receive communication from group participants
- affirm group participants' communication
- create a space for reflection.

To further develop this process, trainee facilitators are asked to make a ten-minute video recording of themselves leading an activity of their choice in a Baby Steps session. The trainee chooses three very short clips from this video that they are pleased to show to their supervisor and peers.

Figure 5.1 VERP supervision session with Baby Steps facilitators

The photograph shows a practice group of trainee facilitators who are, in turn, looking and reflecting on their own film clips. This group was focusing on how reception of clients' comments might encourage participation and increase confidence. For example, there was warm reception of comments from one facilitator when expectant parents were discussing ways to relax, validating suggestions with responses such as:

Yes, that's a good one, I bet that works for lots of people.

That's a really nice one, what a good place to start.

This contrasted with her response when one pregnant woman suggested relaxing by having a cigarette – the facilitator replied neutrally, and without judgement:

You find that works for you, do you?

Discussion among the group centred on microanalysing different ways of facilitating responses and the impact on the clients, while maintaining an open, trusting atmosphere. Baby Steps facilitators have to balance taking a non-judgemental, encouraging stance with ensuring healthy choices are promoted (for example, smoking was raised later in the context of the developing baby, at a time when the parent was able to engage). This first VERP session focused on creating an attuned environment and microanalysing how individuals in the group are 'activated' to participate and how responses are received. The focus for each subsequent group supervision was chosen collaboratively. Reflecting on the video in a small group through the VERP process seems to add to the depth of the learning experience for all concerned.

VERP, firmly situated in theories of intersubjectivity and attunement, helps practitioners to become consciously aware of their own verbal and non-verbal communication patterns and the responses elicited. Observing practitioner–client (including parent and infant) communication on film enables reflection on clients' experiences of the interaction, and how best to engage in work with them. In the first VERP example, the HV was able to explore how she modelled acknowledging the infant as a participant in his own right. By using VERP to aid reflection on their own practice, practitioners can more effectively create a space where parents can reflect on their developing infant's feelings and agency, and how their interactions can enhance this. This is a powerful parallel process for infant mental health practitioners, who seek to support parents to develop a reflective stance and develop attuned interaction with their infants.

CHAPTER 6

Getting to the Heart of Nurturing Relationships in Schools

Exploring Teacher Mind-mindedness through Video Enhanced Reflective Practice (VERP)

Kirsty Quinn

Within schools, there has been a significant increase in the development of relational and therapeutic interventions in seeking to meet the needs of children presenting with confusing, withdrawn or challenging behaviours. Bomber (2011) applies attachment theory to the classroom, with the aim of helping teachers to understand the motivations behind some children's behaviours. She highlights the central importance of relationships in working effectively with young children who have experienced attachment difficulties and developmental trauma, and the need to use daily interactions as opportunities for learning and growth.

Attachment theory (see Bowlby 1988) remains a dominant theoretical framework in understanding children's social and emotional development and emotional regulation. Bowlby proposed that through early child–caregiver relationships, the child develops an internal working model of self, others and relationships which provides the basis of their identity and relationships. Maternal sensitivity (Ainsworth *et al.* 1978) was thought to be the key mechanism through which children's attachment security developed, and how patterns of attachment were transmitted through generations.

However, the empirical link between maternal sensitivity and attachment security has been found to be variable, leading researchers to explore other aspects of maternal beliefs and behaviours that might better predict children's attachment security. 'Parent mentalization' has been presented as a key mechanism (Sharp and Fonagy 2008). Mentalization refers to the parent treating the child as an individual agent, and acknowledging their subjective experience and internal mental states. This involves the adult taking a curious or interpretive stance in seeing the world from the child's point of view and considering what the child might be feeling or thinking.

While mentalizing refers to the parents' 'offline' representations of the child as an individual psychological agent, mind-mindedness (Meins 1997) refers to how the parent uses those representations within an interaction in an 'online' way. Meins refers to mind-mindedness as the parent 'tuning in' to what the child may be thinking or feeling in the moment, and talking about their infant's thoughts and feelings while interacting with them.

> a person's sense of self arises from the experience of being in the minds of others, without which it simply does not develop. (Music 2011, p.7)

Research to date shows that higher levels of maternal mind-mindedness at an early developmental stage (measured by mothers' use of attuned mind-related comments) are linked with a range of positive outcomes including children showing greater theory of mind at age four (Meins *et al.* 2013a), greater emotional understanding (Meins and Fernyhough 2013) and fewer behavioural difficulties in children from lower socioeconomic status families (Meins *et al.* 2013b).

To date, studies into mentalization and mind-mindedness have focused primarily on parent–child interactions. Little is known about the role of mentalization and mind-mindedness with key adults beyond the role of parents. Recent research in early years settings has begun to explore teachers taking an interpretive stance in making sense of children's mental states that may lie behind their behaviours. For example, Degotardi and Sweller (2012) explored practitioner mind-mindedness during one-to-one play scenarios with infants. They found that 19 per cent of practitioner comments referred to infants' mental states, and they highlighted the rich opportunity for attuned metacognitive talk within childcare settings.

What role might teacher mentalization and mind-mindedness play in working with school-age children who might have experienced difficulties related to attachment security? To what extent is teacher mind-mindedness a key predictive factor in the development of secure teacher–child relationships and in how children behave and regulate their emotions? Bomber (2011) suggests that the key adult must work in partnership with the child, taking an interpretive stance in aiming to understand what the child's behaviour might be communicating. The key adult helps to 'translate' what is going on for the child through using a 'reflective dialogue'. This involves the adult observing, commentating and wondering aloud about what the child might be experiencing, thinking or feeling, verbalizing what is usually left unsaid. This reflective dialogue appears to be consistent with maternal mind-mindedness, and is thought to help children in building their self-awareness and in regulating their experiences, sensations and emotions.

This chapter describes a project using Video Enhanced Reflective Practice (VERP) to explore and extend teacher mind-mindedness within a nurture group setting (see Bennathan and Boxall 2000). A nurture group is a short-term targeted intervention for groups of six to ten children presenting with social, emotional and behavioural difficulties thought to be associated with lack of attachment security. Nurture groups are based on attachment theory, and aim to provide a structured, nurturing, learning environment with a key focus on building secure child–teacher relationships. The use of VERP in this project served as both an exploratory intervention tool working in partnership with school staff, and as a research tool to look at changes in behaviours over time.

Using VERP to explore teacher mind-mindedness in nurture groups

The project set out to use VERP to explore and extend teacher mind-mindedness within nurture groups. The first aim was to explore the proportion and nature of attuned mind-related talk by the teachers in the nurture groups, and second, to consider the extent to which this mind-related talk increases over time as teacher–child relationships develop, and in response to a VERP intervention. Finally, consideration was given to the impact of teacher mind-mindedness on teacher–child relationships and on children's behaviour and use of emotional regulation strategies.

The aims of VERP are typically framed in terms of the 'attunement principles' and focus on enhancing greater client sensitivity to another person's initiatives leading to more effective interactions. VERP has at its core the theory of intersubjectivity where intersubjective attunement incorporates the adult's interpretations of the child's intentions, thoughts and feelings that lie behind the child's behaviours. Intersubjective attunement would appear to incorporate aspects of mentalization, where the parent holds representations of the infant's emotions, attention and intentions, and mind-mindedness where the parent engages in a reciprocal exchange with the infant, responding to the infant's mental state. To date, VERP has not been used to focus specifically on client mentalization or mind-mindedness.

The project was carried out across six nurture groups within a local authority in the UK over a period of two school terms (six months). The nurture groups were all within schools identified as having a relatively high number of children presenting with social, emotional and behavioural difficulties and in areas of high social deprivation. The schools had all demonstrated interest in building on nurturing principles and practices at a whole-school level. Each nurture group was run by a teacher and a teaching assistant (referred to throughout as teachers) for children aged four to seven.

The VERP intervention process

The teachers from three of the nurture groups participated in an initial two-hour workshop introducing them to the theoretical and empirical background and to the VERP methodology. Within the workshop, research into parent mentalizing and mind-mindedness was explicitly highlighted, along with Bomber's practice recommendations regarding reflective dialogue. Mind-mindedness was emphasized as a key element of the attunement principles. The group practised identifying examples of attuned mind-minded interactions through analyses of videos of parent and teachers interacting with infants and children. At the end of the workshop the teachers identified key goals that they wished to work on in their own practice.

The teachers from each nurture group participated together in a series of three shared reviews over a three-month period. They prepared for each review by arranging for a short video to be taken during group activities with the children. They reviewed the clips, identified interactions that they were particularly pleased with and highlighted examples of attuned mind-minded interactions in line with their goals.

During the shared reviews, the clips were reviewed and discussed with the VERP guider. The guider aimed to facilitate reflection on how the teachers interpreted the children's behaviours and mental states (intentions, beliefs, feelings) within the interaction, and to identify and further explore teachers' attuned interactions, mind-related comments and behaviours. The guider also extended the reflections to consider how this impacted on how the teacher thought about the child and the representations the teacher held about them (akin to parent mentalizing). At the end of each session, goals were reviewed and aims for the subsequent video discussed.

The research design

As teacher mind-mindedness may well develop over time in line with the development of the adult–child relationships and not necessarily as a result of the VERP intervention, the nurture groups were split into two groups. Three of the nurture groups were randomly selected to participate in the VERP intervention, with the aim of offering the remaining three groups the VERP sessions at the end of the two-term period.

To track teacher mind-mindedness over time, two 12-minute videos of breakfast time discussions were taken in all six nurture groups at the beginning and end of the project period. Breakfast time in nurture groups is intended to be a free-flowing quality discussion time between the adults and children, where personal stories and narratives are shared and explored. The teachers first familiarized themselves and the children with the camera so that it was not a novelty or distraction for either them or the children.

The adult talk in the videos was transcribed and coded with reference to the mind-mindedness coding scheme (Meins and Fernyhough 2010). The scheme seeks to identify all mind-related comments made within an attuned interaction. Mind-related comments are defined as those comments that 'use an explicit internal state term to comment on what the infant may be thinking, experiencing, or feeling' (p.4). All mind-related comments were identified on the transcripts, and then the video was watched again to consider whether each statement was attuned to the child's perceived mental state. Mind-related comments that referred specifically to children's emotions were also highlighted.

Changes in teacher mind-mindedness in the nurture groups over time

There was a high level of engagement and enjoyment amongst the teachers and teaching assistants throughout the project. All reflected on the perceived usefulness of the shared review sessions and the insight and self-awareness they had gained regarding their own interactive behaviours. They also referred to gaining a deeper understanding of how they interpreted children's behaviours and mental states within interactions, and referred to the benefit of having an opportunity to reflect on this in light of their wider beliefs about the children.

The project aimed to consider both the frequency and nature of attuned mind-related comments in the nurture groups. Due to technical difficulties, videos from only four of the nurture groups were available (three VERP and one non-VERP nurture group) from the beginning of the project.

The nurture groups that participated in the VERP intervention showed a greater increase in the use of attuned mind-related comments over time. The frequency of these comments in the three VERP nurture groups increased from a mean proportion of 4.75 per cent of total comments at the beginning of the project to 16.86 per cent at the end. In the non-VERP nurture groups, the proportion of attuned mind-related comments increased slightly from 4.44 per cent (on the basis of videos from only one nurture group) to 7.14 per cent of total comments at the end across the three non-VERP groups.

Teachers in the VERP groups also showed a greater increase in their use of emotions-focused mind-related comments, appearing more tuned into children's emotional states. At the beginning of the project, few of those attuned mind-related comments focused on children's emotions, referring instead to children's cognitions, desires or preferences. At the end of the project, in the VERP nurture groups, the adults were using an average of one emotion-focused mind-related comment almost every two minutes (a total of 33 comments in 72 minutes). In the non-VERP groups, in the final videos, there was an average of one emotions-focused mind-related comment every 10 minutes (a total of seven comments in 72 minutes).

The emotion-focused mind-related comments involved the adults labelling and making commentaries about children's emotional experiences for example, 'I think you're happy today as you've got a really big smile!', and also showed some examples of the adults 'wondering aloud' about the child's experience, for example, 'I wondered if it made you feel embarrassed'.

Changes in child–teacher relationships and children's behaviour

Whilst it is expected that all children will make progress over the duration of a nurture group intervention, for the children in the VERP groups, teacher ratings suggested a greater increase in the level of closeness in the child–teacher relationships (using the Student–Teacher Relationship Scale; see Pianta 2001). Teachers' ratings also suggested that children in the VERP groups were presenting with fewer intense emotions and/or challenging behaviours than the other groups by the end of the project (using the Emotional Regulation Checklist; see Shields and Cicchetti 2001).

This was primarily an exploratory study, and the comparison of children's measures should be treated with caution. There are limitations in using teacher report measures as the participation in the VERP may also have influenced teacher perceptions and interpretations of children's behaviours. Future research would be useful in this area to more fully explore the relationship between teacher mind-mindedness, child–teacher relationships and children's social and emotional wellbeing.

Reflections, implications and future research

The development and value of teacher mind-mindedness

Teacher mind-mindedness based on the use of attuned mind-related comments showed a much greater increase following a VERP intervention over time than without the VERP. It seems likely that VERP helped to accelerate the development of attuned mind-mindedness through reflecting on daily interactions, and focused the teacher's attention on interpreting what children might be thinking or feeling.

Further research is required before drawing any more robust conclusions as to the value of teacher mind-mindedness, over and above teacher sensitivity; however, this project provides some initial support for the hypothesis that teacher mind-mindedness may be a key predictive factor in effective teacher–child relationships and in children's emotional regulation and behaviour. Greater mind-mindedness may lead to the child feeling more understood by the adult, contribute to the formation of closer relationships more quickly and, over time, contribute to the use of more adaptive social and emotional behaviours. This interaction highlights the need to consider children's behaviour and emotional regulation skills within the social, relational and interactional context that they exist, rather than as individual child measures.

In working with the children in the nurture groups there seemed to be a sense of progression in the type of mind-related comments that teachers used over time and that might develop along with the relationship. First, the adults tended to comment on children's cognitions or desires, and later commented on what a child might be feeling. Second, there seemed to be progress in the level of interpretive stance expressed by the adult, first making mind-related comments that related to concrete behaviours (for example, 'you're enjoying that toast!') and later making more interpretations in relation to feelings (for example, 'I wonder if you were feeling disappointed/excited when...'). This progression from labelling and commenting to wondering about feelings and their causes appears to illustrate elements of the reflective dialogue proposed by Bomber (2011).

The value of VERP

While VERP has traditionally focused on sensitivity and attuned interaction, this project provides initial support for VERP as a useful methodology in exploring and extending teacher mind-mindedness within the framework of the attunement principles. Mind-mindedness appears to be implicitly captured within the theory of intersubjectivity and at each level of the attunement principles. As illustrated in this study, there is scope to incorporate teacher mentalizing and mind-mindedness within the VERP methodology in three ways:

- Introducing the concepts of mentalizing and mind-mindedness through initial workshops and providing opportunities for identifying these behaviours within attuned interactions through video analysis.

- Highlighting and exploring attuned mind-mindedness within the client videos during the shared reviews.

- Facilitating reflection on how the client is interpreting the other's behaviours and mental states (intentions, beliefs, feelings) within the interaction, and considering how this impacts on the representations the client holds about the other person (akin to parent mentalizing). This increasing focus on mentalisation within the guiders' comments is illustrated in the diagram below

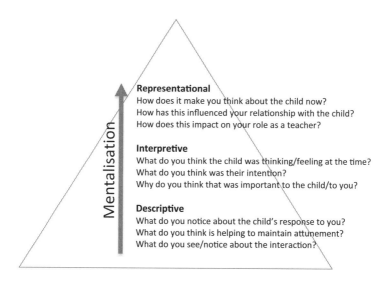

Figure 6.1 Increasing focus on mentalisation during VERP shared reviews

A final reflection refers to the difference between mind-related comments (as measured in this study through the mind-mindedness coding scheme) and mind-related behaviours. During the shared reviews, at times teachers highlighted examples of interactions where they had behaved in a mind-minded way, but had not made a mind-related comment. Indeed, there were occasions where teachers noted that commenting on the child's mental state at that time had felt inappropriate and may have been experienced by the child as intrusive. The absence of mind-related comments in such cases did not make the interaction any less 'mind-minded'. Research that considered both mind-related comments and mind-related behaviours would provide further insight into this distinction. The unique benefit of attuned mind-related comments may be that they help the child both feel secure and attended to whilst helping to make sense of and regulate his or her own emotions and mental states.

Effective, meaningful support and professional development opportunities are essential for teachers working with children presenting with confusing and challenging behaviours. VERP presented as a respectful yet powerful approach that allowed for personal agency, where teachers retained control over their videos and made decisions regarding their own development aims, remaining active partners throughout the process. The VERP process also presented a robust structure for research design, allowing practitioners to explore change over time, and to consider the potential impact of different aspects of successful interactions.

Summary and conclusion

Parent mind-mindedness has emerged as a potentially key predictive factor in children's attachment security and social and emotional development. This project aimed to both explore and extend teacher mind-mindedness within daily interactions in nurture groups with young children through VERP. The concept of mind-mindedness was integrated explicitly with the attunement principles, and brought to life by teachers identifying and building on positive examples of mind-minded behaviours and comments within their daily interactions. VERP appeared to accelerate the development of attuned mind-related comments with a particular increase in teachers' use of emotions-focused comments. It is proposed that mind-mindedness might help strengthen the child's relationship with the adult through children feeling more attended to, understood and valued, and having more opportunities to develop effective ways of recognizing and managing feelings.

VERP provides a sensitive and powerful method for working in partnership with key adults to further explore and understand the role of teachers in children's emotional socialization through daily interactions. Teacher mind-mindedness, as an integral part of the attunement principles, presents a rich and useful framework for those working with these young children that goes beyond teacher warmth and sensitivity, and taps into a professional mindset based on empathy and curiosity.

CHAPTER 7

Making Sure that Teaching Assistants Can Make a Difference to Children

Training that Uses Video Enhanced Reflective Practice (VERP)

Jo Hewitt, Stephanie Satariano and Liz Todd

Teaching assistants comprise 25 per cent of the English school workforce, and yet there remains concern about whether they have any impact on pupil learning and development. This chapter discusses the role that Video Enhanced Reflective Practice (VERP) can play in effective training to enhance the teaching assistant (TA) role of supporting pupils in school. Increased training and support is needed so that TAs can be more child-centred, reflective, strengths-based and encouraging of collaborative problem-solving and critical reflection. We discuss why these qualities are needed and the role that VERP can play in their development. Two small-scale research projects carried out by the first two authors using VERP in the professional development of TAs are discussed. In these examples the TAs reviewed video clips from films of their practice with children one-to-one with a trained VERP guider. The VERP process allows TAs, alongside teachers, to set meaningful goals for themselves and their pupils.

The role of teaching assistants in supporting pupils with special educational needs (SEN)

The 1994 World Conference on Special Needs Education developed the Salamanca Statement, calling for inclusion to be the norm. One way schools attempt to meet the challenge of inclusion is through the employment of TAs. In mainstream English schools, there has been a steady growth in the number of TAs, from 79,000 in 2000 to 232,000 in 2012 (DfE 2013). TAs are often given the most vulnerable pupils to support, yet there is some evidence that they lack the expertise to fulfil this role effectively (Higgins *et al.* 2014). Other research has suggested that TA support for pupils with special educational needs (SEN) has little, no or even a negative impact on pupils' learning and development (Blatchford *et al.* 2009; Higgins *et al.* 2014). The importance of deploying TAs effectively is emphasized by Michael Barber's statement that 'the quality of an education system cannot exceed the quality of its teachers' (Barber and Mourshed 2007, p.16). The Education Endowment Fund, in its evaluation of possible interventions to be deployed using schools' 'Pupil Premium',[1] judged TA deployment to be low-impact and high-cost (Higgins *et al.* 2014). The popularity of TAs with schools and their teachers in the face of research questioning their impact has led to a surge of research to look at when and whether TAs have a positive impact.

A comprehensive review of the research literature on TA effectiveness is beyond the scope of this chapter. However, some key areas may be emphasized. The initial findings of recent randomized controlled studies in the UK using TAs suggest that they can indeed have a positive impact, but not how TAs may best bring about that impact (the projects 'Switching on Reading' and 'Catch-up Numeracy', and from the Education Endowment Foundation 2015). At the heart of effective teaching is quality in teacher–pupil interactions (Webster, Blatchford and Russell 2012). TAs are well placed to develop a strong and trusting relationship with pupils,

---

1 Pupil Premium, UK coalition government policy from 2011 to give additional funding to schools to improve the educational attainment of poorer pupils (those receiving free school meals).

so as to promote all-round development (Blatchford *et al.* 2009; Humphreys *et al.* 2007; Moran and Abbott 2006). They are likely to have more sustained interaction with pupils than is possible for teachers. However, such interactions may be focused more on task completion than on teaching and learning. TAs are likely to have a more positive impact when they are provided with training on the needs of those pupils with whom they are working or on specific approaches and interventions (NFER 2014).

Research suggests that TAs often lack adequate preparation for a more pedagogical role. It is suggested that TA support should add value to class teachers' instruction rather than take on a pedagogical role; this has been described as a 'guide on the side' (Webster *et al.* 2012). Of course, this questions whether the expectations of TAs are realistic, given that guiding skills are indeed part of a pedagogical role. However, guiding skills seem highly likely to be required within a pedagogical role. For example, it was deemed valuable when TAs aimed to activate pupils to become independent thinkers and learners (Blatchford *et al.* 2009; Ofsted 2004), skilfully noting when and when not to intervene so as to guide pupils' thinking to produce meaningful work, rather than supplying answers to complete tasks (Blatchford *et al.* 2009; Moran and Abbott 2006). Thus, it is suggested that the emphasis of TA deployment should be in supporting pupils' development of 'soft' skills, that is, confidence, motivation, dispositions towards learning and collaboration between pupils (Giangreco 2010). The development of such skills requires TAs to show strong interpersonal skills, including empathy, patience and understanding, which we know are key to effective TA support (Moran and Abbott 2006). Such 'sensitive' TA support has been suggested to facilitate pupil engagement in learning and social activities, and to promote their independence (Alborz *et al.* 2009). But how may TAs be trained in this complex variety of 'soft' skills?

VERP as a model of TA training

Training has tended to be through courses covering the many aspects of the TA role (Groom and Rose 2005; Swann and Loxley 1998), and there is insufficient research into the impact of more general courses. However, it is possible that training might need to be focused on key aspects of the entire role. Research suggests that TAs need regular feedback on performance. Ofsted (2010) concluded that the most effective schools have introduced formal observations and regular, formal feedback focused on TA performance rather than pupil performance. Other research finds that specific, strengths-based feedback that takes sufficient account of the impact of TAs on pupil learning seems most valuable (Jarvis 2011; Ofsted 2010). Research also suggests it is important to train TAs to monitor pupils' progress meaningfully as this enables them to acknowledge their impact on pupils' learning and progress (Ofsted 2010).

VERP offers an approach that starts directly with TAs' own practice, involves feedback and supports the development of 'soft' skills. This chapter describes two projects in which the TA works one-to-one with a VERP guider. Together they review clips from a film of the TA supporting the child in a classroom activity. VERP practitioners aim to model and encourage the development of 'soft skills' as well as build a collaborative relationship that activates their thinking. The opportunity to watch and review the video allows for personalized, bespoke training (directly relevant to the needs of TAs and their pupils), and also provides formal observation and specific feedback. VERP has the potential to help increase the sensitivity of TAs. Described as an approach that 'promotes critical analysis, attuned communication and relationships, problem solving and creative thinking' (Glen Strathie Partnership 2014), it places a strong emphasis on promoting effective communication. This is done through analysis of interactions at a microanalytic level. Drawing from theories of mediated learning and intersubjectivity, VERP pays particular attention to the importance of the relationship in learning. Described as an approach that encourages participants to focus on much more than purely academic outcomes (Kennedy and Sked 2008), it aims to be a holistic, child-centred approach to support.

The possibilities for using VERP for TA training are explored in two research projects. Conclusions from these projects are limited by their small scale, the use of self-report rather than more objective measures and the difficulty of attributing causality in complex human situations – more detailed critical rationale for the methods (Project One) can be found in Hewitt (2009).

Project One: VERP with classroom assistants in a primary school setting in Northern Ireland

In 2008/9 four TAs with varying work experience (one to twenty years) working with children with a range of SEN in a mainstream primary setting were recruited for a VERP intervention (also part of a doctoral thesis). The four TAs, each working with one child, participated in five cycles of VERP taking place approximately every two weeks. Each cycle consisted of making a film, then undertaking a shared review. The 10- to 15-minute film was taken with the TA and child (away from the classroom) engaged in an activity of the TA's choice: they were encouraged to think of activities the child might enjoy. A week later, a shared review took place with the TA and the VERP guider (author Jo Hewitt). The shared review consisted of a learning discussion between the VERP guider and TA, looking at three to five very short (15- to 30-second) clips taken from the film, which aimed to highlight areas of strength and key next steps evident from the video. The VERP guider chose the clips. The VERP guider was supervised throughout the study, and consultation took place with Education Board managers.

Methods used to explore the impact of using VERP included:

- semi-structured interviews with the TAs, children and the special educational needs coordinator (SENCo) at the school

- pre- and post-questionnaires completed by the TAs relating to work satisfaction and competence

- pre-and post-questionnaires completed by the TAs relating to child factors (social, emotional, behavioural, adaptive and academic functioning)

- video analysis of the first, third and fifth videos (rated by the VERP guider and by an educational psychologist)

- four months after the cycles had finished, another film was made and further interviews of the TAs and SENCo took place.

Despite methodological limitations, the data suggested that the behaviour and cognitions of all four TAs changed positively as a result of the intervention. Changes seemed individual to the particular TA, having their impact on the greatest areas of need. For example, one TA did not demonstrate a high frequency of encouraging or receiving the child's initiatives (a key principle of attunement: see Kennedy, Landor and Todd 2011, p.28). By the end of the intervention she had made the most progress in this area. By contrast, another TA who was already quite skilled in encouraging and receiving initiatives made most progress in the area of leading and guiding the child – the interaction principle she had demonstrated least at the beginning.

VERP training seemed to impact positively on the relationships between TA and the child. The children were strongly positive about the intervention. They all said they enjoyed the time they had spent with their TA, and felt that their relationships had become stronger as a result of VERP. One TA commented that their child had been through an extremely difficult time in the period between the films. She felt, however, that as a result of the VERP work they were doing, she could help him overcome these difficulties. In fact, all TAs reflected differently about the child they were supporting by the end of the intervention – and recognized that they were doing so. They each felt that they knew 'their' child's strengths better, empathizing and trying to understand them more when problems arose.

TAs all reported benefits for the children in terms of their adaptive skills (becoming more independent), their academic skills, and their emotional and behavioural development. Interestingly, there appeared to be a parallel between TA progress and child progress – the more progress the TA made, the more progress was described for their child. Change in TA and child skills and confidence seemed sustained; indeed, there were slight further improvements in the four-month follow-up film.

TAs felt strongly that time with the child away from the classroom (even just 10–15 minutes once every two weeks) was important in developing a positive, trusting relationship. Rather than isolating children through a 'Velcro effect' (a danger if TAs work solely with one or a small group of pupils, leaving the teacher for the rest; see Balshaw 2010), this actually seemed to improve independence and interaction skills in the children. They thought the VERP training helped to change teachers' views of their role, from one that was purely academic and task-focused to one that was 'relationship-focused'.

The one-to-one VERP training seemed to have an impact beyond the TA and child. The TAs and school SENCo reported that TAs increased their abilities to create and develop sensitive interactions, and that these behaviours had become generalized: not only did the targeted pupil benefit, but so did their classmates. One TA noted that she had shared her personal discoveries about 'what works' with the teacher, and that both of them were learning more – about how to interact with the children and how to support them. The VERP guider also noted that the TAs received support, interest and encouragement from the teachers and school management team that enabled the intervention to be carried out.

Project Two: Using VERP to support pupils with autistic spectrum disorders (ASD)

In 2013 two TAs working with two boys, Chris and Darren, with autistic spectrum disorder (ASD), at different schools, undertook three cycles of VERP with a VERP guider (author Stephanie Satariano). Each cycle involved video recording an interaction between the TA and the boys when they were engaged in an activity of the TA's choice. This encompassed adult-led educational activities and child-led play activities. This was followed by a 'shared review' in which the VERP guider encouraged reflection from the TA on three to five short (15- to 30-second) clips from the film showing moments of positive interaction and connection (according to the principles of attunement: Kennedy *et al.* 2011, p.28). Microanalysis of and discussion of video clips was also underpinned by the SCERTS® framework (Social Communication, Emotional Regulation and Transactional Support), in the hope of enabling TAs to develop their skills and competence to promote the social communication development of pupils with ASD. SCERTS® focuses on building competence in pupils with ASD. It encompasses a detailed framework of assessment and intervention guidelines for professionals working with pupils with ASD. The emphasis is on directly addressing the identified areas of need by developing interpersonal and environmental supports. This is done with the aim of helping a child become a competent and confident social communicator (Prizant *et al.* 2006).

The impact and efficacy of using VERP was explored using:

- video analysis with a checklist combining the principles of attunement and the SCERTS® interpersonal supports
- pupil impact monitoring with the SCERTS® checklists
- confidence monitoring with target monitor and evaluation (TME); this tool uses a rating scale to monitor the development of a target for measuring the perceptions of the impact of intervention (Dunsmuir *et al.* 2009)
- TA's views, sought through a semi-structured interview, post-intervention.

Data analysis suggested a positive impact on the professional development of both TAs as well as the all-round development of the boys. Microanalysis of the video clips and the shared review discussions suggested an increase in the TA's understanding of 'their' child's ability and needs. This finding was triangulated in the post-intervention semi-structured interviews with TAs. They noted that VERP increased their understanding of ways to interact with the boys, based on a clearer understanding of the boys' abilities and needs.

The VERP guider's microanalysis of the VERP video clips illustrated an increase in the frequency and intensity of attuned interactions, particularly in encouraging initiatives, receiving initiatives and building on responses so as to enhance the learning experience. Furthermore, TAs noted that they felt this work facilitated the development of a trusting relationship with pupils.

There seemed to be an impact on the boys' development. Both showed an increased frequency of task completion and engagement with academic tasks. Darren had often been absent from school, and following the intervention, he was back in school on a part-time basis. A significant increase was seen in Chris' social skills, as measured by the SCERTS® assessment checklist. This developed from pure echolalia (repetition of others' words and phrases with no meaning) to spontaneous echolalia (unsolicited repetition of familiar words and phrases) in appropriate contexts, with the addition of his own vocabulary. Furthermore, Chris developed increased competence in securing another's attention prior to initiating an interaction. However, VERP was not the only intervention being experienced by the boys and their parents, so it is not easy to attribute the causality of any pupil impact.

In the post-intervention semi-structured interview, the TAs noted that the microanalysis of the video clips, reinforced by the knowledge obtained by the SCERTS® framework, increased their knowledge of effective strategies to promote the boys' learning and development. They noted an increase in their understanding of ASD and their knowledge of effective strategies, in particular to facilitate emotional regulation and consequent behaviour management. Both noted the invaluable impact video analysis has had on their professional confidence and competence: 'I no longer get overwhelmed when Chris goes into his own world'.

Following the intervention, one TA felt that she had the skills and knowledge to successfully support Darren back into school: 'I have a good understanding of his ability and what engages him… I also feel more competent in adapting these things to get him into school and to get him learning.' Both TAs set targets for promoting the child's development and their own professional confidence; the review of the targets triangulated the above findings, as both TAs met or exceeded their targets. The amalgamation of the principles of VERP with the SCERTS® framework provides promising results.

Conclusion

The findings support the view that VERP as a training tool for TAs deserves further detailed research. In the two projects, training was individualized and seemed to benefit children, TAs and the wider school environment. The aspects of VERP that seem important to the success of the training are a positive, solution-focused approach and sufficiently spaced out training sessions to allow time to prepare videos and put knowledge into practice. TAs noted the importance of assuming a non-expert, collaborative approach, and they all appreciated the highly practical nature of VERP. VERP most often takes place in groups in which the TAs make and analyse their own videos, bringing small clips to a group meeting of other TAs and a guider.

VERP seemed to engage TAs in their own learning and development. By increasing their attunement to them, TAs could help 'their' children develop at a pace and manner that was right for them, accessing support and guidance where needed. The case studies discussed in this chapter indicate that VERP has the potential to provide high-quality training for TAs, and to enable them to provide more valuable, sensitive support for the children they work with. This research also suggests that, with good training and support, TAs can make a difference to children with SEN in mainstream settings.

CHAPTER 8

Connect, Reflect and Grow

Video Enhanced Reflective Practice (VERP) Development in the Early Years

Jo Birbeck, Karen Williams,
Monika Celebi and Annemie Wetzels

Introduction

This chapter is based on the development of Video Enhanced
Reflective Practice (VERP) within early years educational settings.
It gives general reflections on VERP interventions with adults
and children, and practitioners' feedback on the learning process.
These early years VERP courses were developed from the review
of staff development programmes in Dundee (Strathie, Strathie and
Kennedy 2011). Projects from Hampshire, Oxfordshire and the
Netherlands are briefly presented as short case studies. The first
describes the VERP training delivered by Hampshire Educational
Psychology Service for early years practitioners. This exemplifies
their use of 'connect, reflect and grow' as a way to conceptualize
learning within VERP, and describes outcomes for practitioners.
The second briefly describes how VERP in a children's centre in
Oxfordshire has facilitated cohesiveness in the team. The third case
study shows how VERP is used in the Netherlands to coach early
years science teachers, with a pre-test/post-test improvement in the
number of stimulating questions asked by teachers and in the level
of children's reasoning.

VERP engages interest and curiosity in the 'how' as well as the 'what', and in the dynamics of the learning process for oneself, as well as for children, parents and other key adults. It provides a springboard for possible connections and deep thinking, for professional development and change. The VERP model is based on attuned engagement, on trying something new and on reflecting on learning, all of which are integral components of being an active adult learner. The process may be applied to a wide range of educational and training backgrounds, with practitioners at different starting points in their personal and professional development.

Connect, reflect and grow

The essential elements of the VERP approach to learning are captured in the language: to connect, to reflect and to grow. This is a meaningful way to convey the 'how' of learning within VERP.

> *Connect:* This describes the adult's role in the relatedness of attuned interaction, which may be described as a joining of hearts and minds. DiPardo and Potter (2003, p.337) identify that 'emotions are inevitably present in any teaching-learning event'. To connect is to understand the relationship between initiatives and reception, and to recognize that emotions are intimately connected to our thoughts and actions.

> *Reflect:* Through focusing on times of 'connection', there is a fine-tuning of observational skills and analysis of feelings and behaviours within the interaction. While reflecting safely on 'usual or better than usual' moments, one can consider the implications for learning and development (self and others), and the application of this learning to more challenging situations. This is also called 'reflective function' (Fonagy and Target 1997).

> *Grow:* This is the process of change, enabled by connecting and reflecting. It is facilitated by interest, curiosity, following initiatives and a feeling of being energized. It is based on the dynamic interaction within guided learning, and involves engaging with one's own next steps that emerge from the reflective dialogue.

In the independent report for the revised Early Years Foundation Stage (EYFS), Tickell (2011) recommends a better understanding of the quality of interaction in learning and development in the early years. An essential element is 'meaningful interaction between adults and children to guide new learning' (Tickell 2011, p.29). Kennedy, Landor and Todd (2011) provide a detailed framework of the 'principles of attuned interactions and guidance' that underpin VERP courses (see Chapter 1, this volume).

The emphasis on the *quality of interaction* helps to redress the balance from 'what' children can do to 'how' children's learning is facilitated and guided through attuned interactions and mediation in their relationships. The adult adapts dynamically to the needs of individual children and groups of children. VERP focuses on the development of practitioners' self-awareness and their understanding of the impact of their interactions on the quality of engagement and learning of the children or adults they work with.

Early years practitioners, perhaps because of overwhelming pressures of target-setting and recording within their settings, can lose sight of the basic elements that young children need before learning can begin. As Colwyn Trevarthen (2011b) proposes, love comes before play, which prepares for work.

Hampshire project: VERP in mainstream settings

In Hampshire, VERP early years projects were led by Karen Williams, Services for Young Children, and Jo Birbeck, Educational Psychology Service, both accredited VIG guiders. The courses focused on practitioners' and lead professionals' development in working with children with special educational needs (SEN) and in supporting language and communication in mainstream settings (Birbeck and Williams 2013). A training day on attuned interactions and microanalysis of video clips was followed by practitioners taking videos and selecting clips to share for each of three small-group half-day supervisions, finally sharing their discoveries, learning journeys and next steps together. Participant numbers ranged from 12 to 20 per cohort, with preferably two participants from each setting.

'Connect, reflect and grow' (CRG) as a title and explanation was first developed for early years VERP courses for practitioners supporting SEN in mainstream settings (Phillips and Williams 2013). Within these CRG-VERP courses, the fundamental elements of the method enabled practitioners to look carefully at adults' non-verbal communication. They became more aware of how significant their physical position and movements were in their relationship with a child. Through guided analysis of their video clips and reflection in small groups, practitioners recognized that it was essential to all children's emotional wellbeing to be responded to with warmth and fun before learning could be achieved. They learned from their own and others' video clips that children flourish when adults move at a rhythm that is 'in tune' with them, and when language is kept simple and repeated at a pace that the child can process, leaving enough time for the child to have a turn.

In what Paul Wels (2004) calls 'self-confrontation', seeing their successful interactions with a child on video helped practitioners to gain greater insight into their own behaviour. The video acted as a 'neutral messenger, creating a space to jointly (with the attuned guider) examine the possibilities of change' (Wels 2004, p.52). Supported by a VERP guider, practitioners overcame their initial anxiety and self-consciousness as they soon realized that the focus is on successful moments of vitality and connection. Feelings of apprehension changed to confidence and eagerness to make changes in their practice (see the examples below). This positive approach to learning follows the view of Dowrick and Biggs (1983), that showing people videos of themselves failing in problem situations is not conducive to learning and can be destructive.

Examples

By analysing her clips, one practitioner realized how much the child had watched her every movement, and how she had naturally mirrored his body movements, which had helped to keep him on task and extend his play. She then decided she wanted to change her career path and focus more on working with children with SEN.

Another practitioner realized after watching video clips of herself with a child with English as a second language that she wanted to practice 'talking less'. She decided to continue using the principles of attuned interactions, as she had noticed an increase in the child's sounds and vocabulary. She was then able to share her skills with others at staff meetings, thus ensuring a consistent approach was taken across the setting.

Practitioners supporting language and communication development

The Every Child a Talker (ECaT) (DCSF 2008) programme for early years practitioners has been successfully enhanced by a specific and additional VERP development within the Hampshire programme (Keep On Talking, KOT). This enabled a close link to be made between the quality of interaction to support language and communication, and practitioners' development as applied within their early years settings. The initial focus of the programme was on developing the skills of early language lead practitioners, and then involving other early years practitioners. These included nursery and early years workers, childminder coordinators, teachers and teaching assistants.

Evaluation: key themes from the Hampshire project

Qualitative questionnaire data from these early years VERP courses (CRG, ECaT and KOT) have been drawn together under the following three key themes (Birbeck and Williams 2013):

1. Personal communication skills and development: Practitioners were enabled to discover their own individual style and to identify their strengths and the focus for development and change – for example, to do more of, try out, apply to a different context, situation or challenge. These key 'connecting' elements are summarized below:

- encouraging initiatives by watching, waiting and pausing (less talking and fewer questions)
- recognizing a child's initiatives
- repeating and mirroring the child's actions, gestures and facial expressions
- repeating the child's sounds and words
- naming what the child is doing or feeling (tentatively)
- adding something *small* that builds and extends the interaction
- supporting extended turn-taking, creating a 'flow of movement and sound', where turn-taking and cooperation became a natural outcome enjoyed by both.

Looking at their practice on their selected video clips, practitioners learned that they connected best through being emotionally in tune with the children (as described above), which encouraged further initiatives from the child, and created opportunities for sustained shared interest. Practitioners learned that their active reception of children's initiatives enabled the children to initiate even more, and to be active participants in extended turn-taking and in the development of learning. As practitioners' confidence with attuned interactions increased, they were able to give time to connect through naming and to build from where the child was. This led to a greater understanding and depth within their practice. A few practitioners started to reflect on the selective use of open-ended questions.

2. Active adult learning – reflection on the learning process: It is a challenge to create a learning environment where practitioners feel safe enough to be active, to value a 'space to think' and to be inspired in reflective practice within busy working environments. VERP courses helped to energize practitioners, working from a starting point of valuing existing skills and attunement in supporting practitioners' learning. They were engaged in taking and selecting short self-modelling video clips of effective communication linked to new learning and thinking, which enhanced their self-esteem and supported an increase in work satisfaction. They became more motivated and active in creating changes.

Practitioners consistently rated the usefulness of the VERP courses very highly. The spontaneous language of practitioners' evaluations best captures the richness of their engagement, active learning and developing practice:

> It showed me how much more I can see and understand – in myself and in the children, and how to help them.

> Being able to analyse my own skills and use this to improve practice with help from the group sessions.

> A very useful reflective tool – an excellent learning journey for myself.

> It has made us as a setting look carefully at our practice, good for new staff and staff who have been in the setting a long time, it's changed our way of thinking.

Overall, practitioners developed reflective skills that increased their understanding of the impact of their actions on the children's developmental and learning needs.

3. The impact of practitioners' interaction on children's development and learning: By understanding what they did which made a difference, practitioners' development included deeper thinking about the children's developmental needs, tasks and learning. They became more conscious of what children need in order to grow, and this experience was felt as intrinsically uplifting. They valued the time to understand the world of the child better, to become more mind-minded (Rosenblum *et al.* 2008), and to find the language to talk about the child's feelings and needs in different situations. This led to a shift in what was seen as important, and thence to different interactional responses.

Practitioners linked the microanalysis of what they were doing, that is, the specific elements of their interaction, with improved outcomes for children over time. This is an important step in turning Tickell's (2011) recommendation of 'meaningful interaction' into practice. Practitioners' language reporting child outcomes over the three to four months of the VERP courses (see Table 8.1) was grouped broadly into, first, outcomes that relate to the quality of interaction and relationships and, second, outcomes that additionally relate to the identified focus on language and communication.

Table 8.1 Identified child outcomes	
Quality of interaction and relationships	Language and communication
Child: • Feels the adult is interested and listening to them • Feels more confident and is developing trust • Feels enjoyment and pleasure – play and learning is extended • Feels valued and included, that what they are doing is important – shares for longer • Feels understood • Is listening more, exploring and moving on • Is looking towards adult and giving more eye contact • Is copying the adult • Is confident to communicate and express more	Child: • Has increased engagement, attention and concentration • Is given time to think about what he or she wants to say • Joins in, repeats and conversation builds • Extends vocabulary without pressure • Relates words to actions • Is using sentences, not always grammatically correct but improving • Can use language to express feelings • Can express frustration appropriately, which helps to defuse a tricky situation and child finding own solution (emotional regulation was actively supported) • Can take turns and co-operate

Source: Birbeck and Williams (2013)

The analysis of spontaneous language showed that practitioners understood that linking 'hearts and minds' is the foundation for improved practice and better outcomes. The Hampshire VERP project provided experience-based learning that helped them to understand that children thrive on being seen, understood and having their feelings recognized and received, and that this underpins children's emotional wellbeing and educational development.

Oxfordshire project: VERP developments within a children's centre

Monika Celebi, parent–infant psychotherapist and VIG guider and trainer, developed her work using VERP for practitioners' development within children's centres in Oxfordshire (Celebi 2013). This evolved from VIG work with families linked to the centres.

Monika's role as a member of a children's centre team led to a systemic approach, a formal VERP training conducted for all the members of a children's centre team, from the manager to the crèche worker. The team included primary school teachers, nursery teachers and children's centre senior and junior workers. A training day, covering the principles of attuned interactions (Kennedy *et al.* 2011; see also Chapter 1, this volume), and how to microanalyse the video into clips exemplifying these principles, was followed by the trainees videoing each other in their work situation. They then reflected on the videos in small supervision groups over three sessions, facilitated by a VIG guider in training. The feedback was overwhelmingly positive:

> The VERP training can be used in so many different ways. It has been a very positive experience, because we did it as a team. You can watch the clips again and again, and always find something different, and you can look at your interaction with the children in detail and notice things, which you would not remember otherwise.

The VERP training increased cohesiveness in the team. Individual professionals felt empowered and their confidence grew. The centre adopted the language of the principles of attunement to evaluate their 'drop-in' and 'stay and play' sessions. Follow-up training was subsequently commissioned for new team members.

This is an example of how VERP training can enhance the professional development of professionals from many different disciplines, who all have something to contribute and something to learn about themselves professionally and personally, thus improving their interactions with each other and with their clients. It also shows the potential of VERP to encourage a culture change in an organization.

Netherlands project: Video Feedback Coaching for Teachers (VFC-T) – how to teach science to the earliest grades

A focus on developing young children's higher order language and thinking skills in science, through a training programme for teachers, was undertaken in the Netherlands. Annemie Wetzels, Henderien Steenbeek and Paul van Geert (2013) implemented a Video Feedback Coaching for Teachers (VFC-T) programme based on VERP (Kennedy *et al.* 2011) and School Video Interaction Guidance (S-VIB) (van den Heijkant *et al.* 2004). They developed it with the aim of supporting teachers giving science lessons in the early years (pre-school grades 1 and 2, five to eight years old), as a need was identified to support teachers to ask questions that stimulate inquiry by children and to respond to the questions the children ask.

The teaching programme, which is extensively described in a handbook (see Wetzels, Steenbeek and Fraiquin 2011), was theoretically based on the use of scaffolding (van Geert and Steenbeek 2005), the empirical cycle (de Groot 1961) and asking the right questions (Oliveira 2010) in order to stimulate children's science learning. The focus for the project was therefore on developing teachers' pedagogical skills to scaffold and to ask questions that invite children to think within the science framework of the empirical cycle. The participants received information about these elements during the initial training session. After that, the VFC-T provided four coaching sessions with a trained coach using video and microanalysis of teaching moments that encompassed teacher–pupil interaction, teachers' learning goals and questioning. Six elementary school teachers from two schools took part in the programme. With this group, using video coding, two pre-test and two post-test measures were undertaken of children's level of complexity of thinking (skill theory) elicited by the teachers. During the programme teachers asked significantly more questions to stimulate children's reasoning, and the level of children's reasoning also improved significantly. This higher level of reasoning was maintained at both post-test measures conducted two months after the end of the intervention. The teachers positively reported their experience of VFC-T and the guided reflection. They also reported greater confidence and enjoyment in incorporating the teaching of science in their classrooms (Wetzels *et al.* 2013).

When interviewed after the coaching sessions and asked what she thought about the use of the video clips, one teacher answered enthusiastically, 'I think it is amazing. A real eye-opener! You can watch yourself, and if you watch your behaviour, you can see things you normally do not see.' Another responded, 'and then she [the coach]…asked my reaction about the clip, which gave me the possibility for reflection.'

Conclusion

As we have seen, VERP developments in Hampshire, Oxfordshire and the Netherlands seemed to increase practitioners' reflective functioning and create a 'thinking space' for learning and professional development. Within the early years, this model of active adult learning was applied to staff development and working practice with families and early support, SEN, language and communication, and science teaching for young children. Other potential areas for staff development through VERP include supporting social and emotional needs, language for critical thinking and learning, and becoming effective learners (Stewart 2011) – in effect, wherever relationships and scaffolding learning are important components of the adult's role. VERP provides the 'attuned challenge' to bring about change and cultural shifts, underpinned by an authentic enrichment of the quality of learning and development. In essence, this is captured simply as 'connect, reflect and grow'.

CHAPTER 9

VERP (Video Enhanced Reflective Practice) as a Leadership Development Tool in the Banking Industry

Maria V. Doria

Introduction

In recent years businesses have experienced rapid globalization due to the technological revolution of the twentieth century. There have been dramatic changes in the demographics of the labour force and of consumers. The world of business is constantly changing, and business leaders have to adapt to the current challenges in hand. This chapter discusses the theoretical and practical relevance of Video Enhanced Reflective Practice (VERP) as a leadership development tool, and presents a case study applying VERP in a financial banking unit, with the director as the main client of the intervention.

In the past, firms needed to expand in order to attain sufficient scale to develop global distribution networks, attract global talent pools and to create profit and employment. In contrast, an emerging revolution in modern economics means that relatively small firms are able, through technology, to achieve the same scale, giving them major advantages in speed, agility and responsiveness in a competitive world. Now the emphasis is not on size and control, but on flexibility and communication. The good news is that talented people, regardless of gender, race or ethnicity, have a greater opportunity to create and lead global businesses, but entrepreneurs, leaders and professionals in general need to be aware that they are operating in a world that is more diverse, volatile and complex than before. Company success is more closely linked to the ability to respond efficiently to the changing needs of its global and multicultural clients and partners.

Recent literature consistently suggests that organizational leaders with a transformational style, high relational skills and emotional intelligence are better equipped to lead contemporary organizations (see, for example, Conger and Hunt 1999; Lowe, Kroeck and Sivasubramaniam 1996). Whilst the importance of the leader's interpersonal skills was recognized earlier (see, for example, Blake and Mouton 1978), recent research offers evidence-based studies showing that the leader's relational skills and concern for people positively affect team satisfaction and performance (see, for example, Sarin and McDermott 2003). This suggests that truly effective leaders, as well as having the traditional qualities of intelligence, determination and vision, have skills that allow them to relate to people, to lead and to motivate in the face of new situations.

The discrepancy between executives' technical and relational skills may be linked to the false dichotomy, still present in many business contexts, of viewing 'hard skills' and 'soft skills' as mutually exclusive. 'Hard skills' are often thought of as the occupational skills that provide value and are necessary to complete a job task, while 'soft skills' are often thought to be 'all about feelings' and are considered inferior or less relevant to the task. Traditional myths of leadership offer an image of the leader as the captain of a ship, someone above the group and detached from its influence, rather than as an active collaborator with a particular role in decision-making, both influenced by and influencing the system. The challenge of leadership at any level is necessarily about other people, and currently executives seem to demonstrate a greater need for relational skills training in order to communicate more efficiently with their teams and clients (Carter, Ulrich and Goldsmith 2005). In reality, there is nothing 'soft' about the relational skills of leaders, because relating to people is challenging, more so in our present times where organizations, economies and entire societies are increasingly global, diverse and interconnected. All the scientific evidence in this domain seems to suggest that yesterday's soft skills are the hard skills of today's organizational world. However, a relevant question is how relational skills may be developed in an effective and sustainable manner.

Although increasing numbers of professionals are returning to tertiary institutions at various stages of their lives to address these changes in their work roles (Watson *et al.* 2003), education is often criticized for a lack of responsiveness and adaptability to the specific needs of professionals and organizations (Boyatzis and Kolb 2000). In fact, research suggests that the consistent preference of successful executives is for on-the-job coaching or action learning interventions (Carter *et al.* 2005). In response to this, other forms of professional development, such as coaching or mentoring, both internal and external to the organization, have emerged as successful tools for task-specific adult learning within the workplace (see, for example, Ragins and Kram 2007). These relationship-based interventions, involving feedback from experienced workers and psychosocial support, seem to provide greater positive learning and professional performance (see, for example, Higgins and Kram 2001) than traditional training programmes. There is a particularly high demand for training in communication and interpersonal skills in the context of leadership development. Successful contemporary organizations are now beginning to adopt leadership development as a priority strategic measure for enabling organizational change (Carter *et al.* 2005): 'the fantasy that somehow organizations can change without personal change, and especially without change on the part of people in leadership positions, underlies why many change efforts are doomed from the start' (Senge 2003, p.48).

VERP is an intervention to help professionals improve their interaction skills. It developed from Video Interaction Guidance (VIG). VERP, like VIG, works from the premise that attuned responses to the initiatives of others are the building blocks of an attuned interaction pattern (Kennedy, Landor and Todd 2011; see also Chapter 1, this volume). When interpersonal communication skills are lacking, people may give up making initiatives, resulting in very little interpersonal contact and a discordant pattern of interaction. Video clips of the client's 'better than usual' attuned interactions in natural settings are the focus of reflection in a 'shared review' meeting between the guider and client. The same model can apply between leaders and their teams in the organizational context. VERP is evidence-based, cost-effective and cross-culturally applicable. In addition, it is a coaching type of work-based training that can offer businesses opportunities for real and positive change. VERP can be both a preventative and an intervention tool.

The case study

A director of a bank investment unit requested the author's assistance following her presentation on VERP at a business meeting. He wanted to make his communication more effective, as some members of his team were neither performing satisfactorily nor following recommendations. The participating leader and organization were therefore chosen out of convenience. VERP is often carried out in a group setting, but the present example is a single-person intervention. The author, hereafter referred to as the VERP guider, was at the time in training to become a VIG guider. The main goal for the case study was to test the applicability of the VERP method as a leadership development tool in the specific professional context of financial banking, which, in popular culture, is perceived as having low relational sensitivity. Results of this case study will be interpreted, taking into consideration the inherent limitations of generalizability and subjective bias (Mason 2002; Yin 2003).

The VERP client

The VERP client is a 36-year-old male with more than ten years' experience as a financial project manager, currently a director of an investment banking unit in France. He works exclusively with institutional clients in the development of equity business with multicultural teams of financial analysts. The VERP intervention started 18 months after the client assumed this leadership position, and during this time no leadership training has been received.

The intervention procedure

At the first meeting, the client received detailed information about the purpose and procedure of the VERP intervention, and informed consent to participate in the study was obtained. Attitudinal measures (see below) were administered pre- and post-intervention. A one-month follow-up interview was conducted to explore further the effectiveness of the VERP intervention from his perspective, and its potential as a coaching tool for professionals in general and leaders in particular. The VERP intervention comprised two video recordings and two shared review sessions, instead of the three cycles originally agreed, to accommodate the client's schedule. The situations to be videoed were chosen by the client in consultation with the VERP guider, taking into consideration the client's self-set goals (motivating the team and delegating), and the practicalities of daily routines. For example, the first videoed situation was a previously arranged team review meeting. These video recordings lasted approximately 20 minutes and were always undertaken in the usual setting at the office.

It should be noted that in most VERP programmes the client reviews the video and selects examples of their attuned interactions for discussion in the shared review session; however, in this case, pressures of time resulted in the VERP guider taking over this task from the client, making it more like a typical VIG intervention.

Pre-intervention measures

The pre-intervention questionnaire explored the client's personal aims for the VERP intervention, motivation to participate, overall perception of the VERP method, and perceived communication and relational skills. The attitude items were measured using a 7-point Likert scale. Blake and Mouton's (1978) leadership questionnaire was also used to evaluate the leadership style of the participant, and the Inclusion of Other in the Self (IOS) scale (Aron, Aron and Smollan 1992) was used to measure the interpersonal closeness between the leader and his team members. The leadership questionnaire contains 18 statements on leadership behaviour in two main domains: concern for people and concern for task. The level of agreement with each of these statements is measured by a 5-point Likert scale.

Post-intervention measures

The post-intervention questionnaire explored attitudinal measures of general satisfaction and achievement of the pre-established goals, and included the same measures as the pre-test session. It also included three open evaluative questions:

- What were the main factors that contributed to the success of VERP?

- What were the main obstacles to achieving greater success with VERP?

- How could VERP be improved as a coaching tool within your domain of activity?

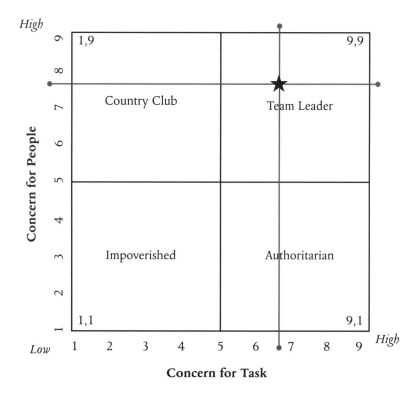

Figure 9.1 Leadership style

Source: Blake and Mouton (1978)
Notes: VERP client's score is indicated by the grey lines and star.

Results and discussion

The client's leadership style scores (people-centeredness score 7.6; task-centeredness score 6.8) suggest a team leadership style that is high in 'task' and high in 'people' (see Figure 9.1). This result confirms that the client is within the effective leader quadrant, but has some room for improvement. According to Blake and Mouton (1978), this score suggests that the client is a person who encourages the team to reach goals as effectively as possible while also working tirelessly to strengthen bonds among the various team members. He is a leader who prefers to lead by positive example, and endeavours to foster a team environment in which all team members can reach their highest potential, both as professionals and as people. Research suggests that such a team leader style positively affects team satisfaction and performance (see, for example, Sarin and McDermott 2003). The client was extremely satisfied with the outcomes of the intervention (giving the maximum score of 7), which was seen by him as effective in the achievement of his two self-set working goals: motivating the team and delegating. He remarked, 'I have learned that by analysing in detail the interaction between myself and the team members there are so many different techniques and strategies that can allow me to improve my role as a leader'. Consistently, the client also indicated he would definitely recommend the VERP intervention to others in the profession, and that VERP was 'an extremely good surprise' for him. Regarding the main factors for the success of the intervention, the client referred to the 'video sessions where certain clips were studied and questioned thoroughly'. The main obstacle to achieving greater success was the 'lack of time'. Finally, in the last item of the post-intervention questionnaire, the client mentioned that the VERP intervention could be a valuable coaching tool in his domain of activity as a 'way of enhancing the intrinsic skills of a leader within his team'. He proposed 'individual video sessions for the leader, but perhaps team members as well, besides maybe a group session with all to better assess how the leader interacts individually and in a group'.

The client already had a positive attitude to the VERP method at the outset of the intervention, as well as a positive attitude about his professional communication and relational skills, as was seen in the pre-intervention attitude measure. Post-intervention results suggested a slight increase in his positive attitude towards the VERP method and a slight decrease in his perceived communication skills.

The client had rated himself at the start as 7 (on a 7-point Likert scale), and at the end of the intervention dropped this to 6. This apparently contradictory result was clarified in the follow-up interview. He justified the downgrade as a consequence of his increased understanding of what communication really is, and the personal challenges he faces in developmental terms. In the client's own words:

> I think this is exactly because when we go deeper in our analysis we understand that we don't know as much we think we know; I now also have a more detailed view on what communication is; I should have maybe ranked myself as a 5 and then gone to 6.

This awareness is a crucial step for change and development, and is consistent with earlier VIG research in family work, where parents score the highest in metacognition and negative self-perception in the second shared review (Doria, Strathie and Strathie 2011).

The follow-up interview allowed for deeper exploration of the client's perspective on the effectiveness of VERP as a leadership development tool. The qualitative statements seem to suggest that the client recognizes the importance of leadership development for everyone's benefit (leader, team and organization), and that he now feels more mature in the leadership role and better able to do a good job. The client describes the VERP as a 'very enriching and insightful experience' that improved his interpersonal skills in many dimensions (for example, positive attitude with team members, encouragement of initiatives, listening and capacity to deal with frustrations) with a long-term impact. In the client's view, the major success factors of VERP were the opportunity to reflect on his practice with the support of the VERP guider and the video. This allowed him to review and understand the situation better than in busy ordinary life, where 'things are rolling'.

With regard to his personal working goals of delegating and motivating the team, the client emphasized that VERP was important to make him a leader with 'better standards'. For improvement to the intervention, the client agreed to the inclusion of team members in the review process, providing 'it is previously negotiated with the VERP guider what information can be shared and what cannot'.

The client also explicitly expressed belief in the potential of VERP as a leadership development and team-building tool. He stated that 'organizations should consider investing time and money in this type of intervention that is highly adaptable to different levels of the organization'. In his view the main challenge for his professional context was the issue of confidentiality and sharing information with outsiders or consultants. As a way of overcoming this, the client suggested that organizations could have a psychologist on the human resources team allocated to do the VERP work. Overall, the client summarized his experience as a VERP participant in this way:

> It has been a very enriching experience…when you use the video and you see yourself, what you are doing and the reactions of others and re-seeing it several times you then understand certain things that you do not understand when things are rolling…the fact that we've studied specific moments of interactions of myself and my team allowed me to assess what is important in my way of working that can be improved to make me a leader of better standards…it helped me to have a more positive attitude with people, the correct posture, encourage initiatives of others, try to listen and to be able to deal with frustration in a calm way…and yes definitely what I have learned still remains with me today.

Conclusion

This chapter contributes to the growing body of VERP literature by offering a new theoretical viewpoint regarding the relevance of VERP as a leadership development tool in today's modern organizational landscape through a practical example from the banking sector. The case study suggests that VERP is a theoretically relevant and effective tool to enhance the interpersonal skills of leaders. Of particular note was the increased level of reflection the manager developed as a result of the VERP process. Despite the limitations of this single case study and the associated challenges, the results open a new avenue for VERP research and practice. Future research should directly test the impact of VERP on improving team dynamics and performance in organizations.

The hardest challenge of leadership at any level is necessarily about other people. Twenty-first-century executives need to develop their communication and relational skills in order to create higher-functioning teams, as societies are increasingly global, diverse and interconnected. The VERP method offers a practical response for leaders who wish to develop their interpersonal skills in an effective and sustainable manner, and top-level management should seriously consider its potential.

Part Three

PROFOUND AND MULTIPLE
LEARNING DISABILITIES

CHAPTER 10

Supporting Interactions with Adults who have Profound Intellectual and Multiple Disabilities as their Skills Deteriorate[1]

Sheridan Forster

Introduction

Adults with profound intellectual and multiple disabilities (PIMD) may be one of the most challenging groups of people with whom to interact. These adults present with PIMD affecting memory, concentration and problem-solving. Additionally, many have severe motor impairments, such that they cannot walk and have limited control of movements, and sensory impairments affecting vision and hearing. Health problems including epilepsy and gastrointestinal problems are also frequently present. Many people with PIMD also take medication to control health conditions, which may contribute to further cognitive difficulties.

1   I acknowledge the financial support of the Windermere Foundation (Australia), the support of the Centre for Developmental Disability Health, Victoria, where the majority of this research was completed, and the staff and residents of Araluen.

Nevertheless, people with PIMD maintain a capacity for engagement with others. They may show interest in a person or objects, and pleasure in the company of another person or in comfort from a familiar hand. They may express a range of emotions in response to experiences. The most frequent interaction partners for many people with PIMD are their caregivers, who are often family members or disability support workers (DSWs).

The innate communicative abilities of people with PIMD have been acknowledged increasingly with recognition that communication involves more than speech. Thurman, Jones and Tarleton (2005) categorized three key approaches to supporting the communication skills of people with PIMD. These are: *profiling approaches* (for example, communication passports or dictionaries documenting the person's communication); *consensus approaches* (processes for discussing and documenting what people believe a person with a disability may feel or want); and *interactive approaches* (strategies and guidance for interacting with people, such as Video Interaction Guidance, (VIG); (see Kennedy, Landor and Todd 2011) and Intensive Interaction (Nind and Hewett 2005)). Important features of interaction between adults with PIMD and their DSWs have often been drawn from the behaviours observed in parent–infant interaction. These include: sensitive responsiveness, joint attention, co-regulation and an emotional component (Hostyn and Maes 2009). These behaviours align well with intersubjectivity and the principles of attuned interactions (Kennedy *et al.* 2011).

Another group of people with complex multiple disabilities, who are becoming more numerous, consists of people with Down syndrome who develop dementia. People with Down syndrome are at particular risk of developing dementia, and do so at a much earlier age than people in the general population (Strydom *et al.* 2010). Prior to developing dementia, people with Down syndrome often present with moderate or severe levels of intellectual disability, may be alert and actively interactive with their environment, and are usually independently mobile (Bittles and Glasson 2004). PIMD is not typically associated with people in this group but, as they develop dementia, their skill deterioration shows similarities with that of people with PIMD, such as reduced cognitive and adaptive behaviours.

They, too, are increasingly reliant on skilled interaction partners in order to have positive interactions with people.

Another similarity between adults with PIMD and adults with Down syndrome and dementia is the necessity for DSWs to adjust their focus on the person's needs. For many in both groups, support needs to be re-oriented to maintaining skills, slowing the deterioration of skills and supporting the person as their skills decrease. DSWs have reported that it is a difficult shift from an ideology of encouraging independence and skill development to that of maintaining or supporting the loss of skills, particularly as the DSWs may at the same time be supporting others who require the former focus of skill building (McCarron and McCallion 2005; Wilkinson, Kerr and Cunningham 2005). The focus on maintenance or support of deterioration is also contentious in an environment in which funding is related to outcomes in the form of improved behaviours by the person with a disability.

Benefits of VERP when working with people whose communication skills are deteriorating

Video Enhanced Reflective Practice (VERP) may be an ideal form of support for people whose skills are few or are deteriorating. Janicki, in his review of quality outcomes in dementia care for adults with intellectual disability in group homes, stated that in quality measurement of dementia care, 'there should be evidence of staff skill sets and functioning, including constructive attitudes towards dementia and the people for whom care is provided, and staff capabilities and resourcefulness to accommodate to resident changes associated with decline' (Janicki 2011, p.772). VERP has the potential to support these quality outcomes.

Supporting discussions of values and culture

VERP provides an environment where the issues of values, power, risk, knowledge and experience can be discussed (Strathie, Strathie and Kennedy 2011). It is an environment in which strategies that align with current paradigms may be observed in practice and named. Alternatively, the lack of fit of the current paradigm with the person with a disability may be carefully observed through real examples, rather than anecdotes, and considered opinion across a group may be developed and advocated with observational evidence.

Staff working with adults with PIMD and adults with Down syndrome and dementia often face many dilemmas in practice (Finlay *et al.* 2008; Forster and Iacono 2008). Both groups are sometimes expected, and indeed may themselves expect, to be able to integrate the dominant paradigms of supporting all people with intellectual disabilities (Bigby *et al.* 2009). Such dominant paradigms currently include enhancing the independence of the person, and having the person direct their own support packages. DSWs may have policies that they are expected to follow, but little support in how to put the policies into practice when supporting adults with the most severe disabilities.

Developing naming skills

When exploring the training needs of staff supporting adults with dementia and intellectual disabilities, Wilkinson and colleagues note that 'while staff might well be doing the right things, they had little confirmation of this' (2005, p.394). VERP responds to this issue by guiding DSWs to see what is working, *naming* this and continuing to do it. The confirmation may come from being more aware of the otherwise tacit skills of support and acknowledgement by colleagues, and can also come from management if they are included in the VERP process.

The development of staff naming skills aids their confidence, as naming can be used to communicate the potential meanings of idiosyncratic behaviours, sharing these observations with people who are less familiar with the person with a disability. This is crucial if the person is unable to express their state clearly in words. The ability to name people's sometimes subtle expressions is particularly pertinent to health management. Since DSWs accompany people with PIMD to health appointments, they are in a position to describe any signs of pain or distress. Regnard *et al.* (2007) have suggested that, while carers may be skilled at intuiting and identifying distress cues, they may have little confidence in communicating their observations. The naming skills acquired through VERP can help to address this issue in populations for whom pain is recognized as an under-reported and under-responded-to problem (Kerr, Cunningham and Wilkinson 2006).

Matching strategies to present needs

No manual will tell you how to work with a person with PIMD or intellectual disabilities and dementia. Their present needs may be quite unlike their needs of ten years or even ten months ago. VERP allows for using the present exceptional interaction as the benchmark for strategies. Rather than asking DSWs to focus on building a person's skills to the next higher level of complexity, the present exceptional interaction shows the person's current highest skills, and supports staff to do more of whatever made it successful.

Conducting VERP over a number of months also aligns with best practice in dementia care training: that training should be delivered over time and respond to the different stages of dementia, as opposed to a single training session (Janicki 2011). VERP, for someone who is using speech and is occasionally confused, may be focused on the higher order skills of guiding or deepening discussions (using the principles of attuned interactions: Kennedy *et al.* 2011; see also Chapter 1, this volume). When the person is in late stage dementia, however, the focus of VERP may be on basic intersubjectivity, letting the person know there is someone attentive to them.

Providing emotional support during a difficult time

McCarron and McCallion (2005) have explored the ways in which DSWs experience stress when supporting adults with intellectual disability and dementia, and their methods of coping. They found that 'observing the loss of skills among individuals with whom they have worked and with whom they have often made huge efforts to help acquire new skills can be trying' (p.143). The deterioration of skills and the change in behaviour can also be distressing. DSWs are aware that they are moving into end-of-life care for an individual, and are supporting the person, and often the people they live with too, through the process of dying (McCarron *et al.* 2010).

VERP provides an opportunity to talk about the interactions that continue to work best, to acknowledge the challenges experienced by all people in a team, and to prepare for the next steps in a person's deterioration.

Case study

VERP was used in a research case study focusing on a woman with Down syndrome and dementia (pseudonym 'Mary'). The aim of the study was to examine the effect of VERP on the interaction between a person with intellectual disability and dementia and five of her DSWs, from the perspective of the DSWs. A university ethics committee approved the study, and informed consent was gained from the DSWs and from Mary's next-of-kin.

Sixty-six-year-old Mary had lived most of her life in supported accommodation, and for more than ten years in her current five-person group home. She had also attended her day service for many years. She had friends both at her home and day service, and occasional contact with her family.

Mary had Down syndrome, severe vision impairment and a hearing impairment. For many years she had walked with a cane. Two years ago she was capable of performing many self-care activities with minimal support, and was very alert to activity around her. However, more recently, she had experienced deterioration in skills attributed to dementia. When Mary became involved in the study she was no longer able to walk independently, and was confused about where she was. She increasingly needed prompting through self-care activities, and was becoming more withdrawn, with prolonged periods of moaning and crying out. She was intermittently alert during short conversations. Her presentation was consistent with mid-stage dementia.

Four DSWs from Mary's home and one from her day service participated in the study. They had supported her for between

18 months and 18 years, and spoke fondly of her, expressing sadness at her deterioration.

The case study was conducted over seven months. The five DSWs participated in a semi-structured interview (audio-recorded), exploring their perception of Mary's interaction skills, the challenges in interactions and their expectation of change. They were given a reflective journal to document their thoughts throughout the intervention. The support workers then participated in a three-hour workshop to learn about the principles of attuned interactions, the processes of VERP and the use of an iPad to record interactions. Subsequently, each DSW made a video recording of their own interaction with Mary, and brought it along to three group 'shared review' sessions, each lasting two hours, facilitated by a trained VIG guider. The gap between sessions was from five to ten weeks and was affected by staff leave periods. At the end of the intervention the DSWs were interviewed again and returned their reflective journals for analysis. In order to ease potential anxiety, and considering the limited parameters of the study, none of the videos used in the shared review sessions was analysed; these remained the property of the DSWs.

During the seven months of the intervention, Mary's skills deteriorated significantly. She became less alert, spending several hours in a drowsy, unresponsive state, screamed during the night and required assistance for all self-care activities. There was increasing uncertainty about the feasibility of caring for her within her group home. However, the DSWs reported that the VERP intervention was very useful. The themes emerging at that time are outlined below.

VERP as a context for discussing practice issues

On my [the author's] first meeting with Mary, a DSW commented on the amount of touch that I used with Mary (in the form of hand holding) during my conversation with her. The DSW said that this had been an area of contention for years, as some said that Mary should be discouraged from engaging with touch with staff, and others used touch with her consistently. Subsequently, the use of touch became a topic of conversation for shared review, leading to staff having rich conversations about its effect on Mary and her DSWs. They became more able to describe why they were doing what they were doing, and sitting holding hands with Mary became a frequently used interaction without reservation.

A shift to intersubjectivity

Prior to the intervention, the DSWs were asked what interacting with Mary was like. Some DSWs appeared to be unable to name intersubjective moments with Mary, describing her only in terms of her current or lost care needs. In the follow-up interview, this shifted somewhat (but not completely), with more moments of intersubjectivity described. For example, in the first interview one person said, 'It's been difficult of late because she really has gone downhill with the dementia part', and then gave further explanation of the behavioural difficulties and deterioration. In comparison, in the follow-up interview, she responded, 'Well, just I muck around with her when I do her toes, and I say, "This little piggy", so just having games with her', followed by a description of the skill deterioration. The VERP process aided an intersubjective framing of interactions.

Appreciating smaller things

The final shared review session touched on whether or not it was all right that Mary would just say 'yes' or nod in response (with no apparent understanding) to what her DSW said to her. While the DSWs acknowledged the desire to have Mary appear to understand and engage further, they also came to a shared understanding that a simple nod was an important response, to be celebrated, in the context of knowing that she would become less responsive over time. This discussion appeared to be quite a shift for several of the staff. One staff member was particularly moved, saying, 'the little things that we thought were just nothing are huge for her, huge, so even splashing her in the bath…not even a minute, and she can have a laugh'. Another DSW said, 'my problem throughout the whole project was that I was looking for far too much… I was trying for a great response, not just the little responses. So I've really got to re-train myself to understand that even those little responses are successes.'

Staying in the moment

In reflecting on the VERP process, one DSW said, 'So if Mary's… being quite responsive to something, just try and stay in that moment by staying on the subject and not moving on. You do sometimes get some really special moments with Mary when you do that.'

'Staying in the moment' was a frequent topic in shared reviews. The DSWs were able to find clips in which there was a more alert, positive response from Mary. They were guided to explore how they could stay in the moment longer, rather than moving on to a different topic. These moments could be as simple as Mary exclaiming 'Oh! Oh!' when she caught her dressing gown on her bedroom door, or delightedly repeating 'chicken' in a conversation about dinner.

Feeling more confident

All the DSWs spoke about how they felt when the guide or another member of staff named an interactive behaviour of theirs. One DSW commented, 'It was actually an ego boost as [guider] really picked some things that I was doing well', and another said, 'You don't like to see yourself, I must say…but when [guider] was pointing out, this is amazing, this bit, and we're thinking, oh yeah'. When asked about the best part of the process, one DSW said, 'Seeing…[that] we are all actually doing the right thing by Mary. It was fairly confirming.'

Team practices

Whilst tension across the team regarding the different beliefs people held about ways of working and their expectations of Mary continued across the seven months, in the follow-up interview this appeared to shift. Staff referred to seeing each other's strengths and what they were able to learn from differences in practice. Several people talked about the humbling shift towards acknowledging that other people interacted well with Mary, when previously they may have been rather more judgemental. One DSW reported that the best part of the VERP intervention was 'receiving encouragement… "Oh yes, you were very patient there and you made her feel at ease"…that was very positive for me'. Several staff also talked about the benefits of seeing the guider interact briefly with Mary: 'Mary was sitting down, and [guider] came down to her level, she just interacted and had a conversation with her about something that was in a magazine. It was really quite effective, so I think my interactions with her [Mary] have completely changed since doing this thing [VERP training].'

Timing of the intervention

Several staff reported that VERP met their needs at the time they needed it. One member commented, 'because at first…when [guider] first interviewed Mary, I felt she's too far gone…and we were having a bad time with her, anyway…but it was good. It was really good, and I'm glad she chose Mary because it has helped us along.'

Conclusion

Interactions with people with PIMD can be difficult when responses are few or idiosyncratic. VERP is an ideal intervention for supporting adults with PIMD, including those with Down syndrome and dementia, and their support staff. It provides an environment in which to examine present communication skills, using the videos to continue best practice in interaction. VERP also gives space to attend to the needs of staff, confirming the good work that they are doing in a team context, and acknowledging the emotional work of supporting people whose skills may be few or deteriorating.

CHAPTER 11

OIVA – Supporting Staff for Better Interaction with People with Complex Communication Needs

Katja Burakoff and Kaisa Martikainen

OIVA is a Finnish model of video-based guidance that aims to enhance the interaction skills of professionals working with people with complex communication needs. 'Complex communication needs' is a term used to describe those of people who cannot use speech as their primary means of communication, or have speech that is difficult to understand, when the primary cause of their impairment is not due to hearing loss.

OIVA: Participation through interaction, translating as 'Succeed, be inspired by using video'

When the work of developing OIVA began, there were no other models of video-based guidance aimed at professionals working with communicative impairments being used in Finland. The Mannerheim League employed the Video Interaction Guidance (VIG) method, but mainly in families. The OIVA principles have been strongly inspired by the teachings of both trainers from the

Mannerheim League and the Scottish pioneers in VIG and Video Enhanced Reflective Practice (VERP).

While the theoretical basis of OIVA and its operating principles share many of the features of VIG and VERP, the contents and emphases have been specifically designed to take into account the needs of the communities serving people with complex communication needs. OIVA and VERP are both reflective practices enhanced by the use of video (Strathie, Strathie and Kennedy 2011). They aim at improving effective communication in naturally occurring situations, and involve video recordings of real-life situations, followed by a shared review of the edited clips in small group meetings with a guider. They are strengths- and empowerment-based approaches to skills in communication, reflection and critical analysis, and are both founded on the belief that successful interaction requires sensitive partnership.

In this chapter we introduce two features of OIVA. First, we introduce the OIVA Interaction Model® in which staff communities develop their interaction using a video-based reflective process. Second, we examine how OIVA guiders are trained to support others in the work.

The Communication and Technology Centre, Tikoteekki, of the Finnish Association of Intellectual and Developmental Disabilities, has been developing the OIVA Interaction Model® since 2005, and training OIVA guiders since 2009. Both these projects are now a core part of the Centre's services. OIVA was initially designed to serve the needs of communities working with adults with severe learning disabilities. However, we found that OIVA is not a diagnosis-dependent model; it is well suited to all types of interactive situations in which a communicative impairment of any degree hinders communication.

There are an estimated 40,000 people with learning disabilities in Finland. Approximately a quarter have complex communication needs whereby, although they may understand language in a very limited way, they can only express themselves by non-verbal means. In 2005, Tikoteekki received project funding from Finland's Slot Machine Association, RAY, to improve the interaction opportunities of people with complex communication needs and learning disabilities. The main objective of OIVA is to start a process through which staff may discover more effective ways of interacting with their clients with

complex communication needs, and the OIVA Interaction Model®
was born as a result of the development work carried out during this
four-year project.

OIVA Interaction Model®

The OIVA Interaction Model® is a 12-month process of guided training
for organizations supporting people with complex communication
needs. Gradually all of the organization's staff are included in the
training, ensuring that the aim of enhancing interaction becomes a
shared goal (Bloomberg, West and Iacono 2003). The staff supervisor
also plays a key role in the successful accomplishment of the training
project, inspiring and motivating staff members, and ensuring that
it is possible for them all to attend the meetings that are part of the
process (Koski *et al.* 2014).

The model includes four phases that contribute to embedding an
OIVA culture in an organization (see Figure 11.1).

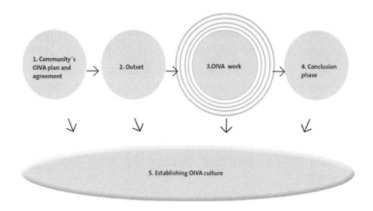

Figure 11.1 Process of the OIVA Interaction Model

Phase 1 and 2: Organization's OIVA plan and agreement, and outset

The OIVA guider discusses the OIVA Interaction Model® with the staff supervisor. Together they plan the schedule of the work and agree on the group of staff from the work community that will take part in the process.

After the initial planning, the OIVA guider begins by getting to know the organization, talking to each participating staff member separately, with a half-day training session to agree on the goal of the OIVA work. The training session focuses on introducing the staff members to the theory behind OIVA, and explaining how they are going to develop their interaction skills by putting the theory into practice.

Phase 3: OIVA work

The main OIVA work phase includes six meetings of video-based guidance. Prior to the meeting, the participants film themselves in interaction with a person with a disability whom they support. In each of the meetings the participants and the guider observe a clip from the video. During the OIVA process, each participant has an opportunity to explore their own question connected to their interaction with their partners with complex communication needs.

The focus of the video-based guidance is on reviewing successful moments of interaction and seeking out elements that support sensitive partnership. A sensitive interaction style has been highlighted in the literature as one of the most important factors supporting communication between people with complex communication needs and learning difficulties and their communication partners (see, for example, Nafstad and Rødbroe 1999; Nind and Hewett 2005; Zeedyk 2008).

A mnemonic is used in OIVA work to guide the focus on a sensitive partnership (Koski *et al.* 2010): LOVIT®. This summarizes the five elements of sensitive partnership by using their Finnish initials. It serves as a tool for the staff and their guide in reviewing the videos, concentrating on the elements that are central to successful interaction.

Attuning to the needs of a client with complex communication needs means that the communication partner:

- *Läsnäolo* – is reciprocally present
- *Odottaminen* – waits and gives time to initiate
- *Vastaaminen* – responds
- *Ilmaisun mukauttaminen* – adjusts their own expressions to meet the other person's communication needs
- *Tarkistaminen* – checks and makes sure that the interaction is not cut off.

Sensitivity in interaction may be observed through the communication partner tuning into the situation and adjusting their own emotional state and pace to the other person's emotional state and needs at that moment (Stern 1985). A sensitive partner constantly observes how his or her own actions are affecting the person they are communicating with (Ainsworth *et al.* 1978; Feeney and Collins 2004), and, if necessary, adjusts them according to the developmental needs of that person, described as 'scaffolding' by Jerome Bruner (Bruner 1981). A sensitive partner ensures that the interaction proceeds at the pace of the other partner, observing and reacting to the other partner's initiatives. Mutually positive experiences of interaction increase the desire of both partners to spend time together, which leads to an empowering, positive cycle of interaction. The construction of this kind of a 'yes cycle' is one of the key goals of VIG (Kennedy 2011).

Throughout the OIVA work, each staff participant makes observations on the filmed situation and develops a practical plan for change in the day-to-day work. On the basis of their observations and the related discussion, the participants agree how to apply what they have learned in order to put their new plan into practice in the coming month.

Phase 4: Conclusion phase

At the end of the OIVA training the group holds a concluding meeting when the participants reflect on their experiences and agree on how to keep up successful interaction practices. The guider has individual discussions with each participant in which they are able to share what they thought about the process, how it has changed their own way of interacting, and the impact it has had on the communication opportunities and skills of their service users. The guider and the supervisor discuss the organization's experiences and new ideas, and what the staff feel they would need in the future for these new ideas to become an established part of the interaction practices in the organization.

Principles of the OIVA Interaction Model®

OIVA aims at a permanent change in the organization's culture of interaction by building a strengths-based foundation. The change is not predetermined, but is developed from the discussions between the guider and the group (Berger and Luckmann 1966). The guider works with staff in a way that allows them space to reflect on interactions together and discover for themselves what kind of practical actions develop interactions. The guidance is delivered through a dialogical, cooperative relationship in which the guider and the trainees meet as equal partners and learn from each other (Isaacs 1999). Through discussing and reviewing the video material together, the community discovers alternative narratives for their perceptions on interactions (McCartan and Todd 2011).

OIVA has many elements in common with how VIG and VERP make use of video. In OIVA and VERP the staff film their own daily interactive situations. It gives them the chance to film the situations that they feel the community would benefit the most from reviewing. However, in OIVA the staff do not choose the video clips to be reviewed in the guided meetings themselves – the choice is made by the guider. This ensures that the reviewed clips bring the positive aspects into focus. The staff then see how they achieve successful interaction with their clients, and how they can steer the situation in a positive direction at points when the interaction is at risk of failing. The discussion of the video clips helps the participants to become more aware of both their own resources and skills and those of their communication partners. This is different from most VERP training, when clients analyse their own videos.

In OIVA, the whole team takes part in the improvement of interaction. Discussion is developed in the group in a way that allows all the participants to share their experiences and views. This kind of interaction produces an atmosphere that encourages learning and creativity. It is easier for the staff to put the new ideas into practice in a framework, where they are discovered and discussed together.

Participant experiences of the OIVA Interaction Model®

According to participants, the OIVA Interaction Model® has improved both their own wellbeing and that of their partners with complex communication needs. When the staff are attuned to the messages of their communication partners and respond to them, the partners are more likely to express their needs and wishes. These successes are reflected in the overall atmosphere of interaction in the workplace and job satisfaction.

The following quotes were gathered from various groups' OIVA training evaluations. Staff working with people with dementia have noted that many aspects of their work take a positive turn when they focus on successful interaction, for example: 'We have started spending more time with the residents and reflecting on how we approach them and encounter them. This has increased the residents' sense of security.' The staff become better equipped to encounter their clients in an unhurried manner: 'Along with the change of skills among us carers, the residents have started to react more strongly in situations of interaction. They tend to live more in the moment, smile, their expressions are open and eyes observant. They are present and react each in their own way to what is going on.'

Experiences in organizations that work with children with learning disabilities have been similar. For example, video has helped the staff to become more conscious and appreciative of even the smallest signs of progress: 'I've noticed from the video clips that the children are much more capable than I had thought. For our students, the steps of progress are small, but it is still progress.' The staff also feel that they have started to give priority to communication: 'I just learned to think in a different way: this individual is expressing something now and I cannot just ignore it by saying that I am busy. I need to stop and listen to him.'

The staff in all the cited organizations report that the OIVA Interaction Model® has increased interaction among the staff members and strengthened the communal spirit: 'Now we listen to each other more and stick to our common agreements.' This has had a noticeable effect on the atmosphere and helped the staff to cope better with the work. Two nurses describe their feelings: 'People feel less burdened by the work. We are all in a better mood.' 'I feel more energetic and happier these days, the work doesn't feel as hard.' The staff's professional skills and awareness of their own competence have also grown: 'I have gained more confidence, found my own style and my self-esteem has increased. OIVA has made me more confident that I am doing my job right. I've come to use my professional skills more consciously in situations of interaction.'

Training of OIVA guides

In Finland, many professionals whose work involves training and consulting staff working with people with communicative impairments feel that they need further training and tools for guiding the staff. Tikoteekki wanted to respond to this need by disseminating the OIVA Interaction Model® throughout the country, so a second project financed by Finland's Slot Machine Association was launched in 2009, during which a training model for OIVA guiders was developed as well as a support network for the guiders and their employers.

The training was designed for professionals with a degree in the field of social work, healthcare or teaching whose work involves consultation to organizations working with people with communicative impairments. During the training, participants learn how to guide the work according to the OIVA Interaction Model® and to use video for strengths-based guidance. They also learn how to enable groups to discuss and reflect on their own practices and strengths for better interaction.

Principles of the training of OIVA guiders

The training of OIVA guiders lasts 13 months and is conducted in small groups (six people). The training includes eight days of face-to-face training, a practical training project, a learning diary and a final written project. In the practical part of the training, the trainee guides a training project according to the OIVA Interaction Model®.

Video is used to support the trainees through their learning process. The trainees film their own work and prepare for training days by choosing a short clip from their guidance videos. They are instructed to choose scenes from their videos that they find successful or that display the kind of interaction they would like to encourage. During the group training sessions, each trainee receives individual feedback from the trainer based on the video clips. The aim of this is to strengthen the trainees' self-confidence about their own skill as guiders.

From the video clips of each student, elements of sensitive guidance are identified, based also on the LOVIT® mnemonic. Sensitive guiders are interested in the group's opinions, and encourage each participant to take part in the discussion. They appreciate different views, answer the group's questions and ask further questions. They react flexibly, according to the atmosphere and needs of the group, and check that there is a shared understanding and that the work is proceeding according to the principles of the OIVA Interaction Model®. LOVIT® thus forms the backbone of the training of OIVA guiders as they reflect on their interactions in the shared review process as in VIG and VERP (Kennedy 2011).

The training of OIVA guiders is an experiential learning process (Kolb 1983). The trainees acquire skills by applying the OIVA Interaction Model® in practical training and by reviewing and reflecting on their own experiences and feelings, both independently and with the other trainees and the trainer. They add the new things they learn to their prior skills, and plan how to apply them in the future. The learning is based on the idea that the trainees discover their own solutions, rather than having the information handed to them.

Participant experiences of the training of OIVA guiders

The trainees report that they find it important that the trainers create a safe and positive atmosphere. It is something they should like to achieve themselves, as OIVA guiders: 'The atmosphere in the training has been open and honest from the very start. It has been easy for us to just come there as ourselves and to even speak out about some of the embarrassing things.' Even very serious issues can be addressed with humour: 'The best thing I learned was the cheerful spirit we shared around the OIVA work. It goes a long way, and makes you feel like you can't wait to meet with your group again.' This also has broader benefits:

> The OIVA training has given me a solid basis for encountering people in my daily life and for providing guidance in constructive discussion. These skills have been useful to me also past and beyond the OIVA work. Focusing on the successes, and on existing strengths and improving them, has had a strong effect on my own way of thinking and I find it a very constructive approach in many of the situations I come across.

The trainees consider video to be an effective tool, especially because it stimulates discussion. On video they can see clearly what successful interaction is:

> I learned to ask the kind of questions that make interaction concrete. The example offered by the trainers and watching the videos under supervision helped me to realize that observing and analysing interaction needs to be restored to the level of practical actions.

The guider enters the situation with an open mind and helps the group come to their own realizations: 'What is especially great about OIVA is that there are no ready answers. It means there are no wrong answers either.'

Conclusion

The aim of OIVA is to achieve a situation where people with complex communication needs have more equal opportunities to participate in interaction. The work towards this goal has proceeded through the long-term development of the OIVA Interaction Model® and the model of training of OIVA guiders.

Three distinguishing features of OIVA and VERP are the person who selects the attuned video clips, the method of training the trainers and the focus on a specialist application. First, the OIVA guiders take the lead in the selection of attuned video clips, whereas in VERP the clients generally are active in their choice of their clips. Second, OIVA guiders are trained in a single year, during which the model they receive in training mirrors the training that they are being trained to deliver to service users. Unlike VERP in the UK at present, OIVA guiders are not VIG-trained before they embark on the OIVA training, although the authors of this chapter and creators of OIVA are VIG supervisors. These first two differences are related. It requires considerable skill and understanding of VIG to be able to work in a VERP group with clips that have not been pre-selected.

Finally, OIVA was developed for the specialist area of enhancing interaction experiences for those with complex communication needs. However, OIVA is now proving successful in training staff for a much wider client group than originally intended. Perhaps it could form the basis of, for example, an enhanced interaction experience for all young children in early education.

CHAPTER 12

The Indispensable Moments of Relating

Marte Meo in Dementia Care

Anna-Greta Ledin

This chapter describes a Marte Meo project carried out in Sweden with staff working in dementia care, on their own work. The term 'own work' refers to professional development, when staff members focus on their own strengths and goals in order to develop their skills further. As in Video Enhanced Reflective Practice (VERP), staff are supported to take and microanalyse video of their own practice in the light of core principles of communication, to set goals for themselves and to share their learning with other team members. They are guided by a Marte Meo trainer. Marte Meo, which means 'on one's own strength', is an intervention for bringing about change in any setting (family, education, social work, health, etc.). It stems from the same roots as Video Interaction Guidance (VIG) and shares key features, basic methodology and values. In the following example the Marte Meo approach is applied to professional development in a healthcare setting, mirroring VERP practice in all respects.

Introduction

A woman with dementia says that her caregiver is competent, then asks if the caregiver works there. What makes her assess that caregiver as competent while not remembering whether they work there or not? What is the woman perceiving and appreciating about her caregiver?

Some 48 studies concerning the experiences of older people in acute care settings were reviewed by Bridges, Flatley and Meyer (2010). Their findings show that older people's admittance to acute care hospitals may elicit feelings of fear, worthlessness and lack of autonomy. Three features of care are linked to positive experiences of trust and safety (Bridges *et al.* 2010):

- creating communities: connect with me

- maintaining identity: see who I am

- sharing decision-making: include me.

Stenwall and colleagues (2008) interviewed older people who had suffered an acute confusional state (ACS) and later regained lucidity. They talked about feelings of loneliness in their perceived reality of ACS, of being an outsider in encounters characterized by inequality and distancing. They experienced a delay in time and space, with difficulties understanding what was happening in encounters. When there was a mutual understanding, they felt supported and safe. Staff perceived the confused elderly as unpredictable. Caregivers were constantly on guard when trying to understand and connect with the patients, and change occurred often and quickly, as if unfolding second by second (Stenwall *et al.* 2007). According to Stenwall and colleagues, 'in order to understand the patient, the professional carers need to find a tool within themselves to get in contact with the patient' (p.519). The interviews show the importance of staff being attentive to what happens in the encounter with the confused person, and of giving caregivers the opportunity to reflect on their own behaviour in their interaction with patients (Stenwall *et al.* 2007, 2008).

Interaction is constantly affected by the initiatives of the participating subjects and their reactions to each other. Emotional reactions are influenced by what is happening in the present moment, and these reflect previous experiences in similar situations

(Stern 2004). In Marte Meo guidance, as in VIG and VERP, events are split into unfolding second-by-second micro-events, which makes it possible to explore what is happening in the interactional moment (Aarts 2008; Hedenbro and Wirtberg 2012; Kennedy, Landor and Todd 2011). In this process of interactional analysis the elusive information that enables mutual understanding, security and trust can be identified.

Marte Meo in dementia care

Örnsköldsvik is a municipality of 59,000 inhabitants where Marte Meo is provided for nursing assistants (hereafter called 'caregivers') in dementia care. After a trial period with caregivers from different units, Marte Meo was provided for entire teams caring for people suffering from medium to severe dementia (hereafter called 'residents'). Since 2002 teams at a day care centre, at a short-term accommodation and at seven residential homes have participated in a cohesive training called 'Marte Meo Core'. The training is run in groups of five participants, and consists of 130–150 tutoring hours over three years. Each year a new unit is invited to start training. Trained caregivers introduce staff, relatives, management, politicians and so on to Marte Meo in many different contexts. The organization now has four Marte Meo supervisors in elderly care, and one of them is learning to run the core training.

The Marte Meo 'own work' programme has three phases:

- Phase 1: Caregivers learn the technical aspects of taking and showing videos and identifying the core principles of communication evidenced in their videos.

- Phase 2: They learn how to microanalyse and edit their video showing themselves using the communication principles with dementia patients; these clips are presented at a 'field day' to other participants and management.

- Phase 3: Caregivers work on their assignments, which are based on each person's individual goal for their own professional development.

In addition, psycho-education is included about biological programming of affects (emotional states), fight-and-flight patterns and how the different brain structures make networks.

In the groups there is confidentiality concerning all information of a private nature. The confidentiality covers both service users and group participants. Caregivers are responsible for storing videos as classified documents, and for deleting them when the training ends. Video recording starts when the family or guardian has given their consent. The wishes of residents who show signs of not wanting to participate at the moment of video recording are respected. This approach to consent is based on the premise that the broader context of video recording is complex and difficult to grasp for those suffering from dementia.

Training process

Important features of the training process are curiosity, learning by doing, exploring needs and capacities of residents, exploring moments of joy and interest, exploring moments of mutual understanding, finding skills of communication, and exploring how to extend the skills to new situations, modelling and self-modelling. The caregivers explore interactional moments step by step, and find out for themselves how core principles of communication support residents. The core principles of communication are explicit, and the constituent elements can be discerned in short video recordings of daily activities (two to ten minutes).

These Marte Meo core principles of communication derive from the same roots as the VIG principles of attuned interactions and guidance (Kennedy *et al.* 2011; see also Chapter 1, this volume) and have many parallels. The core principles of communication and the caregivers' motivation behind their choices of situations to be videoed guide the supervisor when exploring the videos together. Individual assignments cover four videos, and afterwards, the caregiver makes clips showing the process of change and the achieved results. This part of the training increases the caregiver's capacity to use the core principles of communication as tools to accomplish positive change.

The edited video is presented to all team members. The medical nurse and the director of the unit are invited to all presentations.

Table 12.1 Core principles of communication in dementia care	
Creating a positive atmosphere	• Eye contact • A friendly face • An inviting and warm tone of voice • Using names • A welcoming and open body language • Mirroring positive feelings • Positive naming of situations • Using the communication of social rituals: greeting each other positively, telling who you are, please and thank you, etc. • Welcoming people and connecting people
A shared focus of attention	• The resident's attention to surroundings: what is the resident looking at? • The resident's attention to inner processes: what is the resident saying and/or expressing with body language? • Confirming initiatives • Naming feelings
Shared focus of attention, pacing and turn taking	• Looking at the face, waiting and reading the response • Selecting and supporting the most appropriate initiative in the action moment • Repeating/summarizing what the resident says, waiting and reading the response • Mirroring the body language, waiting and reading the response • Adjusting your pace to fit with the resident's pace in movements and speech

Shared focus of attention, pacing, turn taking, naming	• Telling what the person is seeing • Telling what the person is hearing • Telling what the person is doing • Telling what you are doing • Telling what other people are doing • Telling what is happening
Clear leadership through naming	• Structuring initiatives • Naming the action moment step by step • Using micro-pauses in between steps, confirming responses • Clear starters • Clear endings • Clear distribution of turns to different people in group situations • Staying attuned and balancing
Clear leadership through naming and modelling the appropriate behaviour	• Modelling behaviour step by step, being attuned and staying with the pace of the resident while modelling

Evaluation of the Marte Meo core training

To support the implementation of Marte Meo to achieve high quality in dementia care, the following overarching purposes were introduced to the director of elderly care:

- Employees will receive information about actions and reactions in different care situations as well as being provided with guidance about possible action strategies based on needs and capacities of residents.

- The team and the individual employees will increase the ability to design action strategies for *salutogenesis* (successful coping strategies for the creation of wellbeing; see Antonovsky 1988).

- The team will develop a concrete frame of reference as a basis for methodology and a consensus approach for supporting residents.

- Employees will develop their capacity to use the core elements of supportive and reality-coping dialogue.

- Employees will develop their capacity to maintain positive cycles of communication when interacting with residents with cognitive impairment and communication difficulties.

A total of 46 caregivers and one nurse had completed the Marte Meo Core training by October 2010, and 43 evaluations had been submitted. The evaluation questionnaire consisted of open questions, and the caregivers responded freely with their own reflections. They had no knowledge of the overarching purposes mentioned above. Linking the reflections of the caregivers to these purposes may indicate the extent to which Marte Meo Core has achieved them.

Caregivers answered a question on how Marte Meo guidance had affected them. Reflections indicating an interactional viewpoint demonstrate that the caregivers received specific and helpful information about actions and reactions of residents. All the responses showed knowledge of how to align with the needs of the residents. Caregivers said they had more understanding of interactions. They were more aware and considerate of the residents' reactions, and they noticed when support was needed. They thought about what they did and how they did it, seeing what went astray, and were able to correct it. They felt more secure, more reliable, strengthened and calmer in their professional role, and they had more job satisfaction.

> Marte Meo guidance has influenced me in many areas, both at work and in my private life. I have learned to think from multiple perspectives, to wait and observe, seeing when help, support, and bracing is needed.

> Marte Meo has influenced me very positively both in work and privately. I have become more observant of my behaviour in different situations. I also have acquired names of various communication principles, which makes it easier to explain to students and temporary staff.

Salutogenesis is concerned with coping resources that maintain wellness. Wellness is strengthened by a perceived sense of coherence, which includes the components of comprehensibility, manageability and meaning. Comprehensibility is supported when internal and external stimuli 'are making cognitive sense as information that is ordered, consistent, structured and clear' (Antonovsky 1988, p.17). Manageability is the extent to which one perceives that resources are available to meet the demands of different situations. Meaningfulness is associated with the experience of participation: 'a participant in the processes shaping one's destiny as well as one's daily experiences' (Antonovsky 1988, p.18). The caregivers answered a question on how their Marte Meo skills affected the residents. Answers indicating wellbeing of residents are affirmative of the caregivers' ability to design action strategies for salutogenesis. Indeed, all the answers included words about wellbeing – almost everyone mentioned that residents were calmer. Caregivers stated that residents were happier, had a more harmonious and positive life, were relaxed and contented, and were living in a positive atmosphere. Residents were more involved – they listened, made eye contact, were allowed the time needed to understand and to do what they could do and showed improved self-esteem:

> They become calmer, understand better. Seems happier. Manage things better themselves since they get better treatment.
>
> They become more secure. They are cared for with the same approach and that means security. Through our knowledge, we become more confident and can make it easier for them, especially in difficult situations, such as aggressiveness and when speech fails.

Caregivers answered a question about how their participation in Marte Meo training affected the team. Themes such as shared views, shared knowledge, being able to name what they are doing, being more observant of what they are doing and adoption of Marte Meo principles suggest that the team has developed a concrete frame of reference. Caregivers said the team had the same understanding of the residents, had increased knowledge and understanding of the various difficulties facing people with dementia, and were more observant about how they worked. It was easier to talk with each other about different situations. They worked better together and helped each other more. They tried to find common solutions and solved problems in a better way. There was better cohesion, more security and a better understanding of the value of good treatment:

> A more open group; can talk more with each other. More security, more calmness in the team. Less whining about guests with severe dementia. Trying to find a common solution to problems.
>
> Common knowledge has made us work in unison. We understand in an entirely different way. We have been able to use our knowledge and received words [from the training] on our actions! Moreover, it has given us interesting discussions!

Calmness, security, contentment and harmony are the expected effects when Marte Meo skills are practised. Residents and teams were affected in this way as described above. When caregivers mention which principles of communication they practise, they show an established capacity to use them. The principles of pacing and following the residents' focus of attention were mentioned most often by the caregivers. Creating a positive atmosphere with a good facial expression, good intonation and eye contact were also put into practice. Other inherent descriptions of acquired skills were taking one step at a time, clear naming, clear leadership, clear starters and clear endings:

> I understand how important it is to use and clarify these principles: that I have a friendly face and eye contact, a good intonation and to take account of the pace of the elderly.
>
> Pacing and clear leadership. Giving space for residents' initiatives has been very good for me in my work.

Marte Meo guidance investigates present skills as they are played out in the living moment evident in video recordings. When core skills of communication are identified, named and clarified, the ability to use this functional approach consciously grows. Then the employee has the tools to maintain positive communication in complicated interactions. An in-depth ability to maintain the supportive dialogue emerges, when caregivers reflect on their ability to deal with difficult situations.

> There is less conflict when I understand and make myself understood with the demented. With simple means I

can supervise dementia patients so they manage things themselves. Learned a good face that is so important and get many happy smiles back.

I've got another safety in situations I previously thought were difficult. I can deal with things that previously made me completely bewildered. An absolutely fantastic feeling: I can do this!

Summary

Marte Meo Core training supports caregivers to acknowledge present skills in non-reflective behaviour and to acquire a language that describes the elements of communication. This new knowledge is put into reflected practice when caregivers explore how to use their skills to promote change. The caregivers were asked to name three things they truly appreciated with Marte Meo guidance, and four main themes of equal value unfolded. It was most interesting to see that the most appreciated features of the Marte Meo Core training mirror the overarching purposes! They also constitute a beautiful summary of the training:

- Seeing the knowledge in videos with the second-by-second analysis showing what couldn't be detected otherwise; becoming aware how situations are influenced by one's own behaviour.

- Acquiring new knowledge with an increased understanding of the sick, learning the principles and being able to change one's approach.

- Acquiring an everyday tool useful in all situations; the importance of following the pace and initiatives of residents, having a friendly face and good intonation, clear starters and clear endings, being able to support residents to sort things out for themselves.

- Receiving competent guidance in small groups with personal instruction and positive feedback, being given the time and ability to digest information.

Caregivers described themselves as growing, feeling more secure and competent, and valuing the caring profession more highly. Improved cohesion in the working team, with a better understanding of what might go wrong and how to correct it, was another appreciated effect of the training. Feeling more satisfied was connected to receiving positive responses from residents, and knowing that the quality of the residents' lives was improved.

The caregivers experienced Marte Meo Core training as the acquisition of an everyday tool to understand the residents and to make themselves understood. Gudex and colleagues (Gudex, Horsted and Bakk 2008) describe similar results when Marte Meo was implemented at a care unit in Denmark. Staff there considered Marte Meo to be a useful tool to enable them to understand residents' needs, and they believed that Marte Meo contributed to a reduction of problematic behaviour among residents. Instances of reported violence changed from 186 during a 12-month period before Marte Meo, to only a few instances in 2007 (Gudex *et al.* 2008). Furthermore, in Norway 30 caregivers were provided with Marte Meo practitioner training focusing on the core elements of communication. The Person-centred Care Assessment Tool (P-CAT) was used before and after the training. Caregivers experienced themselves as working in a more person-centred way after the training. The change was statistically significant (Lunde and Munch 2012).

The Marte Meo Core training is similar to VIG (Kennedy *et al.* 2011; see also Chapter 1, this volume) and to the Basic Trust method described by Polderman (2007). Skills of communication are emphasized, because the needs of the resident or child require more than regular sensitivity. All these methods focus on strengthening the sensitivity and mentalizing abilities of caregivers or parents. They all teach caregivers or parents how to provide a sense of basic trust so that security is experienced by the resident or child in daily moments of interaction. This sense of trust is dependent on indispensable moments of relating: connect with me; see who I am; include me.

Conclusion

A woman with dementia says that her caregiver is competent, then asks if they work there. What is the woman perceiving and appreciating about her caregiver? One clue might be what the caregiver in question said at the end of her Marte Meo core training: 'I know it may sound strange, but it seems as if I have a video camera inside the frontal bone, and I can see in reality what I previously could see only on film.' Another clue might be found in a letter written to a weekly magazine delivered to all households in Örnsköldsvik:

> I have, against my will, been thrown into elderly care because of the needs of my husband [...] I regularly visit the residential home...which I will try to describe. When I have managed to find a parking lot I pass through the head entrance and go downstairs. I press the pin code. The door snaps. I open the door and when I step into the ward I'm entering a different world...a world breathing calmness, like a merry-go-round slowing down and about to stop...a world where every human being is seen...where every little reaction is noticed and attuned to...where you are met by smiling, positive faces... It may sound like a fairy tale or wishful thinking. But it is a fact that for almost a year now I have been astonished at the ability of the caregivers to move calmly, although I know there is plenty to do, and their calmness brings calmness to everyone in the room. In this pleasant place you are allowed to be who you are, here your will is important. The working method they are using is called Marte Meo, meaning 'On one's own strength', aiming to bring out the positive capacities in every human being. (Friendly greetings, 2013)

Part Four

HIGHER EDUCATION

CHAPTER 13

Just Conversations

VERP as a Tool for the Development of Communicative Skills in Social Work Practice[1]

Robin Sen, Carole Chasle and Bev Jowett

Introduction

This chapter describes the delivery and evaluation of a Video Enhanced Reflective Practice (VERP) course provided for six newly qualified social workers (NQSWs), four consultant social workers and two social work lecturing staff. In this course, VERP consisted of the shared small-group analysis of edited video clips of participants' day-to-day professional practice. The six NQSWs had recently started work in children and families teams in Rotherham Metropolitan Borough Council (RMBC), a local authority in the north of England, and the four consultants had, as part of their role, a remit to provide support, mentoring and developmental supervision to child and family NQSWs in the authority. Robin Sen and Bev Jowett from the social work team at the University of Sheffield were responsible for

---

1 This project was supported by a grant from the Higher Education Academy. Additional funding was provided by Rotherham Metropolitan Council, which consented to be named in this chapter.

coordinating the practical organization and evaluation of the course, and also participated in the course itself.

The six NQSWs undertaking the VERP course were part of a group of 17 child and family social workers who started at RMBC around the same time, none of whom had previous experience of VERP. There have been longstanding questions regarding the readiness to practice of newly qualified child and family social workers, given further impetus by the repercussions over the death of Peter Connelly (Carpenter *et al.* 2011). These questions led to the formal establishment of an Assessed and Supported Year in Employment (ASYE) for NQSWs in September 2012, after the VERP course described here took place. However, the development needs of NQSWs were already on the agenda and RMBC, like many employers, already provided a specific programme of assessment and support for NQSWs. RMBC's programme consisted of training days around key practice areas, direct observations of practice, reflective supervision provided by the consultant social workers, written logs and the submission of an assessed written portfolio. It was agreed that the VERP course would be provided to a sub-group of the child and family NQSWs in addition to this 'in-house' programme.

The importance of effective supervision continues to be highlighted for social work practice (Munro 2011), reflective supervision being considered as the core of the NQSW programme (Carpenter *et al.* 2011). Supervision includes management, development, support and mediation (Morrison and Wonnacott 2010), and, particularly for NQSWs, may provide an opportunity to observe supervisees' practice. Consultant social worker supervisors, however, rarely have the opportunity to reflect on how they themselves undertake their supervisory role, a role that is key to supervisees' personal and professional development and confidence as well as, most importantly, the outcomes for service users. The decision to conduct VERP with both NQSWs and their consultant supervisors gave both groups the opportunity to reflect on their professional skills generally, as well as on the process of supervision in particular.

The VERP course was delivered over five days, spaced over seven months by four experienced VERP instructors (Jenny Cross, Carole Chasle, Hilary Kennedy and Liz Todd). During the course each participant produced and analysed a number of videos of their professional interaction. It was planned that NQSWs would use video footage of their interaction with parents or carers; consultants would use supervision sessions with the NQSWs; and university staff would bring video footage of individual student tutorials. Some of the NQSWs had initial concerns about gaining consent for film involving parents or carers, and it was therefore agreed that footage of them in supervision sessions with their consultant mentor could be used as an alternative. However, by the end of the course most had obtained footage of interaction with a parent or carer.

The evaluation of the course principally consisted of:

- end of VERP course participant feedback from the consultants and NQSWs (short written questionnaire)

- pre- and post-VERP course self-evaluation questionnaires completed by the consultants and NQSWs regarding their job roles

- analysis of NQSWs' pre- and post-course written responses to a vignette about a fictional children and families social work case.

The 11 NQSWs who did not take part in the VERP course were asked to complete the same self-evaluation questionnaires and provide written responses to the vignette at the same times. This provided a quasi-experimental aspect to the course evaluation, and meant the progress of the NQSWs undertaking the VERP course was measured at the beginning and end of the course, and could be compared on the same basis as the progress made by a 'control group' of NQSWs who 'only' undertook the 'in-house' training provided by RMBC and not the VERP course. The hypothesis was that both 'intervention' and 'control' groups would show progress in self-confidence, knowledge and skills between the beginning and the end of the course, and that the intervention group receiving the additional VERP course would show greater progress, particularly in areas related to professional communication. The experience of the social work lecturing staff was not included in the evaluation.

Course content and delivery

The five sessions of the course allowed small group work, based on microanalysis of edited clips of participants' videos under the guidance of one of the VERP instructors. The clips chosen were those giving evidence of attuned interactions (Kennedy, Landor and Todd 2011, p.28). Participants kept a record of self-identified strengths and working points of their communication, rating themselves on a 10-point scale as to how competent they felt in a given area. Participants were also given targeted reading on VERP (see Table 13.1).

Table 13.1 Course overview	
Day One (November 2011, full-day, whole group together)	Introduction to VERP, the principles of attuned interactions, techniques for filming and reviewing. Videos were made of small groups in role play, followed by plenary discussion of filming and a review of films. Core principles of attuned interactions were identified in videos. For Day Two each participant was set the task of obtaining a video of themselves in a professional interaction and selecting three micro-segments of 30–60 seconds' duration. Homework reading provided.
Day Two (December 2011, half-day, small group supervision supplemented by plenary discussion)	Plenary discussion of application of principles of attuned interactions to social work settings, supported by set readings. Small group supervision review of selected micro-segments of each participant. Aim to identify attuned interactions, strengths and working points in the micro-segments. Plans for change discussed. Participants set the task of obtaining at least one further video for Day Three.
Day Three (February 2012, half-day, small-group supervision supplemented by plenary discussion)	Plenary discussion of what makes for 'difficult conversations' in social work led to development of concept of 'just conversations', supported by reading from Stone, Patton and Heen (2000). Small-group supervision review of selected micro-segments for each participant. Plans for getting further video footage discussed, focusing on a more challenging interaction.

Day Four (March 2012, half-day, small group supervision supplemented by plenary discussion)	Plenary discussion returning to concept of 'just conversations' and their application to child protection concerns. Ways of avoiding, reducing and resolving confrontation in these contexts discussed. Small group supervision review of selected micro-segments for each participant, with plans for final filming discussed. NQSWs who had not yet filmed with a parent or carer were encouraged to do so.
Day Five (May 2012, full day, whole group together)	Presentation of selected clips from different films by each participant to the wider group, charting their learning during the course. Plenary discussion of future plans for professional development. All participants received certification allowing them accelerated entry to VIG Stage 1.

Both Video Interaction Guidance (VIG) and VERP share a focus on building strengths and respect for others in difficult situations in order to promote and sustain change. The VERP course offered NQSWs and their consultant mentors the opportunity to reflect on their communication and to build on their strengths and prior learning. Thus both groups were positioned on more equal terms as learners with respect to each other. Furthermore, learning was supported by giving participants an understanding of the underlying theory of effective communication and an opportunity to reflect critically and apply this to a range of practice contexts: mentoring, supervision and conversations with parents. Thus, the first day provided not only learning opportunities relating to the principles of communication and their application to recent research, but also gave an opportunity to consider 'what makes for a good learning conversation – putting principles into practice'. Here the aim was to connect the elements of communication with aspects of 'mindfulness' or 'reflective functioning', and to encourage the participants to ask, 'how do we listen to ourselves...?' (Billington 2006, p.73). Subsequently, small group video supervision sessions built on this introduction by providing a safe forum for the course members to have an open discussion about 'moments of attunement' in their interactions with others, from which targets for personal development of communication were established. Grounded in the approach of the instructors was the concept that facilitating others positions expert practice as an 'art' rather than a 'science', as they coached both individuals and the group towards microanalysis of each interaction pattern brought to supervision.

'Just conversations'

On Day Three the group considered how the VIG principles of attuned interactions and guidance could be applied to the most challenging conversations that social workers and, indeed, other professionals will have from time to time. As an unexpected outcome, the course saw the concept of 'just conversations' as an alternative to 'difficult conversations', developed through group discussion around the work of Stone, Patton and Heen (2000). This concept was co-constructed by both VERP trainers and participants. The concept of managing 'difficult conversations' tends to locate the responsibility with the professional, and positions the service user both as problematic and as an unequal partner in the dialogue. Reframing the conversation as 'just' or 'fair' restores the idea of partnership in dialogue and, whilst the discussion will remain 'difficult', there is an expectation that each party will experience the process of the conversation as 'just'. Table 13.2, developed with course participants and based on their experience of VERP, suggests some specific principles pertinent to having a 'just' conversation and the implications for the communicative dyad/group.

Table 13.2 'Just conversations': Co-constructed principles and implications	
Principles	Implications for Communication
Beginnings:	
Acknowledgement of person, of issue(s)	Showing interest in the other, open to receiving initiatives, awareness around initial conversational turn-taking
Attentiveness	
Engagement	

Checking out perspectives, being aware of context, naming perspectives, naming context (including use of written notes during meeting)	Establishing rapport and common ground; establishing expectations for conversation
Establishing ground rules	Structuring turn-taking in future dialogue; however, if discussion of ground rules too long or formulaic, this can lead to disengagement
Guiding and initiating turn-taking	
Open body language; being attentive (eye contact, minimal encouragers, nods, paraphrasing)	Welcoming, shows relaxed, open to receiving other's initiatives
Receiving, having fun, smiling	Warmth, encouraging other's initiatives, relaxing the other, setting positive tone for conversational exchange
Turn-taking	Sharing viewpoints; fairness in communicative exchange
Active listening; receiving initiatives	Other feels their initiatives have been received
Slowing pace	Allowing message to be received and understood
Calm tone/normal tone	Engaging in register underpinning positive dialogue
Avoiding (too) long turns	Reflecting back understanding other's initiatives
	Checking out understanding if other is taking long turns (e.g. 'can I stop you there for a moment to see if I've got that')
	Awareness of taking too-long turns oneself – encouraging and allowing other to take a conversational turn
Scaffolding	Building on existing strengths within conversation

Agreeing to disagree	Showing that have received the initiative from the other even where there is disagreement
Naming differences of opinion	Recognizing differences of opinion, allowing line to be drawn under areas of difference with possibility of moving on to naming areas of agreement
Naming areas of agreement	
Deepening discussion	Sharing viewpoints, carefully exploring viewpoints, exploring contradictions and conflicts, collaborative discussion and problem-solving, investigating the intentions and interests behind words
Endings:	
Checking out	Summarizing and checking out agreements and differences, emphasizing shared understandings
Summarizing	
Goal setting	Bringing conversation to end in a way that allows for future dialogue and focuses on future actions and tasks

Evaluation of the course

The qualitative evaluation data provided evidence regarding the reception of the course by participants, while the quantitative data gave indications of how the knowledge and skills of both VERP participants and the control group of NQSWs had progressed. An overview of key findings from the quantitative data will be followed by consideration of the end-of-course responses from those participating in the VERP course.

Self-evaluation questionnaires to gauge self-efficacy in a social work role (Holden *et al.* 2002; Scourfield *et al.* 2012[2]) were completed by the four consultant social workers at the beginning and end of the course, eight months later. Strong increases in self-confidence were evidenced in all 13 items, with a mean increase from 22.5 to 30 points. The area with greatest change (*Providing constructive but accurate feedback to an NQSW on their performance*) had clear links to the VERP course, particularly the use of group supervision to provide feedback using a mentoring/coaching approach that encouraged participants to self-identify strengths and working points. Analysis of the six NQSW self-evaluation questionnaires provided some clear evidence to support the hypothesis that the VERP 'intervention group' had made some greater progress during the period of the course. There was an increase in mean self-confidence of the NQSW VERP group between the start and end in 14 of the 15 items, compared to 12 for the control group. The VERP group showed a notably greater increase in confidence in one item (*Challenging parents around safeguarding concerns* – a mean increase of 16 points, compared to 3.3 points for the control group), with clear links to material covered on the VERP course around 'just conversations'. Less straightforwardly, however, the control group increased more in self-confidence in a separate item with links to the material covered in the VERP course, *Communicating effectively with parents* (a mean increase of 8.9 points, compared to 2 points for the intervention group). The reason for this difference is not clear.

The six NQSWs' written responses to the vignettes were analysed according to whether they provided 'strong evidence', 'some evidence' or 'no evidence' of themes related to the child and family social work role. The use of the vignettes was influenced by the approach adopted by MacIntyre *et al.* (2011). The vignette responses suggested there was greater progress for members of the VERP group, who demonstrated greater mean increases than those in the control group in seven of the ten themes. The theme most obviously linked to the VERP course syllabus, *Demonstrates ways of building relationships with*

---

2   Professor Jonathan Scourfield generously provided copies of the self-evaluation questionnaires used in this study.

family members, was one of those in which the intervention group made more progress.

All ten participants (NQSWs and consultants) anonymously completed a short open-ended questionnaire at the end of the VERP course. Basic qualitative analysis of the questionnaire data is described below. The responses cannot be identified as from either NQSW or consultant, as the small numbers involved mean that this could compromise confidentiality.

Usefulness of the VERP course

Responses highlighted, first, that participants valued the fact that the course had sought to identify and build on existing strengths around professional communication, and second, that group supervision was particularly valued, due to input from the instructors and the contribution of colleagues:

> Learning to focus on my strengths. Good understanding of what I do well + my learning points. The principles + how they underpin good communication skills. (Participant 2)

> The group sessions – modelling of VERP skills by the trainers, insights from colleagues. (Participant 5)

> Analysing videos and group reflection. Looking at what things are received. Positive strengths based approach. Has built confidence. (Participant 8)

Impact on social work role effectiveness

Three areas of participants' job roles were consistently identified: communication with families; reflection and analysis of their own practice; and the translation of the course's strengths-based approach to mentoring other social workers or practice with families:

> I am more confident in the relationships I am building, am a true believer in reflection for change but VERP has reinforced this. More aware of the questions I am asking and in that it is ok to name feelings, etc. Although still have a lot to learn. (Participant 4)

> Identifying my own and others' strengths, supporting workers in identifying their strengths and skills in working with parents and children. (Participant 5)

Perspectives on course delivery

Two participants would not have changed anything about the course, while difficulties external to the course – time and workload – were a consistent theme. The duration and intensity of the course were suggested as areas for development: one participant felt changes would have been better embedded had the course lasted longer, while a number felt that meeting more regularly for group supervision would have been beneficial. The technology used on the course presented a difficulty: the video cameras used software installed on the computer on which they were used. Unfortunately, while footage could be viewed and micro-segments selected, restrictions on participants' work laptops prevented the availability of editing functions:

> Although it has been appropriate doing it over the six months, I think it would have been useful to meet more regularly [if able to commit] so as to remain more focused. (Participant 3)

> Workload and balancing this with time for workshops/ course days meant films taken at last min. and then rushed reflection prior to course. (Participant 7)

> The technology to clip videos – didn't work on work's laptop. Time and workload – reduction of workload to allow time to spend on making + analysing videos. (Participant 8)

Appropriateness of VERP for other professionals

All participants recommended the course and some, perhaps pointedly, suggested it would be of use for social work managers. One participant questioned whether the course was best placed for NQSWs, given the other learning required of them in their initial year, and an earlier theme was reiterated, that of the difficulty of balancing course learning against other work demands:

Yes. In fact think all SWs [social workers] and team managers need this. May improve communication and may also change the culture from being a blame culture to far more positive and developmental. Social work doesn't appear to promote professional challenge or group supervision as it should. (Participant 4)

Yes – line management should be given the opportunity to address their interpersonal skills. (Participant 6)

Conclusion

Whilst VERP has been valued in social work settings and areas for its further use are being considered, there is a need for caution in drawing conclusions from this study. Numbers of participants were small, the VERP training was short in duration and the long-term impact was not assessed. Contact between experimental and control NQSWs may have influenced the data. Items describing 'just conversations' are likely to have come not only from participants' experience of VERP, but from social work practice more generally. Videos of participant interaction with children and feedback from children could have enhanced the project and its evaluation. However, there was evidence that VERP encourages the development of skills central to social work practice, including effective communication, reflective practice and critical analysis. It also supports the values and principles of empowerment and a 'no blame' culture (Strathie, Strathie and Kennedy 2011).

The course also illustrated how VERP can allow supervisors to reflect on interpersonal transaction by exploring communication skills and the principles of a 'just conversation' in a safe context. Supervision is generally a very private experience, and it can be daunting to consider sharing clips with other group members and a facilitator, even of something working well. Identifying strengths as well as working points can, however, bring increased confidence and improved communication. Supervisors can build on what works while taking the opportunity to reflect on an area that they have experienced as a challenge. The experience would be of value to new or established supervisors in a range of social work roles, including team managers, consultant social workers and practice educators.

Interpersonal communication is central to the social work role, whether with service users or colleagues, and challenging and difficult conversations can take place in both contexts. Debates have surrounded the use of strengths-based approaches and the contexts in which they are applicable (Haringey Local Safeguarding Board 2009), and consideration has to be given to this in relation to VERP and the child protection setting. As with 'Signs of Safety' (Turnell and Edwards 1999), however, the two need not be in conflict. The principles of a 'just conversation', including showing interest in the other party, naming differences, deepening discussion and turn-taking, are all important elements of positive dialogue. Using VERP to reflect on what communication works well in social work settings may develop practice, potentially improve outcomes and, where differences occur, help achieve mutual understanding of what interests and perspectives underlie these.

CHAPTER 14

Integrating Video Enhanced Reflective Practice (VERP) into Medical Education[1]

Alex Greene, Emma Cartwright and Clare Webster

Introduction

This chapter explores the process of integrating the Video Enhanced Reflective Practice (VERP) method into medical education in a Scottish hospital and medical school. The authors are a medical anthropologist and ethnographer (who is also a VIG guider), a paediatrician (who is undertaking VIG training) and a psychologist (who, as a teenager, volunteered to take part in a pilot VIG intervention in the paediatric clinic). The projects described are illustrations of two VERP pilot studies for medical students. The first is a two-day VERP workshop on developing the consultation skills required for successful 'open disclosure' with healthcare users and their families, while the second is a series of VERP workshops for medical students who are failing the communication element of the Objective Structured Clinical Examinations (OSCEs). The chapter concludes with a look at other

1 We would like to thank the AVIGuk community for the support and materials they continue to provide us with for these studies. We extend a special thanks to Sandra Strathie, Hilary Kennedy, Miriam Landor and David Gavine, for mentoring us throughout these projects, and also to the project participants who gave their time and expertise so generously.

contexts in health where VERP is now being used, and how it might be used to develop practitioner skills in other health arenas.

A nod to the synergy between the theories of anthropology and VERP

Anthropology has a long history of using video in ethnography to film people's activities in their natural setting as a way of making sense of sequences of observed behaviour (Pink 2013). This was encouraged in the 1990s by new visual technologies, the advance of critical postmodern theoretical approaches to subjectivity and experiential knowledge, reflexive approaches to ethnographic fieldwork and the push for greater interdisciplinarity. More recently, in the social sciences in general, video has been used to explore embodiment and the senses, and as a method to promote training in methodology and ethical inquiry (Clark 2012).

In medicine, David Pendleton and colleagues (1984) pioneered the use of video recording for analysis of consultations with general practitioners (GPs) in Oxford. His work used peer review and stressed the importance of focusing on the good aspects of one's consultation skills before tackling anything critical, and remains an important part of GP training and assessment. However, video is increasingly being used with medical students often without any emphasis on the strengths-based approach championed by Pendleton and VERP (see the students' comments below). Video reflexivity is another method gaining credence in the health setting for use by clinicians wishing to explore structural changes to their clinical procedures and communication skills. As a more grass-roots approach, this technique offers health professionals the possibility of problem-solving their own practice difficulties (Carroll 2009; Carroll and Mesman 2011).

With this background, the authors were using the anthropological theories of 'reciprocity' (Greene 2004; Mauss 1993) to illustrate the power of attuned interactions as a way to improve patient safety (Flin, Winter and Sarac 2009). For the purpose of contextualizing our work in the health context, where relationships among multidisciplinary members require understanding between people, reciprocity can be defined as a symbolic expectation, or a gift, where those in a relationship wish to act in one another's best interest, for instance, solidarity.

The idea here is that *reciprocity* requires a mutual understanding between people wanting to be in a relationship, so that those who are given a *gift* (symbolic or material) will want the opportunity to make some return in the future (see Figure 14.1). In this way, the formula for successful reciprocity can be said to be a three-way process that involves someone wanting *to give* (for example, communicate) to someone who, in turn, wants *to take* and potentially *repay* the gift (for example, reply) to the giver in the future. It is this act of *repayment*, and the expectation of it sometime in the future, that forms the keystone to long-term relationships such as those of children and their parents, blood donors and traders. A transaction without the potential of long-term repayment is similar to the purchase of goods (in other words, merely giving and taking), which does not require any lasting and meaningful relationship.

RECIPROCITY

| Want to *Give* | Want to *Take* | Want to *Repay* |

Social solidarity and mutual understanding between people.

Mauss (1993) *'The Gift'*

Figure 14.1 Reciprocity

The act of repayment is important to reduce feelings of hierarchy and indebtedness, and it is why most people prefer to give to charity than accept it themselves. Keeping *reciprocity* in mind, the skill for health professionals is to find a way to build a relationship where they can give, receive and repay in a two-way process with colleagues and patients. This is how trust and mutual understanding are reciprocated (Greene 2004).

Our introduction at a two-day VERP workshop to the theory of 'intersubjectivity' and the principles of attuned interactions and guidance was a method that supported reciprocity and, importantly, offered a teaching approach and intervention for medical students, as described in the studies below. In particular, and compared with the other video methods we were aware of, VERP offered us a unique evidence-based structure to find micro-moments of good communication.

VERP workshops on 'open disclosure' for medical students

Using the platform of the 'patient safety' modules offered to them, the two-day VERP course we developed aimed to give the medical students the chance to reflect on and develop their communication skills in 'open disclosure', described here as the skills needed by health professionals involved in an incident resulting in harm and referenced by the World Health Organization's (WHO) *Patient Safety Curriculum Guide for Medical Schools* (WHO 2009).

Also attendant on other relevant literature, it was important and simple to map the VERP method with the existing 'Calgary–Cambridge Medical Interview – Communication' course covered by all medical students in the UK over the five years of their training (Silverman, Kurtz and Draper 2013). This involves learning to speak to people, gather information, build relationships and explain a treatment plan.

Planning the VERP workshops was done in conjunction with the Tayside Centre for Organisational Effectiveness (TCoE), a health service department responsible for patient safety. Two workshops were run annually: one with second and third year medical students ($\sim n=6$ students), and the other with fourth and fifth year students ($\sim n=6$ students).

The morning of the first day of the two-day VERP course incorporated the recommended Association for Video Interaction Guidance UK (AVIGuk) introductory package, with videos we made of medical actors portraying scenarios of 'open disclosure' and 'difficult conversations'. For example, one scenario showed a doctor letting a patient's daughter know that they had been prescribed the wrong medication.

In the afternoon, students were introduced to the principles of attuned interactions and guidance (Kennedy 2011, p.28). Each was offered the opportunity to watch the simulated videos and microanalyse them by reflecting on when they felt the actors were attuned with one another in the process of open disclosure. Working in threes, one student would use clips to guide the second student, who was playing the professional holding the difficult conversation. The third student was an observer who videoed the shared review and gave examples of when the students appeared to be attuned with one another. All students took turns at these roles.

On the second day, the students repeated the process by role-playing ward situations they had experienced. The second and third year students, with less experience of ward situations, preferred to role-play personal communication problems such as speaking up in student groups or talking to patients.

It is understandable, perhaps, that some students find it difficult to prioritize communication skills over their knowledge and technical skills. As one fifth year student said, 'Is this just more communication training because we've already had plenty?' However, written evaluations and recordings of their discussions with us at the close of the workshops suggest that students learned more than they had expected:

> I don't think I had ever thought of communication being a two-way process. It seems obvious now, I know, but when we learn about communication usually, you get the impression its more about learning a set of skills to apply to a patient to get information, like, for taking a history.

A number expressed how the VERP workshops had allowed them to reflect on the specifics of their communication, with some suggesting how the principles of attunement could be used by assessors to standardize student feedback in the OSCEs. The VERP method, they believed, would support transparency, structure, focus and consistency for these feedback sessions as the VIG attunement principles provide a transparent structure.

> If I were to stick my neck out I would say that the mark you get [in the OSCE assessment] depends on how nice your examiner is. It's really frustrating when someone you know is rubbish at communicating gets a better mark than you, because your examiner is harsher. I think the [VERP] principles could provide a framework so that results were fairer.

> I think the microanalysis is useful because you can see exactly what it is you are doing well. It's not as vague as someone saying, 'that was good, well done'.

This last quote fits very well with Dweck's work on self-image and motivation. She shows that praise is less effective if it is general and about performance (trait praise), and more meaningful when it is specific and focused on effort (process praise) (Dweck 2006).

All of the group believed in the value of VERP's strengths-based approach, with most saying that the negative feedback they usually received was demoralizing:

> I much prefer this way of learning. When you look at videos of yourself in clinical skills [with assessors] we're usually told what we're doing wrong. Most of the feedback is critical, so you end up feeling you've done badly and forgetting the good bits.

However, orchestrating the dynamics of each group was impossible, as their small size prevented us from putting students together who worked well with one another. This meant dealing with the dynamics of each group as it emerged. While some groups' dynamics did inhibit a few from speaking out about their experiences, most of the students were open and, in these instances, felt it was easier when showing the clips to give support, because they could use concrete examples from the videos.

The main weakness of the workshops seemed to be the focus on the mother and baby films in the VERP workshop material. As one student told us, 'I enjoyed watching the baby films, but it's difficult to see how they are relevant to our own work.' On reflection, we should have spent more time explaining how the films were illustrations of the research that had established the principles of attuned interactions. With this in mind, we have now adapted the course so that the purpose of the mother–baby videos is much clearer.

VERP workshops for medical students failing their OSCEs

The referral of medical students failing their communication OSCEs followed on from our 'open disclosure' workshops described above. Two to three VERP sessions appeared enough for students to feel ready to re-take their OSCE exams. The limited time pressure was due to students feeling harassed and wanting to prioritize revision for their imminent exams. The sessions started with some general background to the VIG and VERP methods, which seemed to imply to students that the sessions were part of their professional development, rather than something they needed to do because they had failed an exam.

Again, we made sure the workshops complemented the Calgary–Cambridge courses on 'breaking bad news' and 'taking a patient history', scenarios frequently examined in OSCEs. The majority of the students who had been referred had started their medical training outside the UK, and joined the medical course without the standard communication training offered to home students. In the case of the latter, most were struggling to understand the formula of communication they were expected to use:

> It's difficult to revise for the medical stuff, which is what you need to have as a doctor, because you need to show you can communicate in the way that's expected of you... I'm fine speaking normally, but when I get into the exam I freeze. I think it's because I don't really understand what they're wanting from me, which makes me come across as hesitant and apologetic.

All were relieved that merely watching videos of themselves and learning to identify the 'good bits' gave them the opportunity to reflect on and change their behaviour: 'It's obvious when you see yourself, isn't it? I can see that I can do it, which I didn't know.' Another student commented: 'I find it really useful to watch myself again and again. It becomes glaringly obvious what to do.'

For the majority, grasping the essence of their communication skills allowed them to focus more on the medical revision they were feeling stressed about:

> Guider: You seem a bit more assertive about your knowledge in this session.
>
> Student: Yeah, I think I got the hang of what I should be doing, which meant I could focus on the medical stuff.

In a number of cases the sessions allowed students to voice their lack of understanding and frustration without feeling foolish: 'You get to this stage of your training and you know you're good at the difficult stuff, the science, and then you go and fail on something easy like communication skills. It's humiliating.' What is interesting about this quote is that the VERP intervention focusing on strengths gave this student the platform to speak in an authentic way about his difficulties.

All the students expressed how they felt the VERP sessions had treated them as experts, which seemed crucial for those whose egos were already bruised: 'They tell you [the assessors] that you've failed because you come across with a poor attitude, but if that's how you've always done it, there's no way of knowing what exactly it is that they don't like and how you can change.'

Those coming from outside the UK believed that what was acceptable communication in their own country was not accepted in the Scottish context. As one student told us:

> I think the Scottish way of doing things is that the doctor has to appear humble, a bit held back; asking for the patient's opinion…treating them as experts. That's great, but there's no consideration of how, where I come from, patients don't want this.

Another told us: 'Apparently I can appear curt and uncaring. I wasn't aware of this. It's just how I was brought up.' Humour was a useful panacea and was often employed by students when seeing themselves on video: 'Oops, there I go again, chipping in like a "know-it-all".'

The approach of positive re-enforcement allowed some to drop their guard about feeling they were failures: 'I'm out [of medicine] if I fail again this time. I'm desperate; I feel absolutely rubbish. I've lost confidence; in fact I would say that my communication skills have got worse.'

At the time of writing all the students ($n=8$) who completed our first intervention (around two video reflective sessions) have passed their OCSE exams and have completed or are continuing their studies. The feedback from these students was personal, and suggests the relief they felt at mastering their communication under exam situations:

> I passed and am through to the fourth year! I want to thank you, as I have no doubt that the sessions we had got me through.

> I have made it! Thank you so much for the sessions in communication skill. The sessions reassured me about my abilities, which meant I was able to concentrate on exhibiting my clinical skills in exams. I am confident that the basic principles I've learned can be applied in my upcoming years as a junior doctor.

One teaching lead emailed us to say: 'I was at his [student quoted above] graduation last week. Lovely to see him finally get there. Did you know he got a B in his last OSCE? Massive improvement.'

One of these students volunteered himself as a role model for encouraging other demoralized students to try VERP. He has since referred other students to us.

With the result of these pilot interventions, the medical school is considering using VERP as a preventive measure for students who are struggling, prior to their exams.

Conclusion

These projects, we hope, illustrate the flexibility of VERP in a variety of medical teaching arenas. The success of these pilot studies has led to other leads approaching us for further VERP courses, such as courses for junior doctors wishing to enhance their communication skills in preparation for their specialist exams, which the university believes will increase the pass rate, as well as for multidisciplinary team members wishing to improve the effectiveness of their meetings, for improved patient safety.

To enhance the communication of multidisciplinary health professionals and young people with diabetes, training using VERP and VIG principles has been developed further. This intervention takes place as a two-day workshop for staff and out-patient consultations for the young people, who are given the opportunity to reflect on clips of attunement during their clinics with the paediatric author (Clare Webster). Working with young people with a long-term illness is relatively novel, as the opportunity to enhance communication skills is normally offered to health professionals and not to young people themselves, despite communication being a two-way process and diabetes being a self-managed illness (Greene 2009; Webster, Greene and Greene, in press). Working with Cyril Hellier, an author in this book, we have also developed a six-session VERP intervention for a multidisciplinary team working in acute care for older people, wishing to maximize the effectiveness of their board round meetings on discharge planning.

It should be said, however, that the introduction of these VERP studies was demanding at times, not least because we were trying to promote the idea to teaching leads who felt overwhelmed by other teaching methods being offered to improve students' practice. In this sense, introducing VERP to them was a competitive endeavour, demanding marketing skills, stamina and commitment. Putting ourselves forward for conferences and seminar presentations helped, along with informal conversations and generally 'plugging away' at teachers and top-level managers. Also challenging was the ethical permission and technical procedures we needed in order to use video with staff and patients in the NHS (Caldicott Guardians 1997). In addition, unfamiliarity with the video equipment we were given and the secure storage of video material was an important consideration when organizing the projects.

In contrast to the argument that video-based approaches only add to pressures imposed on clinicians already inundated by audit and risk assessment, we believe that VERP provides clinicians with the opportunity to negotiate understanding, as well as to own and shape their increasingly visible work practices (Rick and Long 2006). This, however, does not take away from the preparation we undertook to familiarize ourselves with relevant NHS policy. Framing the VERP method in current NHS literature, we feel, helped teaching leads to see the relevance it had to their service. Ensuring long-term buy-in by these leads also involved seeking approval from top-level managers in the NHS and the medical school.

CHAPTER 15

Turning the Lens on the Professional Learning and Development of Trainee Educational Psychologists

Michelle Sancho, Helen Upton and Joanna Begley

Introduction

This chapter describes how Video Enhanced Reflective Practice (VERP) is used in the initial training of trainee educational psychologists (EPs) undertaking doctoral level training at both University College London (UCL) and the Institute of Education (IOE). Video Interaction Guidance (VIG) and VERP are used by many EPs as interventions to support clients (parents and teachers) in a wide range of situations. VERP is used at UCL and IOE to help trainee EPs develop their professional competencies.

An applied training programme is fundamentally about the imparting and development of knowledge and skills in order that others learn the competencies needed to carry out a particular role or job.

Learning has most often been described as a process that encompasses reflective activity, whereby we draw on previous experience to understand and evaluate the present in order to construct new meaning and inform future action (Abbott 1994; Kolb 1983; Watkins 2002).

As applied practitioner psychologists, the integration of theory with practice is a fundamental feature of educational psychology training; a challenge for us as training providers is to find teaching and learning processes that enable meaningful reflection on the complex professional activity of the EP.

In this chapter we aim to explain the rationale for incorporating VERP into educational psychology training, and to describe the trainees' experience of VERP as a means of reflection and learning.

Overview of educational psychology

Educational psychology is applied psychology focusing on children and young people, usually up to 25 years of age. EPs work in a range of contexts including the home, early years settings, schools and social care. They promote learning to further the development of social skills and emotional wellbeing, and to support vulnerable children and young people, including those with complex developmental needs. EPs offer consultation, advice and support to teachers, parents and the wider community as well as to children and young people. They use their knowledge of psychology to help analyse and make sense of the real-world situations experienced by children and young people and those who live and work with them. They gather information in a variety of ways including observations, interviews and assessments. The work of an EP can either be directly with a child or young person (assessing needs, gaining views, working therapeutically) or indirectly (through consultation with parents, teachers and other professionals). They research innovative ways of helping vulnerable children and young people, and may be involved in training teachers and others working with children and young people or in delivering interventions. At the heart of an EP's work is the ability to communicate effectively with a wide range of people in a variety of contexts.

Local authorities employ the majority of EPs, although a growing number work as independent or private consultants. Professional competence for trainee EPs is defined by the Health Care Professionals Council (HCPC) Standards of Proficiency (SoPs) and British Psychological Society (BPS) Required Learning Outcomes (RLOs) (2012). Key to both the SoPs and RLOs is the development of intrapersonal and interpersonal skills. Core professional skills to be achieved by the end of training include the ability to:

1. generalize and synthesize prior knowledge and experience and apply to different settings and novel situations

2. develop constructive interpersonal relationships with clients and role partners

3. think critically, reflectively and evaluatively.

Attuned communication – the key to effective psychological consultation

Consultation is a core model of educational psychology service delivery, and usually takes the form of a planned systematic discussion with the people who hold the concerns. The context of consultation creates a thinking environment in which the EP can apply different theories, models and frameworks to assist clients with the creation of meaning and reasoned evidence-based action (Wagner 2008).

The VIG supervisory process has been likened to an art (Šilhánová and Sancho 2011). We believe that the process of EP consultation, with the simultaneous application and integration of a range of cognitive psychological theories, models, approaches and skills in an intersubjective context, is also an art.

Effective psychological consultation requires cognitive, affective and behavioural components to be managed in a way that is congruent to client needs and hopes. The co-constructed relationship is therefore central to successful outcomes (Dunsmuir *et al.* 2009). Without the effective communication that flows from attuned interaction, the opportunities to apply psychology to facilitate understanding and change are likely to be significantly reduced. Learning how to engage and interact in an attuned and meaningful way with clients is a central element of initial educational psychology training.

The programmes at UCL and the IOE have incorporated VERP into their curriculum as a learning tool. We believe that VERP offers a unique process and framework for teaching the art of attunement, and also supports experiential learning, that is, reflection on practice.

VERP and the development of educational psychology competency

As applied psychologists, trainee EPs have to integrate theoretical knowledge with professional practice. Experiential learning is a key part of the teaching and learning of initial educational psychology training programmes. But how do trainees learn from their experiences? Is it enough to have the experience of professional practice in order to learn?

Cheetham and Chivers (2005) suggest that experiential learning needs to be structured, that reflection has a role to play, and that this needs positive assistance. They cite Smith (1988), who comments that 'outsiders can contribute alternative framings', but caution that learners, even those with high self-esteem, can have their confidence and learning capacity undermined by inappropriate responses from tutors.

VERP involves the review of clips from a film of the trainee engaged in professional action. This means that the potential for learning is grounded in the experience. The trainee is encouraged to be an active agent in the learning process. Video self-modelling and reflection by the trainee, combined with reflection with a VIG guider (a tutor who is a qualified and experienced VIG practitioner), means that a coaching element is incorporated into the process. The respective roles of the trainee as reflector and the tutor as guider, as conceptualized in the VERP framework for shared review (Kennedy 2011), exemplify the principles for attuned interactions. The aim is to support trainees in the process of noticing and naming what they see and hear in the film, thereby generating experiential knowledge that can be related to the broader curriculum and thus to the affirmation and development of competence.

Clips are carefully selected by the trainee, assisted by the guider (tutor) and, in some cases, a peer, underpinned by the theory of intersubjectivity and framed by the principles for attuned interactions (Kennedy 2011). These provide the stimulus and the structure for the exploration of professional–client relationships and for the application of psychological theory in this relational context. As an active learner, together with the guider the trainee is able to reflect on how positive attunement is created and maintained in the psychologist–client working relationship; how psychological theory is operationalized in ways that guide and deepen the understanding of the client's presenting concerns; and how this assists the client in the framing and reframing of the situation (see Figure 15.1).

Repeated cycles of VERP mean that learning becomes process-based and formative in nature, informing the trainee's personal professional development plan. In the context of a prescribed curriculum we feel that this enables trainees to discover their own natural and successful style of practice and unique sense of professional identity.

We believe that the VERP process, embedded in the context of a professional training programme, offers trainee EPs an opportunity for professional development and change that moves beyond surface learning to deep and meaningful learning. This involves potential shifts in perceptual position (seeing something in a different way), and an increased understanding of how knowledge and skills integrate and interact in practice, also offering the potential to see oneself in a different way. From this perspective, knowledge and application lead to the important attributes of professional endurance and adaptability (Hay 2004).

The use of VERP at UCL and the IOE

Trainees at UCL use VERP to reflect on their interpersonal effectiveness in educational psychology consultation in the first year of their three-year doctoral training. VERP is delivered in a small group where the tutor acts as the guider and the trainees act as a reflective body. During the following year the trainees receive the initial two-day VIG training, and move on to using it in real situations with clients. This developmental approach enables the trainees to experience VERP and VIG both as a guider and as a client. This supports evolving trainee competence and progression as practitioners.

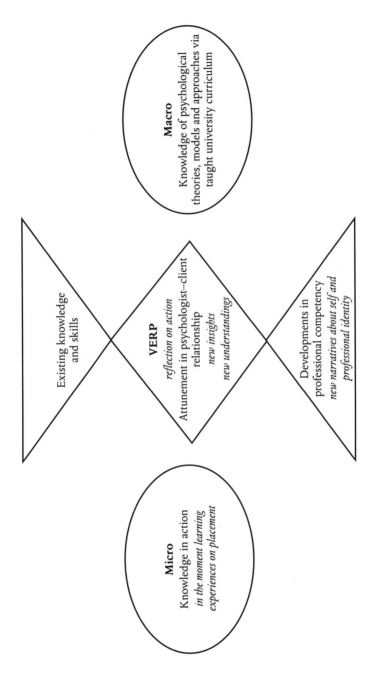

Macro
Knowledge of psychological theories, models and approaches via taught university curriculum

Existing knowledge and skills

VERP
reflection on action
Attunement in psychologist–client relationship
new insights
new understandings

Developments in professional competency
new narratives about self and professional identity

Micro
Knowledge in action
in the moment learning experiences on placement

Figure 15.1 How VERP supports the professional development of trainee EPs

Similarly, trainees at the IOE use VERP to reflect on their interpersonal effectiveness. The tutor team at the IOE has worked to integrate the profession-specific features of educational psychology consultation, where appropriate, with principles for attuned interactions. Over the course of three years, trainees complete five cycles of VERP with the aim of supporting their development from foundation to mastery of advanced level practitioner skills. This supports trainees' ability to apply psychological theory, models and approaches in ways that are accessible and meaningful to clients, thereby promoting and sustaining attunement in the psychologist–client relationship.

So how do our learners experience VERP?

An overarching theme in trainee feedback is that VERP leads to heightened cognitive and emotional self-awareness, both positive and negative, throughout the process. Trainees' perspectives of VIG at UCL and VERP at IOE have been explored and documented (Begley 2013; Hayes, Dewey and Sancho, in press). Perspectives from current trainees on VERP across both institutions are outlined below. We have found a commonality in trainee experience, despite the different approaches taken by the courses.

Anticipatory thoughts

Anticipatory thoughts are a feature commonly associated with forthcoming experiences. Trainees report a mix of positive and negative anticipatory thoughts about being filmed and the process of VERP. Positive thoughts and feelings associated with 'curiosity' and 'hoping to learn' by imagining a positive or useful opportunity for 'self-discovery and self-development' are in contrast to negative anticipatory thoughts about being filmed and the potential for viewing the self as less than competent: 'I just thought this is only going to serve to highlight what I don't know and what I'm not good at.'

It is natural for trainee practitioners to want to be 'seen' to be competent. VERP is a method that allows the trainee to 'see' themselves in practice and, in taking this third person view of themselves, to notice and reflect on an experience. Much has been written about the value of reflection as a learning process (Eraut 1994; Schön 1983; Watkins 2002) and the professional growth that can arise from considering espoused theory and theory in use (Argyris and Schön 1974). However, within the literature there does not seem to be much discussion about possible negative aspects of reflection that may act as barriers to development, for example, increased self-consciousness, loss of confidence and negative perceptions of professional self (Cheetham and Chivers 2005). Feedback from trainee EPs indicates there is potential for VERP to be perceived as a threat to a sense of professional competency. A training programme incorporating VERP into the curriculum as a learning tool needs to consider how VERP learner characteristics (current state, previous competence, previous experiences and beliefs about self and learning) may influence the trainees' engagement with VERP in the present (Watkins 2002), and to remain mindful of this. Trainees identify the provision of a clearly articulated rationale and explanation of the process cycle of VERP as important to managing feelings about the learning experience and their motivation to engage with the process.

Relationship between trainee and guider

Attunement and trust between guider (tutor) and trainee are named by trainees as necessary features for the creation of a thinking space that feels 'safe' (emotionally and cognitively) and offers the experience of 'self-confrontation', 'self-affirmation' and 'challenge', alongside a more skilled other, to facilitate their professional development:

> It forces you in a nice way to try and address some of those things that you could improve on...[tutor] didn't dismiss that or say yes but what else and move on, [tutor] gave me loads of space to talk it through... I didn't feel [tutor] was probing me that much I just felt like I'm going to try and think of everything and I really did.

This emphasizes the central importance of guiders (tutors) using the principles of attuned interactions during shared review, and reflecting on their own interactional style so that the whole process becomes reflexive in nature. Trainees report that knowing this heightens trust and strengthens 'the authenticity' of the learning experience.

Integration of different skills and processes

Trainees talk about the fact that VERP brings to consciousness the challenge of managing attunement in their interactions with clients whilst engaging in cognitive analysis of the information received. This seemed to enable trainees to reflect on the benefits and challenges of responding in a way that maintains congruence with the client. In this way the momentum of the consultation continues and moves forward in terms of the psychological analysis of the situation. 'You're trying to concentrate on the consultation, but trying to think about how you come across…you end up considering a lot of different things at once and that can be quite difficult.' Such reports suggest that VERP does expose the trainee to a learning experience that facilitates their reflection on the multifaceted complexity of educational psychology consultation and the challenge of integrating a number of different skills and processes. However, trainees report that being filmed may add an additional sense of challenge relating to the potential for being evaluated: 'You kind of think of what you're doing…but I'm also thinking about how it looks to someone as well, so there are a lot of different kinds of mental work going on.'

As practitioners in training, trainees are conscious of being assessed. Evaluation of competency is inevitably a feature of an applied training programme, but we would argue that VERP needs to be considered as part of the formative (educative) aspect of the curriculum and that this needs to be clearly communicated to trainees.

Film as a medium for reflection through self-confrontation

The visual self-confrontation and potential to access and reflect on 'lost moments' afforded by reviewing oneself on film is highly valued by trainees. Trainees highlight that, without access to film, the high cognitive demand on especially working memory arising from the integration of different skills and processes during educational psychology consultation means these moments may be easily forgotten or simply elusive in the actual moment of interaction or in a post-situation reflection.

They describe that the opportunity to 'relive' experience virtually a second time enables them to explore the degree to which they were 'present' with the client, described most often as the quality of attunement between them and the client in the moment. They also talk about the value of reflecting on the intentions underpinning their use of psychology in the moment, and how this was received and responded to by the client. This ability 'retrospectively' to step back into the interaction supports Vermuelen, Bristow and Landor's (2011) link between mindful awareness and VERP.

It is not uncommon for people in training to have a bias towards negative evaluation in respect of their competency, as they become increasingly aware of the demands of the new role. This can result in cognitive dissonance and threaten self-efficacy and self-esteem. Accessing visual evidence of practice within the 'strengths'-oriented framework of VERP offers the potential to contrast potential feelings of low competence during and after the consultation with feelings of greater competence that emerge from the carefully managed context of shared review. In so doing, trainees reframe their assumptions and beliefs as a practitioner.

The value of scaffolding and mediation of learning by a more skilled other

Consistent with literature identifying the value of the scaffolding and mediation of learning by a more skilled other (Bruner 1996; Cheetham and Chivers 2005), and research into the role of the guider in VERP (Cave, Roger and Young 2011), trainees report that their learning is enhanced by the opportunity to hear another perspective during shared review: 'Things have been pointed out that I didn't notice...which shows levels of competence that I probably wouldn't have recognized in myself.'

Connecting existing and new facts encourages deep-level learning that facilitates the increased transferability of knowledge and promotes professional endurance. Akin to what is reported in VIG interventions (Kennedy 2011), using film as an object of shared interest, the guider (tutor) is able to build attunement with the trainee, and in doing so exemplify the 'principles of attuned interactions'. Trainees value this opportunity to experience modelling of core professional skills from a more skilled other: 'She [tutor] was very good at looking at the video clip in which I'd been trying to guide and deepen discussion and then in the shared review she was guiding and deepening the discussion in the same way.'

The contribution of VERP to professional progression

Whilst highly valuing the noticing and naming of examples of competency, trainees also report the value of contained and managed 'challenge', looking at examples that provide the opportunity to consider 'even better if…' moments: The '[VERP] process is challenging but provides valuable insight and highlights both strengths and working points.' Thus it would seem that, for the EP trainee, constructive learning and professional development emerge from recognizing current competencies and strengths alongside consideration of how to develop competency in the future.

The ability of the trainees and their guider (tutor) to chart professional progression and needs over time through repeated cycles of VERP holds value for trainee EPs. This links to the central tenet of VERP, that a meaningful way to promote and chart development is represented by starting from where the learner is at in terms of knowledge and skills, and using video (Strathie, Strathie and Kennedy 2011).

Conclusion

Our experience of reflecting on using VERP with trainee psychologists indicates that the experience of VERP exposes the trainee to potential 'dangers' (threats to competency and sense of self) and 'opportunities' (to notice and name competencies, to see the professional self in a new light) as a learner. The components of the VERP process need to be carefully managed by training providers if the dangers are to be contained and the opportunities for learning and professional growth maximized.

Part Five

SYSTEMIC APPROACHES

CHAPTER 16

Systemic Change in Schools using Video Enhanced Reflective Practice (VERP)

Ben Hayes, Lucy Browne, Liz Todd

Bringing about systemic change in schools through teacher development is far from easy. The dissonance between models of professional development that focus on reflective practice and the standards discourse makes it hard for schools to provide space for staff to innovate. The learning opportunities offered to teaching staff are rarely characterized by what we know makes for effective professional development, such as learning over time within a community of practice.

This chapter discusses the application of Video Enhanced Reflective Practice (VERP) to bring about change in an infant school at individual, group and systems levels. This is a process of sustained reflective learning together that uses video. VERP training at the school involved ten members of staff (teachers, teaching assistants and head teacher) in a process of group reflection on small video clips of classroom practice, under the guidance of an external trainer. We suggest VERP provided a sustained collaborative process of challenge through dialogue, reflecting on day-to-day experiences, supported by school management. Research is needed to look in more detail at the process and at the possibilities for systemic impact on schools.

Professional development, systemic change and schools

A school, as a system, has an ethos or culture that comprises the perception by children, staff, parents and, indeed, the wider community of what the school is 'like'. These qualities go beyond the contributions of individuals, but all individuals contribute to them. Schools have hierarchies, and people in the school system have roles relating to the way it is organized. There is much communication, both formal and informal. A human system involves people, all of whom are part of and connected to the system as a whole. Systems thinking places emphasis on personal change and individual learning. For Schein (1999), it is the self-concept of individuals in the system; for Dalin (1993), it is the quality of staff development and how individuals can achieve real learning; and for Checkland and Scholes (1990), it is how individuals come to see or understand the system in new ways. Changing a system must engage with individuals in that system. As Michael Fullan has noted, 'The crux of change involves the development of meaning in relation to a new idea, program, reform or set of activities. But it is individuals who have to develop new meaning' (Fullan 1992, p.128).

Change for individuals, however, is a complex process. Individuals are not always ready, willing or able to change. Senge (2000) describes an approach to systemic change in schools that has at its heart the notion of 'deep learning'. Learning can simply involve deciding to do something different. This can be called 'single-loop learning'. Double-loop learning is a deeper form of learning and will, Senge argues, create improvements in the system as a whole. For double-loop learning, the learner should reframe or reconsider key ideas about what they are doing. This might involve reconsidering basic values or beliefs, or looking at what they do from a different point of view.

A synthesis of international evidence found that effective contexts for promoting teacher professional learning opportunities that impacted on a range of student outcomes were characterized by: sufficient time for extended opportunities to learn; external expertise to deliver the training; teacher engagement in the process of learning; the challenge of problematic discourses; opportunities to interact in a community of professionals; content consistent with wider policy trends; and leaders who actively support the professional learning opportunities (Timperley *et al.* 2007). The importance of a collaborative community of practice for teacher development is well supported in the research literature (Cordingley *et al.* 2005; Erickson *et al.* 2005; Meirink *et al.* 2010; Stoll *et al.* 2006; Timperley *et al.* 2007).

In recent studies of teachers' reports on learning activities that they engaged in and that supported their professional development, five general categories of learning activities were identified:

1. doing

2. experimentation

3. reflection on experiences

4. learning from others without interaction

5. learning from others with interaction (Meirink, Meijer and Verloop 2007).

Dalin (1993) argues that the development of new learning can be best achieved by undertaking challenging tasks relevant to the individual. Such learning tasks are, it seems, more effective than the next best learning activities, such as reading, learning from colleagues or peer discussions (Dalin 1993). These, in turn, are more effective than custom-made training courses, while the least effective activities are standard 'off the peg' courses. The idea that individuals learn most effectively through a process of problem-solving and facing real challenges is common to much thinking about adult learning (see, for example, Savin-Baden 2003). Leat and Higgins (2002) point out that different scales of professional development demand different models:

> At the medium scale, perhaps a department or primary school builds a number of strategies into schemes of work to allow a more consistent targeting of curriculum objectives. At the macro-scale networks of teachers create knowledge collaboratively through the sharing of pertinent craft skills, action research outcomes and research literature which throws light on their endeavours. (p.78)

They draw a contrast with '"tinkering" to describe what experienced teachers do as they engage in cycles of experimentation to improve their routines in their teaching repertoire' (p.79). They suggest the response of pupils is the most critical factor driving the teacher change process.

McArdle and Coutts (2003) suggest that teachers who are able to grow in practice are those with a common core of qualities that include: possessing the ability to act; taking responsibility; making discriminating judgements; and staying with one's values. These qualities are consistent with Edwards' concept of relational agency that, she says, is required by professionals as they work with others (Edwards 2007; Edwards and D'Arcy 2004; Edwards and Mackenzie 2005). Relational agency is defined as the capacity to offer and give support and more specifically as:

> an additional form of expertise which makes it possible to work with others to expand understandings of the work problem as an object of joint activity, and the ability to attune one's responses to the enhanced interpretation to those being made by other professionals. (Edwards 2010, p.13)

Watson (2014) finds that teacher development opportunities often seek to regulate and circumscribe professional development, with goals given in advance. This contrasts with ideas of learning as situated and ambiguous, and with assumptions that inquiry supports the practical deliberation of means and ends. The dissonance between models of professional development that focus on reflective practice and the standards discourse is well documented (Lingard 2007; Priestley, Biesta and Robinson 2013; Thomas 2010).

VERP offers an approach to professional development that seems consistent with many characteristics of effective professional development suggested in recent research literature. Among other characteristics already summarized in this chapter, it involves interaction in a community of practice sustained over time, and learning from and with others. VERP also uses video in training, but in a manner not usually adopted in teacher professional development. Timperley et al.'s (2007) review finds video used not infrequently in teacher professional development. Its main use is to model some aspect of classroom practice, usually not the teacher's own practice.

Where the teacher's own practice is the subject of the video, the aim is usually to identify problems in relation to particular classroom practice, and such an approach is used most often with trainee teachers. VERP, however, uses film clips from teachers' own practice. The purpose of VERP is not to look at models of teaching practice, but to improve communication within the classroom.

There is little robust data on the most effective way for teachers to use video for professional development. However, existing research literature comments on the unique capacity of video to capture the complexity and social fabric of classrooms, highlight what might be overlooked, record small group interactions, and allow pause and review (Borko *et al.* 2008). Video can support collaborative learning that is focused on reflection. There is some evidence that videos need to be watched with a clear purpose, and that teachers find their own videos stimulating (perhaps more so than that of a model lesson) (Borko *et al.* 2008; Danielowich 2013; Seidel *et al.* 2011). Loosely guided contexts in which student teachers watch their own videos alone and with peers have also been effective in supporting teacher learning (Danielowich 2013). Lofthouse and Birmingham (2010), talking about school-based mentoring of student teachers, suggest that the use of video has the potential to change the balance of power in mentoring relationships, and can facilitate genuine inquiry about the development of practice.

We suggest that VERP provides both effective professional development and effective use of video within that development. The possibilities for using VERP for systemic school change are explored in a case study, a small-scale project carried out by the authors (Lucy Browne and Ben Hayes), and reflections on the project are those of the authors. This is described in detail to enable theoretical discussion of the possibilities for professional development as an agent of systemic change.

VERP training in an infant school

An infant school approached its local authority educational psychologist (EP) team, having identified a group of children with whom it was experiencing difficulties. As part of the initial consultation, a theme was identified regarding communication and interaction. Particular points included how to engage quiet or shy children, supporting children to talk more, and managing difficult behaviour. It was agreed to carry out a programme of VERP with a range of staff from different roles in the school. This is a large school with 270 children, mostly of White British heritage, and a school population within the national average for the proportion of children with special educational needs (SEN) and below average for the proportion eligible for pupil premium. The school has achieved a number of awards, many more than once, including Healthy Schools, Active Mark, Artsmark Gold, Gold and Platinum Travel Plans and Basic Skills Quality Mark.

Before starting the VERP training the EP (author, Lucy Browne) established firm commitment to the process from the outset, particularly in terms of fully implementing all elements of VERP. The EP had open discussions about who should take part, making sure that no staff members did so under duress or unwillingly. Where there was reluctance, time was taken to explain the approach fully. Involvement was encouraged from different roles within the school, particularly seeking the involvement of leaders and managers to promote value in the process, and to try to bring about a 'ripple effect' in any changes.

A half-day VERP training course delivered by authors Hayes and Browne introduced ideas from child development to do with the nature of interactions that help children develop positive and reciprocal relationships with their caregivers. The principles of attuned interactions (Kennedy 2011, p.28) were introduced (that is, being attentive, initiating interactions with others and receiving initiatives from others, interacting and scaffolding). The final part of the training involved participants watching video footage of several different adult–child interactions to consider aspects of positive interaction according to the principles of attuned interactions. Ten staff members took part in the training including teachers, teaching assistants and the head teacher. This was only a proportion (approximately a quarter) of the whole teaching staff.

Staff identified individual goals, referred to in VERP as 'helping questions', on which they would like to focus, relating to a child or group of children with whom they worked. The question was related to how the adult could interact with and support the child with an area of need, such as 'How can I (adult) support X (child) to talk more?'

Staff took a video of themselves with a child, a group of children or a whole class, and then identified key moments in the video that addressed their 'helping question', as well as moments that demonstrated the principles of attuned interactions in action. Participants were asked to prepare the film by reviewing and selecting up to three clips. It was hoped in this way to promote ownership and ensure that only selected clips of positive practice were shared in a focused way.

'Shared reviews' then took place, involving a group of three to four participants and an EP (author, Browne), referred to as a 'guider', to facilitate the sessions. These reviews consisted of a 20-minute session in which each participant shared their clips with their group, with appreciative comments made about principles of attuned interactions. This process was repeated three times at fortnightly intervals. A specific seat was used for each person when they took their turn, for example, to encourage individual engagement. Staff were reminded of the new language of VERP (for example, the principles of attuned interactions) from time to time. Opportunities were also sought for ideas, values or beliefs to be expressed and shared in the group. Staff members all kept logbooks to record their films and shared reviews.

Confidentiality and the staff's sense of security were particularly important to creating a containing environment. Staff were reminded that the conversations were confidential to the group. Staff were also advised to keep their videos and clips in a secure place, and to use only the school password-protected computers to edit and show their video clips.

Systemic change

EPs' (authors Hayes and Browne) reflections are provided on the systemic change that they observed in the school at multiple levels, from the individual staff member, to change in the group discussion, and to changes at an organizational level.

Individual staff level

As is often found when using VERP in schools (see Chapter 2, this volume), staff participants reported that VERP made them more aware than usual of positive aspects of their interactions with children, such as reporting what they had not realized before, that they mirrored the child's body language. Participants described feeling more consciously competent in their skills in interacting with children. The processes involved in this appeared to be multifaceted. Participants readily embraced the time to think and talk about their skills in interacting with children by talking in terms of strengths when considering their own prowess. Participants seemed to understand quickly that the main focus was on 'what works', as introduced at the initial training sessions and emphasized by the VERP guider throughout the shared reviews.

Participants seemed to take on board being in charge of their own learning journey during the VERP project, as well as showing a desire to support each other in reflecting on their practice. This was demonstrated in their willingness to set their own goals and also proactively to support each other when looking at the clips, making and receiving suggestions from each other. They were guided in developing their own goals/helping questions and their selection of video clips. It seemed evident that individualized learning experiences were created.

Participants reflected on their own beliefs and values. For example, expectations surrounding children's interactions and communication with adults were discussed. Through addressing participants' beliefs, change was observed with several individuals having a 'light bulb' moment in their own learning journey. For example, in addressing the 'helping question' of 'how can I support a child to talk more?', the construct and belief about children's talking as an indicator of engagement was discussed by all in the group. Importantly, participants were able to note how this conscious awareness affects their practice and outcomes for children.

Group processes and dynamics

The first session seemed important for participants in shifting their reflections to think about 'what works' in interactions. The change took place in a group, and so a genuine collegiate process seemed to be involved that maintained an ethos of individual group members owning their video and using their 'helping question' to guide their reflections. The guider's role emphasized working in collaboration with their group as it reviewed the video clips, supporting individuals on their learning journey with other members of staff offering thoughts and their own reflections.

The approach taken throughout VERP interventions such as this means that participants adopt a strengths-based approach in contributing to group discussions, highlighting strengths as opposed to critiquing practice. Experiencing scaffolded collegiate discussion where (a) change in personal practice is the focus and (b) participants give each other feedback is something participants often comment on as being a rare experience. It is also noteworthy that participants see benefits to feedback from colleagues in this context, as opposed to other forms of collegiate support.

In this intervention participants were prompted and reminded to refer to their training handbook for key language and, in particular, the 'principles of attuned interactions' to structure and guide both their clip selection and their discussions. This provided both a structure and shared language between group members.

Change at organizational or systems level

Change at either the individual, group or organization level had an impact on the other levels. VERP learning was supported over time. This led to the creation and sharing of new thoughts and ideas (in the form of values or beliefs) about what the system did and what it was there for.

The project was made possible and supported by the pre-existing ethos in the school regarding reflective practice. The involvement of senior managers provided management support and modelling for other staff, showing reflective practice at multiple levels within the school system. Staff demonstrated positive working relationships and embraced the emphasis on 'collaboration' introduced at the initial training session.

The experience seemed to provide a space for individuals to reflect on the purpose of their system (i.e. the school and their role as a senior manager, teacher or teaching assistant). Sharing positive practice and interactions not only supported the individual but also others in the group to see effective practice physically in the videos, as understood via social learning theory. VERP appeared to involve a ripple effect, starting with the individual's own personal learning journey, yet also touching the reflections of others through reflective practice and group collaboration.

Staff supported each other within their sub-system (i.e. the shared review groups) and wider system (i.e. all those involved in the VERP course). Further, the importance of VERP as an individual personal learning journey was understood and embraced by the groups. This highlights a particular view, and possible change of view, of continuous professional development (CPD) at a more meaningful and individual level (as suggested by Dalin 1993 and Savin-Baden 2003), rather than at a generic and potentially de-personalized level.

Conclusion

It was interesting that change in a large infant school was perceived at all levels – individual, group and organizational – even though the focus was on interaction, communication and relationships rather than some specific aspect of the curriculum or teaching practice. We suggest that this is because VERP implementation is and was characterized by several aspects of effective teacher professional development.

Conditions seemed to be created that allowed individuals to think about themselves differently, to develop relational agency (Edwards 2010), and so to think about the system they were in from a new perspective. Staff were given the opportunity for change to take place and 'permission' to do things differently. Dialogue, central to VERP, is understood as central to professional development when conditions allow supportive challenge of existing beliefs, and the opportunity to contest prevailing discourses and assumptions (Senge 2000; Timperley et al. 2007). It is not easy to bring this about in today's standards-driven schools. What provided the support was the creation, in a relatively short time, of a collaborative group – a community of practice – that offered peer support (Cordingley *et al.* 2005; Erickson *et al.* 2005; Meirink *et al.* 2010; Stoll *et al.* 2006; Timperley *et al.* 2007). It is possible that a degree of levelling of hierarchies was also important, as teachers and teaching assistants engaged in an activity together as peers, an activity that was both personal as well as professional, reflecting together on clips of their own practice. At the same time as being personal and reflective, VERP is also practical, grounded in what participants are doing now, and generates ideas for action. The learning from VERP was directly linked to the day-to-day challenges and tasks that staff experience and, although a group activity, these were relevant to the individual (Dalin 1993). The involvement by the school management in the initial VERP training day is likely to have been crucial to systemic impact (Timperley *et al.* 2007). Given the systemic nature of the VERP process, it is not surprising that we claim systemic change. Perhaps, however, we need to look again at our theorizing of change in schools. Since VERP is relational, to talk about *individual* change may make little sense; maybe *group* and *systemic* change are one and the same. We suggest the need for robust research and further theorizing in this area, the potential of VERP for systemic change in schools.

CHAPTER 17

Evolving the Delivery of Children's Services

Video Interaction Guidance (VIG) and Video Enhanced Reflective Practice (VERP) Supporting Organizational Change in Glasgow

Sandra Strathie, Fiona Williams and Liz Todd

The delivery of children's services in the context of high levels of disadvantage is a challenge to cities, both nationally and internationally. This chapter is about strategic professional development as a driver of systemic change. It looks at the role played by the training of professionals to enhance communication and relationships in an ambitious programme of transformation in how one city, Glasgow, delivers an aspect of children's services: educational psychology. The planned use of Video Interaction Guidance (VIG) and Video Enhanced Reflective Practice (VERP) is discussed for a large educational psychology service, to facilitate and equip educational psychologists (EPs) to deal with and implement change across the city.

Glasgow context

In the years since the decline of heavy industry, Glasgow has developed an economy strong in the financial, education and hospitality sectors, including growing strengths in specialist manufacturing and renewable energy engineering. There have been improvements, too, in Glasgow's education of its almost 70,000 children. The 2011–12 figures show that attainment at all levels is increasing, with a rate of improvement for Glasgow better than the national rate (Glasgow City Council 2012). The proportion of young people going to higher and further education has continued to increase, and by 2012 was 57.6 per cent. School exclusions continue to decrease. However, considerable challenges remain. Some 33 per cent of all children in the city (over 36,000 children) in 2012 were estimated to be living in poverty, and there is a substantial gap in attainment between rich and poor. There are high levels of adult alcohol and drug abuse. In 2012, 22 per cent of children lived in workless households, 8 per cent above than the Scottish average. Glasgow has the largest proportion of looked-after children in Scotland.

Government policy aims to meet these social and educational challenges for children. Getting It Right For Every Child (GIRFEC) (Scottish Government 2009) set out a vision for developing learners, with skills beyond the formal curriculum, for schools where differences are valued, for multi-agency commitment to planning for individual needs and for viewing the child holistically. GIRFEC, amongst other things, is about a broad focus on outcomes for children beyond narrow attainment goals. Scotland's new Curriculum for Excellence (CfE) (Scottish Government 2002), formally implemented in 2011–12, is about promoting wider achievement in schools so that all children and young people achieve as successful learners, confident individuals, responsible citizens and effective contributors, regardless of dis/ability, gender, ethnicity or social class. The focus of schools is not to be merely on educational attainment, and the context in which learning takes place is not only school.

For Glasgow's children, one major change as a result of CfE is greater inclusion of children with additional support needs (ASN) within mainstream schools. This was instigated in recognition of the role of poverty in the children's learning difficulties (Raffo *et al.* 2007) and the multiple benefits of being part of an inclusionary community. The implication for Glasgow's Psychological Service (GPS) of such a change was a move away from decontextualized assessment of children (focusing on standardized assessments) and a refocus on work with schools. Strands now include: consultation (with teachers); direct work with children; capacity building (in schools); listening to children; and triangulation of support (and assessment) to look at the case for additional resources.

There is much research literature evaluating the many initiatives that different schools, areas and governments have put into place effectively to deliver education and other services to children and families in the context of various forms of disadvantage (Cummings, Dyson and Todd 2011; Edwards 2011; Raffo and Dyson 2008; Raffo *et al.* 2009). What this literature suggests is a need for both targeted support and a more coordinated response. It can be argued that the changed focus of GPS strands represents a move towards both a more targeted and coordinated response to children and young people. Professional training using VIG and VERP were very important to the development of these strands. What is interesting is the manner in which the improvement of communication through VIG and VERP contributed to an improved collaborative culture. In this way VIG and VERP contributed to cultural change. At the end of this chapter we reflect on how and why such an approach might be effective.

VIG and VERP are defined next, as these approaches were combined to assist GPS in the effective delivery of the new strands of work.

Context: VIG and VERP

Video Interaction Guidance is an intervention by which a practitioner aims to enhance communication within the relationships of others (Kennedy, Landor and Todd 2011). When the same method is used by professionals to reflect on their own communication with service users, it is referred to as Video Enhanced Reflective Practice. In both versions, the aim is to give individuals a chance to reflect on their interactions, drawing attention to elements that are successful, and supporting clients to make changes, where desired.

Furthermore, the training for VIG enables work on the practitioners' own communication skills.

VIG guiders make a film of better than usual interaction (for instance, of a teacher and child in the classroom, or a carer and young person in the home), and then review three to five very short clips (13 to 30 seconds) in which elements of attuned interactions (Kennedy 2011, p.28) can be perceived. The skill of the VIG guider is to work collaboratively with the teacher or carer to enable them to see things in the clip that demonstrate strengths. Although the focus of VIG is on client change, VIG also enhances professional skills, since guiders take short clips from their VIG practice to supervision to look at the impact of attuned interactions on the client.

VERP uses the same principles, but the focus is on professional development. Usually in groups, guiders bring short 15- to 30-second video clips of their own work (managing a meeting, talking to a young person or a consultation meeting with a teacher) for a group conversation in which aspects of attuned interactions are noticed (e.g. enabling the taking of short turns in conversation, receiving someone's idea, eye contact or waiting for someone to speak). Repeated sessions over two to four months support a sustained reflective conversation about the way that such communication supports the parent or teacher, for instance, and enhances the purpose of the interaction.

Managing change in GPS: Roll-out of VERP and VIG

Training and supporting staff to implement a number of preventive capacity-building strands of work in an organization with more than 50 EPs is an ongoing challenge for GPS.

One EP (author, Fiona Williams) had been using VIG in practice for a number of years and sought a way for it to be used by other EPs. First, VIG had to be adopted by GPS. Following reports from schools in Glasgow that they valued educational psychology work with individual children, a therapeutic intervention service (TIS) was created by GPS. Until then, it had not offered individual therapy to any great extent. In keeping with existing policy, it would only use therapeutic approaches with a strong evidence base (Dunsmuir *et al.* 2009) consistent with implementation science. This requires: management support; use of the existing workforce; provision of effective training; time to establish new practice (within a coaching model where possible); and a robust feedback loop that changes practice and impacts on the plan for a child (Kelly and Perkins 2012). VIG has a strong evidence base (Kennedy *et al.* 2011); is recommended by National Institute for Health and Care Excellence (NICE) guidelines for autism, attachment and social and emotional wellbeing; and the requirement of frequent supervision was consistent with the coaching required by implementation science. Glasgow's TIS therefore included VIG as one of the core therapies (Williams 2014).

Interest in training in VIG was high, but the roll-out was limited by the availability of GPS staff qualified to supervise its use. VIG training is only of two days' duration but must be followed by three stages, each involving seven to eight one-to-one supervisions at roughly six-week intervals, usually taking about two years. VERP was a solution to this difficulty, providing shorter courses with group coaching to develop communication within professional practice. VERP training is (usually) delivered to groups of about eight people over three to four half-days, spread over three to four months.

Not only did VERP provide training for those waiting to start VIG training, but it also proved beneficial in its own right. It quickly became apparent that VIG both fulfilled the 'micro' of a therapeutic intervention for the individual child, and had the potential for a more 'macro' implementation in larger school systems. Used together, VIG and VERP would provide a way for EPs to offer support for schools to fulfil national policy (GIRFEC and CfE) at a time when the EP role was undergoing change. VERP allowed EPs to reflect on the difficult conversations that were sometimes needed with head teachers, teachers and parents about the policy move towards inclusion. GPS evaluated both VIG and VERP courses, with questionnaires and data gathered from evaluative comments made during the participant presentations. Evaluation has been extremely positive, and comments from GPS VERP participants include:

I opted in because I like to set goals and reflect. As a new EP I was concerned that my tone can be misleading. It was a challenge to record and watch yourself on video but once you got over that you see there is a real depth of learning. I feel more in control and people listen more. It has had an impact on difficult conversations, I've learned from other people's techniques.

I came with the question 'is it me?' in relation to struggling to have constructive conversations with the SMT [senior management team] in a school. It helped me to identify strategies to use to be more active in the conversations.

I think I have always been able to reflect on my practice, but perhaps mostly in a critical way, this helped to remind me of my strengths.

GPS used the skills and training present within the service and set a time scale to train others, thus building capacity and ensuring sustainability. At first a consultant external to GPS (author, Sandra Strathie) supported the VIG and VERP development and the quality assurance of work. From 2011–13 Williams, supported by Strathie, delivered initial VIG training to around eight EPs per year, to set the EPs on their way on the two-year VIG programme. At the time of going to press, 32 EPs are either fully trained or in the process of VIG training. VERP programmes started in 2011 with a group of eight managers from the Inclusion Support Service (ISS). Two VIG-trained EPs participated in that course, and cascaded the knowledge about how to run VERP courses by working in pairs with other EPs. Altogether 16 EPs and around 16 ISS practitioners have been trained in VERP from 2011–13. GPS is now approaching VERP training for its own workers more strategically, that is, using VERP as part of the induction for new members of staff. Most EPs trained in VERP have gone on to undertake VIG training. There are now enough EPs fully trained in VIG to run their own VERP courses in a range of settings, for instance, in nurture groups and in early years centres.

VERP fitted well with implementation science and the capacity-building or coaching model that was valued by partners. From the pilot it was clear that VERP could evidence change in a brief time period. Since course material can be flexibly re-used and delivered to groups over four half-days, it was the best value approach for the local authority. VERP allows professionals to choose their own goals and to edit their own films to communicate these goals. It develops ownership of strengths and working points in a strengths-based model. Expertise can be at a high level, and personal goal-setting ensures that VERP clients make progress appropriate to their level of understanding. The 'seeing' and talking about a clip does more than just talking about something. VIG is a methodology that focuses on strengths and exceptions to the difficulty (Myers 2007; Pattoni 2012), and witnesses the journey of peers who are similarly identifying areas of strength.

The principles and values of VIG have always resonated with the culture of GPS, and VERP allows these to be explored and applied more widely. VERP became a 'tool' that could be used in the move away from traditional models of training staff through 'transfer of information' towards coaching, which 'exemplifies the emotional intelligence competence of developing others' (Goleman, Boyatzis and McKee 2002, p.62). This ensures that there is accountability to the service users, 'who are often with us in the room on video and therefore do not slip from our minds' (Knott and Scragg 2007, cited in Strathie, Strathie and Kennedy 2011, p.175). Overall, VERP can provide an organization with a rich opportunity for development whilst discovering 'people's commitment and capacity to learn at all levels of the organisation' (Senge 2006, p.48), and 'creating a space for caring, thinking and questioning to develop' (p.47).

Challenges

VIG and VERP enhance the role of EPs but, as their everyday role constantly involves working with people from other professional groups, complex discussions are ongoing around partners from other services in Glasgow City Council joining the training. Numbers are still small. Each VIG course from 2011–13 has had representation from other professionals: three social workers, five ISS workers and five speech and language therapy teachers. Due to there now being many VIG-trained EPs, for the first time this year VERP courses are taking place in a range of different areas besides GPS (e.g. two with nurture groups and two with ISS workers).

It is worth drawing a comparison here with the joint VIG/VERP training rolled out in a very different council, Cornwall, where legislation in education, health and social care is based on English law.[1] Unlike those in Glasgow, Cornish EPs have been working for many years in the multi-agency Team Around the Child Early Support System (Granger 2014), and EPs and children's social services have merged within the same organizational structure. Not only have VIG and VERP been used strategically in Cornwall Educational Psychology Service to bring about systemic change, but it has also been easier in this multi-agency context for EPs to involve other professionals in VIG/VERP training. In Cornwall, VERP courses sit within an extensive multidisciplinary VIG project, with VIG supervisors and trainees from health, social work and education. Initial VIG interventions, with school staff as clients, by VIG trainees and a VIG guider (Granger 2014), all EPs, have led to VERP shared reviews with several groups of practitioners. These include a small, specialized special educational needs (SEN) support base (Key Stage 2); a designated SEN specialist school for young people (Key Stages 3 and 4) with communication and interaction difficulties; and a child development centre (CDC) working with preschool children with a range of complex difficulties. VERP has grown up organically as an integral element of VIG training and is now used, as in Glasgow, for staff development and training in a range of working contexts.

There have been ongoing challenges in Glasgow. The GPS VERP project managers have looked at obstacles to implementation as well as ongoing evaluation. They continue to review progress and challenges on a regular basis with GPS strategic managers. As with any work embedded in implementation science, there are vital issues that need to be regularly considered: management support; embedding in staged intervention; ensuring protected time; and providing regular feedback on impact. VERP has allowed GPS to develop its own practice, to introduce the principles of VIG to a wide population and to support the workforce of children's services in developing their own reflection and practice. It has continuing potential and, used with VIG, could be integral to meeting the ongoing needs of a large local authority.

---

1   Many thanks for this example to Maureen Grainger and Clare Lowry.

Conclusion: VIG and VERP as cultural change

'In the realm of management and leadership many people are conditioned to see our "organizations" as things rather than as patterns of interactions' (Senge 2006, p.25). For organizations aiming to develop professional skills to promote multidisciplinary working across a workforce, VIG and VERP provide the means to engage professionals at both an emotional and intellectual level, whilst evidencing outcomes that show change in practice. Through reflecting on video of the micro-moments of attuned interactions, which can be difficult to perceive in daily working life, VERP methodology gives workers at every organizational level the opportunity to reflect on and build on the skills of attuned interactions, drawing on their own effective style. This makes VERP adaptable to a range of working contexts, for example, managers chairing meetings, teachers with pupils and supervision of staff.

The use of VIG and VERP in Glasgow has contributed to culture change for GPS and education, as well as for partner agencies. It has assisted the aim of actively supporting inclusion, and it offers staff, parents and young people a real opportunity to explore behaviour, social interactions and professional skills, so effecting change. As VIG principles became embedded in workforce skills, there has been potential for it to impact on everyday interactions. Clerical, management and generic staff have become interested in professional development for themselves, beyond being trained in delivering the VIG intervention. VERP has allowed the development of bespoke courses for different participants, and so developed a shared language and ethos. When promoting VERP with partners, GPS has been deeply aware of both its potential and the challenges of self-reflection and self-modelling using film. Both VIG and VERP, used together in GPS, facilitate 'expansive learning' so that participants are able to develop new ideas about themselves and others and new ways of working (Nummijoki and Engestrom 2010). In using peer conversations of video of people's own practice, a mode of communication is practised whereby participants are able to reconceptualize shared objects of practice (Nummijoki and Engestrom 2010). Participants have the opportunity to develop 'relational agency', the capacity to engage with others to interpret and act on the object of their actions in enhanced ways (Edwards 2005, 2007, 2009).

Small groups of workers, reflecting together on their real-life work, are given time to be together and to develop their own strengths and style of interactions through illuminating processes of communication and allowing for critical analyses in a supportive setting. The VIG-trained guider ensures a democratic process through attuned guidance of the group. In the Netherlands, where the original theory was developed, the Dutch term for guidance is *leiden given* – 'giving the lead'. In practice, this means the guider is modelling a constructive, democratic and participatory session. It ensures that everyone is interacting to build co-operation in the group, which can filter throughout the organization. It acknowledges that everyone has *equally* valid experience to share, both those new to the role and experienced workers. Discussion is deepened through exploration of opinions and beliefs to include problem-solving and the recognition of strengths and challenges. This can be particularly helpful in understanding different perspectives and values in multidisciplinary work situations.

Within these different reflective practice groups, with the video film to support the exploration of real-life working interactions, differences of opinion may be explored through naming conflicts or contradictions, summarizing the differences, and making explicit the conclusions or decisions. Helpful suggestions can be offered to members of the group, and support is often given through positive feedback and similar shared experiences. The VIG guider, through attuned guidance, is coaching to build on the skills and knowledge of the individual and on the shared experience of the group. As stated by Lishman, 'writing about communication cannot do it justice… it has to be practised' (Lishman 1994, p.143). Rather than the organization looking for 'external fixes' that, Senge writes, 'can lead to a sense of powerlessness' (Senge 2006 p.312), in VERP we see a model of practice that focuses on the organization and its individuals for strength and problem-solving.

CHAPTER 18

Supporting Professional and Organizational Development in Post-school Work

Cyril Hellier

Introduction

This chapter documents the use of Video Enhanced Reflective Practice (VERP) over a ten-year period in the development of post-school psychological services (PSPS) in Scotland (Hellier 2009; MacKay and Hellier 2009). Two projects are described. In the first project VERP in its earlier form as Video Enhanced Communication (VEC) was used for ten years in the work of PSPS with 22 Careers Scotland keyworkers and managers in their national strategy at the time. This led to the setting up of a VEC network and further manager training in Careers Scotland using VERP. In the second project VERP was used for two years as Video Enhanced Reflection (VER) with 12 further education (FE) lecturers in two FE colleges. This led to VERP training with five members of the National Access and Inclusion Team for Scotland's colleges.

The work emphasized reflective dialogue and the consideration of organizational effectiveness. It used the added power of VERP to improve engagement and effect. VERP, like appreciative inquiry (AI), uses a generative process, the co-construction of an alternative future, 'creating momentum towards action' (Dogget and Lewis, 2013). Cooperrider, Whitney and Stavros (2008) describe AI as a 'collaborative search to identify and understand the organization's strengths, its potentials…and people's hopes for the future' (p.151), which promotes energy, affirmation, renewal and movement toward hopeful change. The psychology of 'confidence' involves optimism and a sense of hope, connecting personal agency and goal development (Hellier 2008). Key constituents of solution-focused work (Hellier 2006) are a positive focus, taking time to reflect and review, and seeking improved outcomes.

Project One: Careers Scotland keyworkers and managers

PSPS have become mainstreamed in Scotland. Publications now include the post-school stage (see, for example, Arnold and Baker 2012) and interagency working with organizations including careers services. In 2003, following pilot activity, an adapted Video Interaction Guidance (VIG) was negotiated for key workers within the national strategy for 'peer support'. The term 'Video Enhanced Communication' (VEC) was coined for the purpose, anticipating VERP. The specification ensured that the purposes of supervision were clarified, differentiating the role of peer support from management. VEC was offered to individuals within small groups that were facilitated by VIG-trained psychologists. In order to realize the goals of peer support, the VIG principles of attuned interactions and guidance (Kennedy, Landor and Todd 2011; see Chapter 1, this volume) were used to provide a meta-cognitive framework. Two managers worked together in a separate sub-group. Some 22 participants undertook six sessions, each filming interaction with colleagues in their national role. Clips were then reviewed in the light of individual goals and ongoing working points. Collegiate involvement included opportunities for group comment and discussion; individual summaries of key strengths and working points from supervision were written by designated group members. This group activity was intended to amplify experiences, reinforce learning and build collective efficacy (Maddux 2005).

The initial apprehension about being videoed was quickly overcome as the value and power of the training became apparent: staff commented, 'after being anxious, I became quite natural and confident' and that it was 'extremely helpful'. The impact was measured by a pre-/post-questionnaire and the results interpreted through grounded theory. Evaluation was very positive, the framework and experience of training being seen as accessible and reinforcing 'deepening understanding and skills'. It was described as 'creative', tailored to each participant's starting point(s) and goals, enhancing reflective practice. Participants valued positive relationships, identifying individual working points and developing communication 'choices' to realize goals. Also mentioned were awareness of humour and empathy in communication, attentiveness and attunement, pacing, allowing time for reflection, asking good questions, turn-taking, reflecting back and addressing conflict. There was no negative feedback.

Overall, considerable benefits were perceived by the key workers and managers, including:

- increased relaxation and confidence
- opportunities to reflect and to apply a framework
- understanding processes of communication
- allowing exploration of feelings and issues
- a focus on what colleagues are 'really saying'
- balancing organizational requirements with staff needs
- realizing 'management' can be supportive *and* meet its goals.

Managers who undertook this initial training were highly appreciative, commenting that 'the culture of self-reflection tends to get missed out in a hectic target-driven environment' and that 'those who are prepared to take time to be reflective would stand to gain most.'

The group process was seen as 'very powerful', promoting peer interaction to share practice and building positive individual learning. Furthermore, the individual written summary of strengths and working points helped action planning and progress tracking.

The issues that were raised highlighted many strengths and needs of the organization. Staff morale was a recurrent theme, as a minority of supervisees and supervisors reported feeling dissatisfaction with their role, support and relationships. The colleagues filmed were addressing the needs of an extremely challenging client group. Topics included coping with structural changes, the induction of new staff, workload management, industrial action, IT and organizational skills.

Managers placed greater emphasis on case management, checking progress and action planning, as well as on multidisciplinary working, organizational change, coping with maternity leave and determining priorities. The need was identified for management training to help reduce stress levels and staff turnover and to address self-esteem issues. Considerable differences in the perceived quality of management were reflected.

VEC network

A national network (three meetings a year) was subsequently set up by PSPS strategic officers in negotiation with Careers Scotland management, for those trained in VEC to share continuing practice in using VEC. Aims included to:

- maintain and develop VEC

- continue personal peer support and supervision

- facilitate a national strategy, reflecting on ongoing practice (as sampled in video clips)

- promote VEC across the organization

- support solution-focused training.

Over a ten-year period, the organization underwent three national reorganizations and several bouts of 'downsizing'. During four years of the national network, membership remained stable, and the network addressed numerous issues. Discussions confirmed the:

- importance of making time to reflect

- high quality of supervision and support provided by the network (contrasting with that available elsewhere)

- shared relevance of the issues raised

- potential value to wider colleagues.

Significant concerns were identified, including feelings of being bullied at work, uncertainty about personal effectiveness, difficulties in personal health or mental health and coping with new challenges at work.

Finally, client-specific issues were common, associated with key workers questioning their competence in meeting needs. For example, these included profound disability when not previously experienced, dealing with teenagers when staff were more used to adults, or over-identifying ('she is just like my sister'). Strong feelings were expressed involving shock, lack of preparation or experience, inadequacy and lack of perspective. The value to participants of the process of reflection and support was clear. Frequently the 'safe' group process helped to correct overly negative thoughts associated with video content. Despite relatively high levels of training of participants, the general view was that there was no equivalent opportunity to self-reflect and to improve practice.

Supporting quality management

Subsequent manager training (six sessions for one regional Careers Scotland team) took place within the national strategy to promote the 'reflective practitioner'. Training was voluntary, aimed at individual skill and team development, and designed so that all team members could participate in the reflection process. Each session included filming staff supervision or a manager chairing a meeting of an area team or a full regional team. In most sessions two videos were reviewed, covering a wide range of situations. Active participation by those in attendance was evident from the outset.

Six managers completed evaluations evidencing increased awareness of communication relevant to their role such as attentiveness, turn-taking, appropriate body language, eye contact, praising, giving content, and so on. These included facilitating group members, better questioning and actively considering others' feelings. All participants appreciated the individualized supportive process, which raised awareness of existing and new strategies: 'It has really acted as a framework to take time to reflect how I communicate'; 'It looks at actual/real footage of you in a specific management role. It is not role-play or theory – it is about genuinely looking at your own performance and how it can improve.'

All participating managers reported a positive impact on team working: 'The process of sharing/discussing our own behaviour has helped us to strengthen open communication with each other,' and 'We were not giving each other their place and not chairing as effectively before.'

The received emphasis on co-operative and collaborative processes was evident in the comment: 'Working as a team with a co-team leader – now more aware of our strengths and how we can complement each other.'

The balance between directive or non-directive strategy, assertiveness or facilitation was something that participants had clearly thought about, realizing they had more opportunity to make choices in their communications. Changes in behaviour reflected individual goals, which included active listening, appropriate assertiveness, reflecting back to achieve shared understanding and ensuring fuller participation.

For the whole team to benefit from VEC's future application, participants felt that the engagement of all relevant team members was critical. Overall there was a desire to continue to apply VEC to individual learning, to hold periodic team meetings for reflection and to encourage colleagues to participate in such activity in order to develop an improved organizational leadership culture.

Unfortunately, further PSPS dissemination was interrupted by organizational restructuring and downsizing.

Project Two: VERP in FE

VERP was delivered to FE by PSPS using a similar, adapted, but renamed version of VEC that was embedded in a national strategy of active learning. The initial pilot of VER in two colleges trained 12 lecturers over two years, and demonstrated that applying the principles of attuned interactions and guidance to lecturer–student interactions was highly relevant to staff support and development, anticipating Cave, Roger and Young (2011). After six sessions, significant personal developments were reported. The framework was seen as a creative and relevant extension of existing video use that was applicable to staff and student development. Once again, the shared group process was valued.

A consequent request to train the National Access and Inclusion team for Scotland's colleges was accepted. Objectives were set within the overall development planning processes for the organization. Working across both a wider national team and colleges provided an opportunity to reflect on practices of communication within individual settings (management or supervision) and group management or facilitation. Five team members were trained over six sessions, each participant receiving personal CPD in the context of a shared team process. Aims included developing as a reflective practitioner, building self and peer observation and reflection strategies, identifying and evidencing best practice of communication for learning and teaching, and adapting initial VER training for future use.

Training was delivered that was consistent with the Fukkink and Todd (2011) and Fukkink and Helmerhorst (2013) findings on effectiveness. The PSPS model included the flexibility to suit organizational purposes and roles. Six sessions were delivered in realistic time scales (half a day each month) to an optimum group size of between five and eight, including approximately 30 minutes of individual reflection. Participants selected their clips, usually having spent time beforehand considering the working points. The discussions of these were recorded and summarized for each individual by a nominated peer. These were useful for individuals to self-assess and reflect, being aligned with pre-/post-measures of distance travelled, ongoing working points and perceived future needs.

In addition, the use of relatively brief, focused intervention (five to six sessions) and the connection between microanalysis and wider goals (allied to organizational priorities) were central to reflection. Finally, there was a focus on positive aspects, correcting negative perceptions by reframing and reviewing, or simply naming what was working well. Previous experience had associated video-work with negative behaviour as part of micro-teaching or critical analysis of interview technique. The affirmative experience was universally welcomed.

The group process clearly added value to individual development and helped to overcome the initial fears about being filmed. In one session it was possible to review one's own recording and to reflect on several others in similar circumstances. Collective efficacy should be explored in developing a delivery model for VERP; this requires additional skills to those used in individual supervision, but it is reassuring to realize that the principles of attuned interactions and guidance appear to be just as relevant.

All participants reported significant improvements. The videos included: presentations to colleges, national groups, planning meetings; chairing or facilitating groups (individually and jointly); ongoing problem-solving; and dealing with criticism or conflict. Evaluation demonstrated raised awareness of strengths in communication, including increases in personal insight and learning such as how to name feelings, intervening rather than ignoring, building relationships to support group engagement, and so on. From the comments, it is clear that VER represented a new experience: 'such fine scrutiny of communication activity was new to me – having a conceptual framework within which to identify structural responses was very useful'; and 'a tool to use which complements work we are involved in continually'.

The value of reflecting on group processes and personal strategies in meetings was a common theme: 'VER has reinforced that I am very much a team person and I do "turn take", listen effectively and contribute assertively.'

A valuable contribution to team development was recognized, improving understanding of team functioning: 'We were enabled to publicly recognise skills which we were unaware of and [which were] often taken for granted.' Another noted:

> We all assume an implicit set of skills to communicate at work, to manage presentations, chair meetings, problem-solve, make collective decisions and resolve conflict – this is highlighted explicitly in VER, with the aim of identifying strengths and building individual development.

Improved skills and knowledge included understanding group processes and how to maximize outcomes from them, for instance, actively promoting turn-taking and pacing of activities, and including the less active members. Participants greatly appreciated the capacity to name differences in behaviour, having observed themselves in work settings. They identified working points to build on learning and further application including new settings, delivering workshops or formal meetings and specific projects for including disengaged learners, and other national priorities. It was clear that the value of organizing 'time out' to reflect should not be underestimated given the extremely demanding work settings:

> One of the most valuable aspects of the training was having time with colleagues in a structured situation to review my skills and receive feedback that was well structured, so that it became clear what my strengths are and what I still need to work on.

VERP can add value where staff may feel relatively unsupported and where processes of supervision and support could be improved. VERP also provides a relative oasis of opportunity to reflect in a safe place with colleagues, when hectic work schedules mitigate against this.

Challenges of widening delivery

Developing VERP is in effect the mainstreaming of VIG, taking it beyond a therapeutic milieu to suit differing contexts. The first international conference on VERP (in Newcastle-upon-Tyne in 2013) evidenced growing application on, for example, effective interdisciplinary working, patient safety and assisting innovative change implementation in organizations, with seemingly endless potential. The chapter in this book by Doria, for example, applied VERP to a bank finance manager (see Chapter 9, this volume). However, this raises the question of how to present its relevance to such new settings. Training must correspond with organizational objectives and be the result of 'buy in' at management level, which can be challenging in the face of competing pressures. The presentation of relevance to a context is important, and key words such as 'reflect' and 'review' help to communicate the purposes of training.

Engaging management – whose initiative?

Management's involvement was important in the VERP training delivered by PSPS in both projects discussed in this chapter. Many well-intentioned interventions in the literature do not have the impact hoped for. Implementation science (see Kelly and Perkins 2012) emphasizes that the way an initiative is implemented is critical to its ultimate success: 'promoting change…has to take account of social, perceptual, attitudinal and value-based characteristics as well as existing frameworks for action, such as ethics, resources and policy directives' (p.6).

Preparation, specific to context, can only serve to improve the outcomes and ground any intervention in the real world. It is crucial to spend time in joint formulation with an organization, ideally shaping a training initiative from it that meets its needs. PSPS made considerable efforts to negotiate training, using existing structures to discuss wider psychological input, and suggesting adaptations to suit organizational priorities; this was based on previous pilot work. Such long-term work highlights the challenges of engaging organizations to commit to, receive and follow up intervention, and also the real-world factors that have an impact on sustainability. Positive practitioner take-up may not match the responses from distant or changing managers, and alterations to national and local structures, as well as funding streams, all have an impact.

VERP as a qualitative intervention

Automatic acceptance of qualitative approaches to staff development cannot be assumed. However, building communicative competence has wide potential relevance and should not be left to chance. The British Psychological Society (Dunsmuir and Leadbetter 2010) distinguishes between reflective, reciprocal and balanced communication. Clearly the balance between these is important and will vary according to role, relationship and context. Table 18.1 offers a perspective on how training may be received.

Table 18.1 Using VERP as a qualitative approach to management and leadership

Pros	Cons
Growing evidence of impact of quality of leadership on individual and team engagement in corporate purposes	Seen as 'too hard to tackle' as cultural or system level change is never a quick fix
A neglected yet key aspect of delivery	Competing need to focus on 'hard' outcome measures
Signals a 'caring'/emotionally literate organization that can connect internal relationships, staff support and output	Viewed as potential criticism or threat by management without such training
Raises profile of staff being valued and listened to	Increasing democratization perceived as threat to institutional authority
Can help prevent stress, mental health problems	Seen as sign of weakness – this was not needed in the past, so why now?
Contributes towards improvements in individual and team communication	Unwelcome by managers as it suggests need for change at all levels

Source: Hellier (2010)

An assertion of the benefits should help in discussions about setting aims. Cairns and Alexander (2013) highlight the benefit of improving the wellbeing of staff to maintain morale, while Braun (2011) suggests that successful organizations are premised on an understanding of social interaction. Rock (2009) cites nurturing emotionally intelligent leadership, while Lawson and Cox (2010) emphasize trust, confidence, relationship and team in any organization, especially the development of people for the long term, rather than a singular focus on short-term goals: 'By doing this, innovation, improved quality, greater customer care and higher productivity will be achieved' (p.12).

Unfortunately, in the experience of PSPS, economic challenge can promote cycles of restructuring, shorter-term thinking, emphasis on performance measures and swiftly changing priorities.

Conclusion

An ideal model guarantees sustainability, as far as possible, and PSPS work only went so far: over time, attempts to cascade the training fell foul of external challenges! However, the project added support to the view that VERP can bring about significant improvements for professional learning and development across new settings. The need to improve quality of communication continuously at all levels within any organization, including the client interface, provides an opportunity to consider how VERP may be delivered efficiently to assist in the process of meeting organizational need. The maintenance of good relationships with management and their continuing ownership of emerging findings will be critical. It is also important to adapt training methodology to align with organizational objectives and diverse structures. This requires the capacity to provide flexible input that is both credible and of a high standard, consistent with emerging accreditation.

CHAPTER 19

Sustaining Change in Complex Systems

VERP and the SPIN® Systems Change Assets™

Jane P. Nestel-Patt and Terri E. Pease

Introduction

There is general agreement that, to be sustainable, programme changes must affect more than individual practitioners; they must also address the systems — the interlocking and mutually influencing parts of schools, agencies and larger structures — where services are delivered (Fixsen *et al.* 2005). To accomplish this goal SPIN®USA introduces Video Interaction Guidance (VIG) and Video Enhanced Reflective Practice (VERP) simultaneously at all levels in educational and social services organizations. We call this comprehensive approach to organizational change the SPIN® Systems Change Assets™[1] (SCA) model, hereafter referred to as the SCA model or SCAs.

---

1   SPIN®USA is the non-profit national training institute for SPIN® Video Interaction Guidance™ (SPIN VIG™), VERP, and related models in the US. SPIN®, SPIN Video Interaction Guidance™, SPIN VIG™, Systems Change Assets™, SCAs™, SPIN Basic Contact Principles™, SPIN BCPs™ – these are legal trademarks of SPIN®USA, Inc. All rights reserved.

The SCA model brings three branches into one organization at the same time: VIG at the practice level (helping parents improve interaction and attunement with their children); VERP for supervisors (focused on the coaching and mentoring skills of social work supervisors in regular supervision with programme staff); and VERP for managers (coaching leaders and managers in team building, meetings management and organizational change strategies). In this chapter we describe how introducing a full SCA project in an organization generates changes in organizational culture and leadership as well as in practice and supervision.

SPIN® VIG and VERP share a common practice framework and core constructs, based on the original Netherlands 'basic contact principles' (Biemans 1990) (see Figure 19.1). These contact principles form the basis of the Association for Video Interaction Guidance UK (AVIGuk) 'principles of attuned interactions and guidance' (Kennedy, Landor and Todd 2011; see Chapter 1, this volume). Together, the SCAs' shared vocabulary and tools allow all parts of an agency to develop a coordinated organizational culture to implement and sustain improvements.

We based the SCA model on our early experiences in child welfare and early care and education, beginning in 1996 when we first implemented programmes in VIG for parent coaching and family therapy along with an early form of VERP for staff development. We learned that sustaining broad change in an organization is improbable, at best, if we train staff only at the direct service level or the supervisory level. Like more recent writers in the emergent field of implementation science, we realized the importance of a system-wide approach (Fixsen et al. 2005; Weiner 2009):

> The goal of implementation is to have practitioners base their interactions with clients and stakeholders on research findings (evidence-based practices or practices within evidence-based programs). To accomplish this, high-fidelity practitioner behavior is created and supported by core implementation components (also called 'implementation drivers'). These components are *staff selection, preserved and in-service training, ongoing consultation and coaching, staff and program evaluation, facilitative administrative support, and systems interventions.* (Fixsen et al. 2005, p.28; original emphasis)

BASIC CONTACT PRINCIPLES™
Developmental Pathways

CLUSTERS	PATTERNS	ELEMENTS
1 INITIATION AND RECEPTION	BEING ATTENTIVE	*turn toward someone* *look at someone* *friendly intonations* *friendly facial expressions* *friendly postures*
	ATTUNING ONESELF	*join* *nod* ***NAME*** *affirm*
2 INTERACTION	FORMING A GROUP	*activate each member* *look around* *check reception*
	MAKING TURNS	*give and take turns* *evenly share turns*
	COOPERATING	*collaborate* *help one another*
3 DISCUSSION	FORMING OPINIONS	OPINIONS: *give* *accept* *exchange* *investigate*
	GIVING CONTENT	TOPICS: *raise* *develop* *discuss in-depth*
	MAKING DECISIONS	AGREEMENTS: *propose* *accept* *amend*
4 CONFLICT MANAGEMENT	NAMING CONTRADICTIONS	*investigate intentions*
	RESTORING CONTACT	*return to Clusters 1,2 & 3*
	NEGOTIATING	*restate perspectives* *make agreements*

Figure 19.1 SPIN Basic Contact Principles™

Source: © SPIN® USA 2000 revised 2013, reproduced under license from AIT, based on Deker 1994

The SCA approach enables schools, social service agencies and similar systems to use VIG and VERP simultaneously to tackle three main tasks required to sustain new programmes (Bradach 2003; Fixsen *et al.* 2005), to:

- improve the competency of staff and the efficacy of programmes and services
- strengthen the quality of supervision and staff development

- improve leaders' ability to develop and sustain programmes, policies and organizational cultures that nurture and develop staff so that they are better able to strengthen the children and families they are funded to serve.

When all parts of an organization apply the common VIG/VERP tools and vocabulary, they create a continuous growth work environment and an organizational culture:

In California, as across the nation, public child welfare agencies struggle in their charge to institute system improvements in response to the [federal] mandate. SPIN® VIG-VERP is critical to our charge as a training academy to equip the supervisors and managers of these agencies with the skill to lead system improvement efforts. (David Foster, Director, Central California Child Welfare Training Academy)

VERP process

Following an orientation session by the VERP group leader (VIG-certified guider) that introduces participants (approximately four per group) to the core frameworks and constructs of the method, the process is as follows:

Step 1: VERP group participants each video about 10 minutes of their own work (clinician–client; supervisor–staff; leader–team).

Step 2: Prior to a group meeting, this source tape is reviewed with the VERP group leader to select best-practice clips (based on frameworks and constructs of the method) to share with colleagues in the VERP group.

Step 3: Participants share their respective clips with their colleagues (discussion guided by the VERP guider).

Step 4: Following the first or second group meeting, participants may opt to select their own clips for sharing without prior discussion with their guiders.

The number of sessions varies between 8 and 12 depending on the setting, skills or requests of the participants.

Applying the SCA model to practice: Two case studies

Fundación JUCONI, Mexico

SPIN®USA and AVIGuk jointly introduced VIG/VERP to Fundación JUCONI in Puebla, Mexico, to support families and to prevent family violence as well as to support supervision and staff development. Fundacion JUCONI is a 25-year-old non-governmental organization (NGO) serving street children and their families. At the same time, the organization's leaders began using the model as an executive coaching, leadership development and team-building tool. Certified VIG guiders at JUCONI learned to conduct individual and group VERP for colleagues and other staff to support supervision, improve the quality of practice and enhance the therapeutic element. The implementation of VIG (for parent coaching and family therapy) in conjunction with VERP (for staff development, supervision, leadership development and meeting management) enabled JUCONI to create a shared language and way of operating that shaped all its practice, programmes, policies and leadership principles. The SCAs brought about improvements across the entire organization.

VERP for supervision and meeting management at JUCONI began with a one-day orientation introducing the multiple theoretical strands that underlie VIG/VERP, describing how the model and principles apply to individual professional growth. Coaches introduced the distinction between the *whats* (goals for leadership success, such as 'facilitate productive team meetings') and the *hows* (items from the basic contact principles such as 'form a group by ensuring even and equal turns') (see Figure 19.2).

This was followed by an introduction to the model-specific supervisory, team building and meeting management process. After this, individual and group VERP coaching (eight to ten sessions) formed the programme. In these sessions, videoing, clip selection and shared review were informed by:

- the basic contact principles

- individual participants' skill levels and their own aspirations for growth and change

- core goals for leaders (refined by participants during their orientation session).

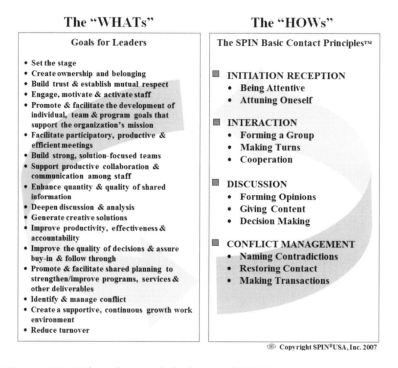

The "WHATs"

Goals for Leaders

- Set the stage
- Create ownership and belonging
- Build trust & establish mutual respect
- Engage, motivate & activate staff
- Promote & facilitate the development of individual, team & program goals that support the organization's mission
- Facilitate participatory, productive & efficient meetings
- Build strong, solution-focused teams
- Support productive collaboration & communication among staff
- Enhance quantity & quality of shared information
- Deepen discussion & analysis
- Generate creative solutions
- Improve productivity, effectiveness & accountability
- Improve the quality of decisions & assure buy-in & follow through
- Promote & facilitate shared planning to strengthen/improve programs, services & other deliverables
- Identify & manage conflict
- Create a supportive, continuous growth work environment
- Reduce turnover

The "HOWs"

The SPIN Basic Contact Principles™

- **INITIATION RECEPTION**
  - Being Attentive
  - Attuning Oneself

- **INTERACTION**
  - Forming a Group
  - Making Turns
  - Cooperation

- **DISCUSSION**
  - Forming Opinions
  - Giving Content
  - Decision Making

- **CONFLICT MANAGEMENT**
  - Naming Contradictions
  - Restoring Contact
  - Making Transactions

Copyright SPIN®USA, Inc. 2007

Figure 19.2 The whats and the hows of VERP

Source: © SPIN®USA 2000 revised 2013, reproduced under license from AIT, based on Dekker 1994

VERP for executive coaching and leadership applies the basic contact principles to team building, programme leading and policy decision-making at the organization's highest levels. This parallels VERP for staff development, shifting the focus to videoing and microanalysing team meetings and individual supervisory sessions.

The following report was written by JUCONI's Director General, Alison Lane:

> JUCONI's initial interest in VIG was as a tool to help improve relationships within the deeply troubled families

with whom we work and especially as a means of preventing family violence. The SCAs enable us to achieve greater coherence by using VERP (in conjunction with VIG for families) to reinforce our strengths-based culture, improve the therapeutic milieu that is central to JUCONI'S programs and mission, and strengthen organizational capacity.

The JUCONI team has for years described our approach as 'strengths-based'... As we progressed, our understanding of 'strengths-based' deepened to include being able to use the approach to name and discuss contradictions. One of the valuable outcomes of this has been to empower staff to more readily identify and manage challenges and inconsistencies – not only in their work with clients, but as a team. We now have a common language and techniques – VIG's principles of [attuned] interactions – which provide a robust framework within which to be able to safely tackle potentially difficult and threatening issues arising between staff members and between staff and the organization.

The introduction of VERP to support leadership development has led to several important, if unexpected, benefits, which are clearly illustrated in the experience of the administration team. The administrative director, who had recently joined the organization, led the work here. The administrative, accounting and operational logistics teams worked largely independently of each other in that they did not see themselves as one team or hold a regular team meeting. This disjunction was reflected in the myriad frictions between areas, the delays and difficulties in finding workable solutions and the amount of time he spent adjudicating disputes. He himself had reservations about introducing a weekly meeting and building a team comprised of members who didn't believe that their work would benefit from collaboration.

Through VERP we learned...to make the purpose of a meeting explicit and provide a motivational and forward-thinking framework; we identified key principles that would make meetings more effective. In the words of one initially reluctant participant, 'Slowly, we moved from testing one another to resolving specific problems to developing innovative proposals together and to co-creating better policies, programs and events for the benefit of JUCONI.' There was a palpable reduction in friction between areas, improving productivity and freeing up the administrative director's time since he was no longer needed to mediate conflicts.

The Director describes how VERP helped him to achieve more strategically focused and efficient team practices: 'I... tried my hardest to speak less and listen more. At first I realized I was just waiting for the other to finish speaking to then make my point, but as I genuinely practiced receiving everyone else's contributions and making them part of my reflections, we began to have deeper, more meaningful conversations and to come up with more creative ideas and solutions.'

Using VERP to develop leadership as well as to help clients provides us with a means of aligning the whole organization and keeping us moving forward together. We have seen a shift in mindset from seeing leaders as decision makers to seeing them as facilitators and promoters of others. We have a more participatory culture where successful leadership is understood in terms of promoting discussion, growing autonomy and pushing decision making down the line.

Northeast Parent and Child Society, New York State

The SCA model also allowed Northeast Parent and Child Society, a large child welfare programme serving 11 northern New York State counties, to remake its approach to serving children placed in foster care because of abuse or neglect. A certified VIG guider coached the six- to eight-session VERP groups. Groups comprised staff with comparable roles and responsibilities: for example, distinct groups for caseworkers and for casework supervisors. Individual and group goals were identified during the orientation day.

Following the orientation day, subsequent VERP sessions followed the structure and process described in the previous case study. In Session 1 the coach (VERP guider) explained the basic contact principles, emphasized the strengths-based framework and introduced two key concepts: the helping question (the change a coachee hopes to achieve with VERP), and naming (positive responsive descriptions of the initiatives that are seen in a video clip or in a live interaction). Coachees selected, presented and discussed video clips that demonstrated their capacity to invite and respond to initiatives, and group members explored the learning points that emerged from the discussion. Each session concluded with a review of the assignment for their subsequent videoing and clip selection.

Next, Deputy Chief of Services Kimberly Cummins, LMSW, and Director of Recruitment/Training Coordinator Julie Lindh, LCSW, describe their experience of using the SCAs at Northeast Parent and Child Society:

> In 2008, the Therapeutic Foster Family Program (TFFP) at Northeast Parent and Child Society sought to build a program culture and common treatment lens that would more effectively support the hundreds of youth and families we served. We sought a model that was based on the foundations of strengths-based, trauma-informed, family-focused and client-centered practice.
>
> We selected VIG/VERP specifically because we could involve staff at multiple levels: caseworkers and clinicians (who use VIG to support client families); supervisors and leaders (VERP supports their ability to guide staff, and to lead the programs and organization as a whole). Having video as an integral piece of the SCA model allowed for a tight focus on client engagement, relationship building and staff development/skill attainment. This was critical to providing a more consistent treatment approach. It also ensured that those same core values – building effective and productive relationships by identifying and utilizing individualized strengths and developing attuned interactions were reflected in our supervision and leadership.
>
> The SCA model offered three key things:
>
> • a common language and parallel process to guide and inform practice across the entire division
>
> • a manualized model for transforming/improving practice and programs

- an integrated strategy to support those changes.

Among the most exciting pieces of this approach was our implementation of VERP for professional development in groups. Our certified VIG practitioners and trainers have run VERP groups for case workers, clinical social workers/ therapists and program coordinators. Each person who participated was able to identify patterns in their practice that led to the development of more effective practices to improve client engagement and client outcomes.

Video interviews illustrate participants' experiences:

Jesmarie, a seasoned program manager, participated in a six-week VERP group with three colleagues who also supervise direct care staff working with foster children, foster parents and birth parents. Initially she had reservations about participating in a training that required sharing video clips of her work. After just one session, she was fully engaged, articulating its value and eager to continue. As a result of this work, Jesmarie says her staff feel more empowered and come to supervision with ideas and solutions, not just seeking direction and answers. She, in turn, feels more effective as a leader, able to build increasingly confident and competent staff. Jesmarie points specifically to her use of the detailed support for structuring supervision meetings as having helped her set the stage for ensuring that staff get their needs met in supervision while also focusing on practice and ongoing professional development.

Jesmarie has participated in numerous trainings aimed at improving her supervisory and management skills. She reports that she fell short when expected to implement the new skills covered in those trainings, even when she saw their value and benefit. Changes were difficult to sustain, and she quickly slipped back into old patterns. The VERP group enabled her to see, specifically and concretely, the changes she was implementing. This helped her replicate and sustain them. Additionally, because of our systemic integration of VIG/VERP, Jesmarie also benefits from being supervised by a manager who has also received VIG/VERP coaching.

Benefits of the SCA model

Model independence

Because the SCA approach focuses on turning the *whats* of a model (a specific curriculum or programme protocol) into *hows* (the way that practitioners actually interact when implementing the programme), the SCAs may be used to support the effective implementation of any evidence-based practice. The VERP practitioner uses the basic contact principles and other constructs of VERP to ensure that the qualitative aspects of practice are supported as strongly as the structured elements of the programme.

> While an abundance of credible consultation, information and training exists around strengths-based practice with individuals and families, the SPIN® [VIG-VERP] methodology provides a level of knowledge transfer that is, in my professional experience, unparalleled…clearly an impressive, measurable return on our investment in SPIN® USA's training. (Linda Holman, Human Services Manager, County of San Mateo, CA)

Explanatory theories integrated into a single theory of change

The analytic framework and practice constructs of the SCAs may support intervention programmes built on many explanatory theories. The basic contact principles and other core constructs of the model operationalize concepts from: attachment theory; theory of adult learning; systems and organizational theories; knowledge of cognitive and social development; and new knowledge in neuroscience relevant to education and social services. As model- and theory-independent constructs, the basic contact principles may be applied to healthy development at every developmental stage and to every job function that requires effective human interaction for success. They support:

- group formation (team building) and sustained cycles of mutually productive, reciprocal interactions

- collaborative, participatory in-depth discussion, analysis, accountability, planning, decision-making and follow-up

- attuned management of contradictions and conflict.

Wrap-around support for sustainable change

As an intervention that supports implementation, the SCA model can be 'wrapped around' the introduction and adoption of any programme, curriculum, policy or 'best practice' with fidelity to the original evidence-supported design. The SCAs advance the practice of implementation science (Fixsen *et al.* 2005) and support sustainable change, instilling the gains from new programmes into self-replicating practices and culture – the 'DNA' – of the agency.

Staff and leaders develop a common culture and a new way of working that holds leaders and supervisors to the same practice standards as direct service providers. The same theory of change and set of principles for learning and human development are applied to service delivery, to the running of the institution, and to the supervision and development of staff. Practitioners, programme leaders and executive staff work within a single explanatory system and employ a single change model. Thus, an organization may use the SCA model to move beyond aspirational, strengths-based mission statements (for example, 'We believe that clients have strengths, resources and the ability to recover from adversity'), and build an organization and practice culture that actually produces strengths-based workers, supervisors, leaders, programmes, policies and practices.

Conclusion

At every level of the system it is the team members who must implement changes in policy and adopt new content knowledge, curricula or programmes. Real systems change can only occur when the relational and interactional skills of all these members improve. Bringing the SCA model to systems change efforts transforms not only *what* organizations intend to do, but moment by moment, and interaction by interaction, *how* they actually do it.

Part Six

EVIDENCE

CHAPTER 20

Effects of Video Enhanced Reflective Practice (VERP)

Current Evidence and Future Challenges

Ruben Fukkink, Sanne Huijbregts and Liz Todd

Introduction

Video feedback is a well-known instructional method applied in various programmes in tertiary education and postgraduate professional training to improve the communication skills of a broad group of 'interpersonal professionals' (Hargie, Saunders and Dickson 1983). These include teachers, psychologists, social workers, doctors and nurses, and professional caregivers, for whom effective communication plays a vital role in their work. This chapter discusses evidence for the effectiveness of video feedback (VF) for reflection on professional practice.

Video Enhanced Reflective Practice (VERP) is a specialized form of VF being defined for the first time in this book, so as yet there is no established evidence base. However, its similarity to much VF provides the evidence for many aspects of VERP. The two chapters that follow present some of the first small-scale semi-experimental evidence for VERP. The chapter by Gibson, Elliott and Archer (Chapter 22) evaluates the impact of VERP on burnout, self-efficacy and attunement for staff in a secure forensic in-patient service for young people aged 12–19. The chapter by Ferguson (Chapter 21) is an evaluation of the impact of VERP on a three-month preschool literacy intervention.

Various researchers and trainers have explored the new educational opportunities offered by video. In its infancy, the use of video for instructional purposes and professional development was labelled a micro-training paradigm. It focused on specific, concrete behaviours with a relatively brief duration, usually studied with behavourial counts (for example, head nodding, frequent eye contact, allowing the children to take turns). Later, VF research programmes have focused on more holistic skills such as like sensitivity, developmental stimulation or empathy. In other programmes, trainees are instructed in client communication according to a professional communication model with distinct phases (for example, initiating the session, gathering information and closing the session). VF has increasingly been used to stimulate reflection (see Tripp and Rich 2012), particularly with pre-service teachers, building on the paradigm of the reflective practitioner (Schön 1983).

Feedback in general plays a vital role in skills teaching and in different learning theories (see Thurlings et al. 2013 for an overview). VF functions as a catalyst for critical reflection and provides trainers and trainees with a tool to engage in a dialogue (Fuller and Manning 1973; Hargie et al. 1983; Hosford 1980). Furthermore, it allows an in-depth analysis of the behaviour of interest and the provision of constructive feedback related to verbal aspects (the content of what is being said), paralingual aspects (intonation, speaking pace and volume) and non-verbal aspects (for example, body posture, eye contact and use of gestures). VF may focus on receptive skills (for example, looking at the other person and use of silences), informative skills (for example, explaining things in a comprehensible way and speaking calmly), and relational skills (for example, asking about the other's experiences and displaying empathy) (see Duffy et al. 2004; Hulsman et al. 1999).

Reviews of experimental study into VF

Various VF interventions have been evaluated in different experimental studies. In a number of reports the effects of different training formats have been summarized, although not every review had an exclusive focus on VF (see Fukkink, Todd and Kennedy 2011 for a review). In a recent meta-analysis with a specific focus on VF for professionals, Fukkink, Trienekens and Kramer (2011) showed that it is effective for improving professionals' key interaction skills; more accurately, interventions that include VF appeared effective, because it is always integrated in multimodal and multifaceted interventions with other instructional components. The aggregate effect size, based on 217 experimental results from 33 studies involving a total of 1058 people, was 0.40 standard deviation (se=0.07). This aggregated outcome is equal to a medium effect size. For the verbal, non-verbal and paralingual domains, the effect sizes were 0.42, 0.35 and 0.39, respectively. The aggregated effect sizes for receptive, informative and relational skills were 0.44, 0.47 and 0.35, respectively. To conclude, VF is an effective method that contributes to the development of a wide range of key professional skills including verbal, non-verbal and paralingual aspects. VF is also able to improve receptive, informative and relational skills of trainees. Experimental effects are somewhat smaller for the relational skills domain and for non-verbal aspects of interactional behaviour.

Moderators of the effects of VF

After many years of VF research, various authors such as Hargie *et al.* (1983), Hill and Lent (2006), Hosford (1980), Hung and Rosenthal (1981) and McLeod (1987) have already emphasized that research should identify key variables that moderate the effectiveness of VF. This recommendation has not lost its relevance today. Empirical research has so far suggested only a small number of possible moderators of the effects of VF.

Outcomes of VF are considerably greater if a standard evaluation form, giving participants an overview of the desired target behaviour, forms part of the training programme (Fukkink, Trienekens and Kramer 2011; effect size=0.55 for training with coding form, a medium effect, versus 0.21 for training without coding form, a small effect). A possible explanation for this finding is that such a form structures the observation, thereby focusing the participants' attention on aspects of their own behaviour that are central to the programme. Structured observation forms enable participants – to use a metaphor borrowed from VF – to zoom in and focus on the professional target behaviour that is practised within the training programme. No relationship was found with the presence of other forms of instruction supplementary to VF. The use of observation forms during the feedback sessions, which is very much at the heart of VF, therefore emerged in this meta-analysis as more effective than other instructional components such as explaining, modelling and practising the target skills. Two other moderators were methodological. First, effects were larger if the outcomes were evaluated with a measure of a positive trait (for example, respect for autonomy), as opposed to a negative trait (for example, intrusiveness). Second, effects were also larger if the outcome measure measured a molar (that is, holistic) skill (for example, sensitivity of a professional caregiver) instead of a micro-skill (for example, receiving initiatives of a child).

More research is needed to reveal which factors facilitate or hinder learning in VF interventions. Meta-analytic research can only find associations between the effects of VF and coded study characteristics, including VF-related variables. However, these correlations do not indicate causal relationships. From a research perspective, associations found in a review indicate only possible, tentative relationships that should be put to the test in an experimental study.

Outcome measures in experimental research

Different measures have been used in VF research to determine the experimental effects of VF for various professionals, reflecting the different professional contexts and programmes with their unique quality dimensions. Depending on the VF programme, the measure may focus on verbal aspects (i.e. the content of what is being said), paralingual aspects (i.e. intonation, speaking pace and volume), or non-verbal aspects (for example, body posture, eye contact and use of gestures), or a combination of these. Furthermore, the measure may relate to receptive skills (for example, asking open questions, looking at the other person and use of silences), informative skills (for example, explaining things in a comprehensible way and speaking calmly) or relational skills (for example, asking about the other's experiences and displaying empathy). The review study of Fukkink, Trienekens and Kramer (2011) showed that the measures involved predominantly verbal skills (82 per cent), and to a far lesser extent, non-verbal (33 per cent) and paralingual skills (17 per cent); these numbers do not add to 100 per cent because some measures pertained to more than one aspect. The outcome measures can be broken down into interpersonal-affective (54 per cent), receptive (47 per cent) and information skills (31 per cent); again, the numbers do not add up to 100 per cent because a single outcome measure may cover more than one domain. In addition, the selected measures may capture positive behavourial aspects (for example, contingent reinforcement, confirmation of client signals or affective mutuality) or negative aspects (for example, not responding to an initiative or intrusive behaviour).

An important distinction is the difference between micro-measures and molar skills. In VF research, micro-measures have predominantly been used. A detailed assessment using micro-measures occurred in 70 per cent of cases, with assessment of molar skills occurring less frequently (30 per cent). However, these figures also reflect the fact that studies with a fine-grained analysis of trainees' behaviour often use several micro-measures, whereas studies with a focus on molar skills usually select a single central outcome measure.

Experimental designs for future VF research

A typical feature of many experimental group studies into VF is that small to very small sample sizes have been used in the evaluation (see, however, Groeneveld *et al.* 2011 and Helmerhorst *et al.*, submitted). The studies in the review of Fukkink, Trienekens and Kramer (2011) had an average sample size of the experimental group of 20 participants, but there was serious variation, and some studies included even fewer than ten participants. The small sample sizes may well be explained by the extensive training format for trainers with the selection of video materials and subsequent discussion with trainees, often in a one-to-one scenario. The experimental evaluation of VF programmes, which very often involves videotaped assessment of trainees' behaviour, is also extensive, particularly when a fine-grained analysis of the video footage with various micro-measures is involved (see Derry *et al.* 2010). This may also explain why sample sizes are often small in the evaluation in the context of VF (see Fukkink, Trienekens and Kramer 2011); sample sizes are small, too, in many VF studies with families (see Fukkink 2008).

Different designs that require smaller number of participants may be interesting for researchers with an interest in VF. A different experimental methodology that has received only scant attention from VF researchers is experimental single-subject research. This type of design has been applied in some experimental VIG studies in the context of family research (see, for example, Juffer, van Ijzendoorn and Bakermans-Kranenburg 1997; Meharg and Lipsker 1991). However, also for VF, some interesting single-subject design studies have been published (see Damen *et al.* 2011; Robinson 2011; Williams and Gallinat 2011). In particular, multiple baseline designs are an interesting candidate for future experimental evaluation. A multiple baseline design is a type of research involving the careful measurement of multiple persons, traits or settings both before and after a treatment. In a multiple baseline design across participants (see Robinson 2011 for an example), the start of treatment conditions is staggered across individuals. An experimental effect is demonstrated if the performance of the first trainee improves after the introduction of VF, and the performance of the non-treated trainees does not improve. The treatment subsequently shifts to the second trainee, and performance should now improve for this person. The same pattern should be observed for the third trainee when VF is finally introduced for the last trainee in this design. It is also important that the interaction training for a participant only begins after a stable baseline has been recorded, and only finishes when measures regain stability after VF. In a multiple-baseline across-behaviours design (see Williams and Gallinat 2011 for an example), different behaviours of the same individual are treated in a staggered fashion, following the same logic as the multiple baseline across participants. An experimental effect is demonstrated for this design only if the treated behaviours improve individually after introduction of VF, while the non-treated behaviours remain stable. These designs allow further investigation of the effects of VF in small-scale, but interesting, experimental studies.

Future research: VF and VERP in practice

The effects of VF have been evaluated in several publications. Less attention has been paid to the actual practice of VF, and such studies should shed light on the actual practice of VF. This line of study may also reveal possible moderators of the effects of VF, thereby linking descriptive and experimental research, and adding further insights for VERP practitioners.

Meta-analytic and other review studies have shown that feedback in itself does not improve performance, and may even produce negative outcomes (Hattie and Timperley 2007; Kluger and DeNisi 1996; Shute 2008). In addition, working with a video camera and watching oneself certainly does not in itself guarantee a successful intervention (Brophy 2004; Hargie *et al.* 1983). The question, then, is how VF programmes realize a systematic and effective use of VF, thereby creating a supportive and analytical environment (Borko *et al.* 2008). How do different trainers and trainees make systematic use of the video and engage in meaningful reflection during a feedback session in order to reach effective and high-level skills? With the focus of the camera on the trainer, as well as on the trainee, research should show how video actually enhances reflective practice. For example, how do experienced trainers succeed in constructive dialogues with their trainees? And how do trainers blend instruction, video feedback and verbal feedback? Process studies of VF may, for example, shed light on how they stimulate the gradual shift from the self-centred and instrumental thinking of pre-service teachers to pupil-centred thinking and a deeper level of reflection (see Lamb, Lane and Aldous 2013; Tripp and Rich 2012).

A basic, descriptive model, which we describe below, may guide the description and analysis of the shared review conversations in VERP. This concise model intends to capture the basic elements of the dynamics of VF. First, we distinguish between structural aspects of VF interventions, distinguishing between empirically motivated characteristics of the trainer, trainee and the video. Following Hosford and Mills (1983), we distinguish between specific modes of showing the video clips in VF. Instruction is also included, because VF is usually part of a multicomponent treatment with different instructional elements (see Hargie *et al.* 1983). Other basic categories include the training and working experience of the trainee (see Huhra, Yamokoski-Maynhart and Prieto 2008). We have also included the use of a structured format for observation of the video materials (Table 20.1), because this relates to learning effects (Fukkink, Trienekens and Kramer 2011). This observation format, which guides participants during the VF sessions (often called 'cueing'), provides an overview of the specific target behaviours, and thereby links instruction to feedback and practice in a systematic fashion.

The central feedback component of the model is embedded in educational theories of professional development and (video) feedback. The model allows an analysis of different types of content from the shared review sessions and the interaction, the different roles of trainer and trainee, and the interplay between trainer, trainee and the video images. The model may also be applied for the analysis of learner's content in video annotation tools (see Rich and Hannafin 2009).

We adopt a broad definition of feedback, fitting in with the comments of several authors who have emphasized the richness of the feedback in shared review sessions (see, for example, Doria, Strathie and Strathie 2011). The model distinguishes key elements in order to categorize the various elements from both trainer and trainee in VF studies. First, we distinguish between skills, attitude and knowledge as related and complementary learning domains. This dimension, which is derived from valid and well-known educational theories of professional competencies (see, for example, Baartman and de Bruijn 2011; Ellström 1997; Weinert 2001), is included to emphasize the important context of professional development of VF studies. The major focus in VF sessions may be related to trainees' behaviour, because this is what is visible in the video clips. However, both the trainer and the trainee may relate the professional behaviour, as demonstrated in the video clip, to professional knowledge and professional attitudes.

Table 20.1 Structural and process features of VF		
Structural features of VF	Process features of VF	Outcomes
Trainer features • Working experience • Training (train the trainer) • Demographics	• Actions prior to (shared) review • Nature of film taken • Identity of person taking video (trainer or trainee): whether or not video is analysed prior to review • Identity of person analysing video prior to (shared) review • Feedback and communication during (shared) review sessions (see Figure 20.2) • Role taken by trainer and trainee (who has responsibility to make comments on video) • Nature of the comments on the video (relating to an agreed list of behaviours, strength-based comments, critical comments) • Video play: length of video excerpts • Video techniques: slow motion or accelerated; freeze-frame; split-screen; picture- or sound-only video feedback; serial viewing • Video annotation • Timing of feedback: before, during and/or after viewing • Use of a structured form for observation (related to instruction)	• Behaviour • Attitude • Knowledge
Trainee features • Previous experience with VF • Training: pre-service/in-service • Demographics		
VF features • Sessions: number of sessions, period, follow-up or booster session • Individual or (small) group sessions, supervision and/or peer review • Time between filming and viewing		
Instruction (complementary): Verbal: written instruction, prescriptive model or description of target skills Visual: video exemplars, video annotation tools, discrimination training, observation of others, role-playing, workplace or classroom visits		

Building on educational theories of feedback, we distinguish between the dimensions of feed up, feedback and feed forward (see Hattie and Timperley 2007). These concepts have also been labelled as *Where am I going?* (What are the goals?), *How am I going?* (What progress is being made toward the goal?) and *Where to next?* (What activities need to be undertaken to make better progress?). Feed up involves the information given about the attainment of learning goals related to the task or performance. They may be related to specific attainments or understandings or to differing qualities of experience. Different authors have listed or described categories that fit in with this category. For example, negotiating the goals, as mentioned by Ŝilhánová and Sancho (2011), fits in with the feed up category. Feedback is information relative to a task or performance goal, often in relation to some standard, to prior performance, or to success or failure on a specific part of the task, also referred to as performance feedback. Frequently mentioned categories in the literature such as 'evaluating' and 'critiquing' fit in with this category. Finally, feed forward means providing information that leads to greater possibilities for learning, including enhanced challenges, self-regulation over the learning process, more strategies and processes to work on the tasks, for example. Categories such as summarizing strengths, formulating the working points, making the bridge (Ŝilhánová and Sancho 2011), giving suggestions (Borko *et al.* 2008) and goals and change (see Doria *et al.* 2011) are examples from previous studies that fit in with the feed forward category. In addition, the distinction between feedback alone and feedback, complemented with antecedents, goal-setting or the behavourial consequences of Alvero, Bucklin and Austin (2001), is related to this last category.

The three distinguished types of feedback may relate to knowledge, attitude or skills, including receptive skills, informative skills and relational skills in professional development (see Hulsman *et al.* 1999). It is to be expected that comments related to behaviour are frequently observed, because the interactions centre on the analysis of videotapes. However, in the discussion of these video excerpts, trainer and trainee may also discuss professional knowledge and beliefs (see also Blomberg, Stürmer and Seidel 2011). In addition, combinations of these categories (indicated with arrows in Figure 20.1) are also possible.

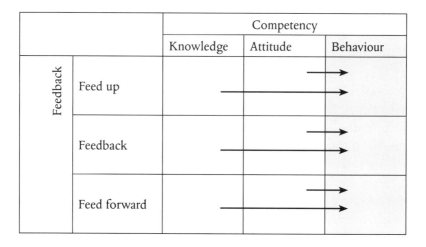

Figure 20.1 Overview of categories for the analysis of shared review conversations for VF studies

Theoretically, four combinations of the three competency categories are possible (KA, KB, AB, KAB, where K=knowledge, A=attitude and B=behaviour). In a shared review conversation, for example, the beliefs of a teacher (i.e. the attitude domain) may be explicitly related to practices (i.e. the behaviour domain).

Depending on the specific research question and taking into account different theoretical perspectives on this topic (see Thurlings *et al.* 2013), it is interesting to add specific feedback characteristics that distinguish other key elements within a broader category for analytical purposes. Depending on the specific focus of the study, it may be important to distinguish between general pedagogic comments content and specific content-related matters (see Borko *et al.* 2008). Fitting in with the evaluative dimension of feedback, the difference between positive and negative feedback may also be distinguished (see, for example, Doria *et al.* 2011; Fukkink, Trienekens and Kramer 2011). This category may be complemented with the frequently mentioned distinction between respectful or neutral feedback, and feedback that threatens self-esteem (see, for example, Kluger and DeNisi 1996; Thurlings *et al.* 2013). Coding whether feedback is related to a coding sheet or a previous instruction is also an interesting category, as this type of feedback is associated with more positive outcomes (see Fukkink, Trienekens and Kramer 2011).

Different authors have emphasized the communicative context of the shared review sessions with interactions between the trainer and trainee and, possibly, other people (for example, in a video club a small number of students may watch videos of themselves and other students in a small learners' community: see Borko *et al.* 2008, for instance). This interactive nature has been given different labels such as co-creation or even 'the dance' (see Kennedy 2011). Also, various categories from VF studies refer to the interactive nature of the sessions (for example, appraising, challenging and negotiating). The model may possibly be supplemented with basic speech acts that occur often in any discourse, for example, a researcher may include the categories of question and answer as basic categories of communication. Other categories that structure the conversation are the suggestion of further observation of the video (Doria *et al.* 2011), for example.

Fitting in with the interactive nature of VF review sessions, it may be valuable to take into account the sequential nature of the interactions. This type of analysis may reveal typical trainer–trainee sequences in turn-taking during the review, such as questions from the trainer and responses from the trainee. At a higher level, Ginsburg, Cami and Preston (2010) hypothesize that a review starts with a descriptive phase, followed by a reflective phase and finally, a critical phase. Sequential analysis may also make clear whether reviews typically follow a specific pattern with distinct phases. It may also be possible that this pattern is found at a lower level with recurring cycles of description, reflection and a critical analysis. Finally, the descriptive model suggests some hypotheses that may guide future research and may be put to the test. Following Hattie and Timperley, feedback has a more powerful impact if the three types of feedback are combined.

Conclusion

VERP is an effective method in professional development for various 'interpersonal professionals' (Hargie *et al.* 1983). The central hypothesis 'Does VF work?' needs further investigation in experimental research with the experimental validation of new innovative formats.

Specifically, follow-up measurement of trainees deserves more attention in future experimental studies, because we currently have relatively little knowledge of the retention of training effects. In addition, possible moderators of VF effects need further investigation.

An interesting theme for the experimental study into the effects of VF is what trainers and trainees do during the VF sessions. These sessions, which are at the heart of VF interventions, are still a 'black box' in the scientific literature, and future process studies should reveal the dynamics of VF. It is important to determine whether VF is able to change dyadic interactions in a qualitative fashion. For example, do professional conversations follow a different sequence of stages after training? Is there a shift from repetitive question-and-answer cycles with a child, following the lead of a caregiver, towards more balanced turn-taking? Although we have educational categories to capture well-known structural aspects of training (for example, number of sessions, working experience of the trainer) and some specific VF-related variables (for example, average number of minutes for video excerpts and emphasis on positive feedback), a thorough categorization of the different programmes is not yet possible. This descriptive line of study should shed more light on the practice of VF in the professional development of pre-service and in-service trainees.

CHAPTER 21

Improving Interactions, Improving Literacy in Early Years[1]

An Evaluation of a Video Enhanced Reflective Practice (VERP)/Literacy Pilot

Nancy Ferguson

> This training was very enjoyable and beneficial to my own personal and professional development and my practice within early years. I have embedded these new skills, and hope to continue using VERP within my nursery centre as part of a whole-team approach. Thank you for the opportunity. (Early years worker, June 2013)

This chapter documents the introduction of Video Enhanced Reflective Practice (VERP) to a large local authority. VERP is a flexible training model that can be used to enhance communication skills in a number of contexts. In this project the following question was asked:

---

1 Pamela Bell and Marianne McLafferty were the Research and Development Officers working on this project. They were supported by Victoria Smith, Iain Walker and Linzi McCorkell.

Does Video Enhanced Reflective Practice improve staff skills in the early years sector, with particular reference to literacy teaching behaviour?

Background

In common with all local authorities, North Lanarkshire Council has a strong commitment to reducing inequality and narrowing the attainment gap. An evidence-based active literacy strategy has been operating in the Council for eight years (for children aged 5–12). Intervening early in an appropriate way to support emerging literacy skills is considered crucial in providing learners with the best start in learning.

Research indicates that focusing on key areas in literacy can produce gains for young children. These areas include interventions in the areas of language (National Early Literacy Panel 2008) and phonology (Snow, Burns and Griffin 1998), in the skills developed through interactive book sessions (Weitzman and Greenberg 2010), and in home–school partnerships (Effective Provision of Pre-School Education [EPPE] Project, University of London IOE 2004). Furthermore, the role of the adult is considered crucial in supporting early literacy development. For example, Howe (1981) noted that adults are more likely to facilitate vocabulary growth when they are willing to listen, watch and interpret the child's behaviour, to follow rather than to lead, and to show tolerance of the child's wrong words.

Within North Lanarkshire establishments, children benefit from opportunities to engage in child-directed play. Staff were interested in exploring ways of making short group sessions child-centred and effective. Wasik (2008) suggests that in the preschool context this type of session should be playful, engaging and tailored to the interests of individual groups; its organization should allow the adult to plan specific achievement goals for children that are developmentally appropriate, whilst maintaining flexibility of response.

It was with these thoughts in mind that the Psychological Service and the Quality Improvement Service embarked on a literacy pilot using VERP.

Intervention

Combined literacy and VERP training was introduced to six nurseries (three nursery centres and three nursery classes) in North Lanarkshire during 2013. Each head teacher was asked to identify a volunteer from their senior management team and a member of staff who worked directly with children to undertake the training. It was considered important that managers of the establishments had a thorough understanding of VERP and the literacy elements in order to support staff and to embed this approach.

The 12 staff members came together for the sessions, along with three Video Interaction Guidance (VIG) supervisors. They were joined by two literacy tutors for the initial training day, making a cohort of 14. An additional half-day training session covered the use of iPads for taking and editing video.

The VERP component consisted of one full day of training, three subsequent half-day group supervisions, and a final half-day for sharing, celebration and accreditation. The full-day training provided staff with background information on VIG and the principles of attuned interactions (Kennedy, Landor and Todd 2011; see Chapter 1, this volume), as well as hands-on practice in analysing brief video clips of themselves with children (or with other staff, in the case of the managers), which they had brought with them. Each of the following VERP group supervision sessions started with some whole-group work in which the practice of focusing on attuned interaction and keeping clips short was consolidated. For example, in one session the theme 'Managing difficult conversations' was explored by microanalysing film footage provided by the guider. In another session, a VIG supervisor supported the whole group to microanalyse a clip of a parent and child in order to identify what made the conversation more successful, using the principles of attuned interactions. The trainees then split into three parallel groups, each with a VIG supervisor (VERP guider), in order to share the clips that they had filmed of themselves in their work context.

The majority of the participants were, as intended, looking at their interaction with children in learning contexts, and so the relationship between attuned interaction and the teaching of literacy featured in the group discussion. In order to help the staff see more clearly the relationship between these two features, they were presented with a further half-day training course entitled 'Nurturing Young Readers'. This course had been prepared by a working group comprising early years practitioners, educational psychologists and literacy development officers. It offered guidance on sharing books with children, and was based on the 'three read approach' advocated by Weitzman and Greenberg (2010). In this approach, an adult shares the same book with a small group of children on three separate occasions, with a different focus each time.

Careful consideration was given to the timing of the literacy course. The project team was keen to ensure that the staff had a good grasp of the principles of attuned interactions before applying this understanding to a literacy strategy. However, if the literacy aspect was delayed, the staff would not be able to obtain feedback on their use of the technique. In the end, it was decided to insert 'Nurturing Young Readers' between the third and fourth VERP session. This decision seems to be vindicated by the results.

The timetable for the project is outlined in Table 21.1.

Table 21.1 Timetable for VERP pilot project
Action
January Make proposal to head of service/education officer. Approve project.
February Identify pilot establishments. Hold initial meeting with head of service and heads of establishments. *NB Purpose of this meeting is to provide a brief overview of VERP and invite heads of establishment to opt into the pilot.*
Send letter to pilot establishments (providing details about VERP).
Secure trainers and establish dates for training.
Order iPads and arrange iPad training.
Plan information meeting and VERP sessions with trainers.
Inform pilot establishments of training dates.
Prepare parental consent forms.
Access and prepare log books for participants.

March Deliver iPad training. Provide brief overview of VERP training and encourage staff to take video to bring to VERP session 1.
Start to deliver VERP sessions, ideally two to three weeks apart. VERP Session 1 – full-day training Participants receive: • training on VIG background and principles of attuned interactions • hands-on practice analysing brief video of themselves with children (or with staff/parents in the case of the managers) in small groups.
VERP Session 2 – half-day Short 'teaching session' after which participants meet in small groups to micro analyse clips.
April VERP Session 3 – half-day Short 'teaching session' after which participants meet in small groups to micro analyse clips.
Deliver Literacy training 'Nurturing young readers'
May VERP Session 4 – half-day Short 'teaching session' after which participants meet in small groups to micro analyse clips.
VERP Session 5 – half-day Accreditation: A final half-day for all to reflect together on their learning, to share clips, to forward plan, etc., and to celebrate achievement.

Evaluation

METHOD

The project was evaluated by research staff from the Psychological Service. They carried out a pre- and post-intervention comparison between the pilot establishments and a matched control group of establishments. The control group received no intervention at the time of the pilot project, but was subsequently able to access VERP training in line with the project's ethical principles.

The establishments were selected to represent a cross-section of socioeconomic index and establishment type within the local authority. Information about type of establishment and deprivation (based on the Scottish Index of Multiple Deprivation; see Scottish Government 2010) was gathered from North Lanarkshire Council and was used to match control and pilot establishments.

The video data for the evaluation were obtained from one member of staff at each of the six pilot establishments and one member of staff at each of the six control establishments. Book reading sessions with a small group of children aged three to five in each nursery were filmed with the same staff member at pre-test (March/April 2013) and post-test (June 2013).

Video observations focusing on staff behaviours were analysed using event sampling. The categories were selected to combine behaviours of effective literacy teaching (see, for example, Topping and Ferguson 2005; Weitzman and Greenberg 2010) and elements of effective interaction (see, for example, Dickinson and Tabors 2001). They included:

- *General adult behaviour:* for example, giving information and instruction, interaction, questioning, non-teaching activities.

- *Specific literacy behaviours:* developing children's emergent literacy skills and understanding of stories. Sub-areas included: developing literacy skills (for example, concepts of print, vocabulary and use of illustrations); narrative story elements (for example, character, setting, actions and problem resolution); aiding comprehension (for example, prediction, inference and summarizing).

- *Adults' question types:* for example, knowledge questions (about print and literacy), literal questions (about information explicitly stated in the text) and inferential questions (which go beyond the text).

- *Turn-taking: Strive for five:* Dickinson and Tabors (2001) suggest that adults should receive children's verbal initiatives and seek to engage the child in five turns during interactions. This type of interaction was included in the analysis.

Qualitative information was gathered from pilot staff following the video observations using a self-complete questionnaire with a combination of open-ended and scaling questions. The open-ended questions were studied using a thematic analysis approach (Braun and Clark 2006). A focus group was later conducted to allow participants to expand on their responses and to ensure that the initial analysis of the data was accurate.

QUANTITATIVE RESULTS

The results of analysis showed that the VERP/Active Literacy intervention had a significant and positive impact on the behaviours of early years staff in all areas explored in the research. Non-parametric tests were used to analyse the data. Due to the small sample size, the Mann Whitney U statistic is reported only where significant. Difference scores (measuring the positive or negative distance between a pre- and post-score) were calculated to measure whether there was a significant difference between the VERP/Active Literacy and control groups.

Analysis of general adult behaviour showed a greater shift in the behaviours of VERP/Active Literacy group staff (see Figure 21.1). The VERP group decreased in the time they spent giving information and instruction compared to the control group who increased in this area.

Comparison of Difference Scores for Nursery Staff Behaviours

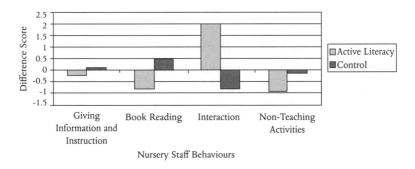

Figure 21.1 General adult behaviour

Time spent engaging in interactions with children increased for the VERP group, and possibly as a result there was a decrease in the adult reading aloud. The opposite trend was observed in the control group. There was a decrease in non-teaching activities in both groups, with the VERP group displaying a greater reduction in this area. This positive result suggests that in the pilot groups staff spent less time, for example, dealing with issues of poor conduct and more time engaged in the literacy activity.

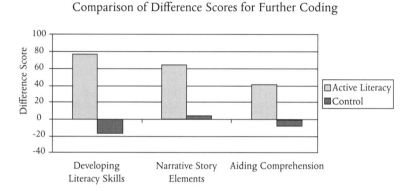

Figure 21.2 Specific literacy behaviours

Further video coding was conducted to concentrate on 'giving information' and 'instruction' with specific focus on literacy teaching behaviours (i.e. developing children's emergent literacy skills and understanding of stories) (see Figure 21.2). The purpose of this was to ascertain whether a staff development programme that focused primarily on building skills in attunement (VERP) could also improve literacy teaching behaviours. The VERP group increased in 'developing literacy skills', 'narrative story elements' and 'aiding comprehension'. The control group's scores decreased for 'developing literacy skills' and 'aiding comprehension'. An increase was seen for 'narrative story elements', although this was smaller than the increase in the VERP group. These results demonstrated that literacy teaching behaviours could be improved through this model of staff development.

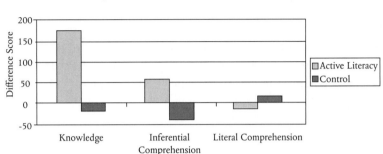

Figure 21.3 Adults' question types

All questions asked by nursery staff to children were noted and categorized (see Figure 21.3). The VERP/Active Literacy group increased in the number of 'knowledge' and 'inferential' comprehension questions they posed, while the control group decreased. There was a reduction of literal comprehension (or testing) questions (for example, 'What colour is this?') by the VERP group, and an increase of this type of question by the control group. These results suggest that, as a result of the intervention, the VERP group asked more open, challenging questions than the control group.

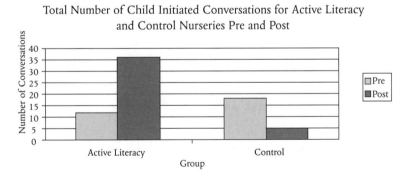

Figure 21.4 Turn-taking: Strive for five

In the VERP/Active Literacy group there was an increase in the number of child-initiated 'Strive for five' conversations, compared to the control group where there was a slight decrease (see Figure 21.4).

This means that at post-test the VERP group staff members were receiving more verbal initiatives than they were at pre-test, and the control staff were receiving slightly fewer of these cues at post-test in comparison to pre-test. This category is very closely linked to the VIG principles of attunement, and suggests that VERP participants were generalizing their learning from VERP into literacy teaching.

QUALITATIVE RESULTS

VERP certainly helps you to become more reflective and better at listening. I am very grateful to have received such valuable training. (Nursery teacher, June 2013)

The following categories were constructed through thematic analysis of data from the questionnaires and focus group.

Initial views of participants

Although all participants were volunteers, some initial anxieties were reported at the beginning of the intervention. These included concerns about using technology, viewing themselves on film, and feeling vulnerable and open to criticism. Although the one-day training helped to allay these fears, it was not until the second VERP session that the participants started to realize that this approach was quite different from others they had experienced. Many said they previously had negative connotations of being observed in order to be graded during teacher training.

Views of participants at the end of the initial training day

Arguably, effective application of the principles of attunement by VERP guiders should ensure that participants find VERP helpful. In this project, summative written evaluations from questionnaires and a focus group were used to investigate whether staff had, in fact, found the training helpful.

Fourteen participants completed the written evaluation. All said they would recommend VERP to a colleague. On a scale of 1 to 5 (with 1 being 'not at all helpful' and 5 being 'very helpful'), 13 people rated VERP training at 5 and one person at 4. Comments included:

> Easy to slot into practice. Trainers were very accepting, positive and encouraging – it made the practice seem manageable to implement and the group trustworthy in their reviews.

> Very useful advice to enhance awareness and knowledge of 'quality interactions' – a term used and heard over and over again in early years but not clearly understood.

> Having information about the principles of attuned interactions and guidance on how to use them helped to extend and refresh my skills.

When asked about 'What I found most useful for my work' comments included:

> More awareness of listening skills, non-verbal communication and waiting my turn – using these to guide and scaffold for children.

> My confidence has grown therefore interactions are more positive.

> The principles of attuned interactions – it helped me know what I was trying to achieve. Watching the clips obviously helped me identify the principles in action. The emphasis on strengths was very positive and effective. I feel it has had a great impact on my work and on the children I work with.

Participants were also asked to consider what could be done to improve training in the future. A number of staff felt the half-day iPad training could have been longer. Others suggested that all staff in the establishments should be trained to ensure a more consistent approach.

VERP guiders' views

Three VIG supervisors took part as the VERP guiders (all were educational psychologists). All found the experience hugely rewarding. The lead supervisor had previously been involved with VERP. Two of the three were themselves training to be VIG supervisors. They found that supervising a group of trainees presented new challenges, mainly in managing their varying learning needs, as they all had different skills and levels of understanding. A number of strategies were employed to meet this challenge. To ensure that each VERP trainee received an equal amount of time to view and reflect on their video clips, it was explained to the group that during each person's turn the other group members would play a supporting role only. This was one way of ensuring that other group members did not dominate during the 'focus' person's turn. One trainee was also nominated to be the timekeeper. This allowed the supervisor to stay focused on the clips and to remain attuned to the trainee. The groups became very supportive and adept at identifying strengths and significant 'tiny moments' in clips. For this ethos to be created, the VERP guider must model the principles of attuned interactions.

Limitations of research

The control establishments were selected to match the experimental establishments on deprivation levels and establishment type (for example, freestanding nursery centre or a nursery class within a school). However, establishments were not matched in terms of child or adult characteristics. The filming of the control group staff could be argued to constitute an intervention. Along with the small sample size, these points represent limitations of the study.

Discussion

When supporting children's literacy development, findings from research indicate that a number of key areas should be considered. These include the role that the adult plays in mediating learning (Howe 1981), the inclusion of evidence-based literacy content (National Early Literacy Panel 2008) and the planning of learning experiences (Wasik 2008). The VERP/Active Literacy intervention presented opportunities for staff to develop knowledge and skills in all these areas. It differed, however, from a more traditional literacy training model in a number of respects. For example, the intervention:

- provided frameworks for literacy 'teaching' and also for attuned interaction

- encouraged staff to appreciate the relationship between these two frameworks

- gave staff the opportunity to integrate these elements into their practice and to reflect on their behaviours during VERP sessions.

Thus it appears that VERP is a mechanism that helps adults generalize key aspects from theory into their own practice.

Conclusion

The aim of this research was to evaluate a VERP/Active Literacy intervention lasting three months in North Lanarkshire Council, through pre- and post-video analysis. Self-report data were also explored through questionnaires and focus group. The impact of the intervention was highly positive. Statistically significant results for the VERP/Active Literacy group were found in a number of areas, for instance, improvement in the literacy content of sessions, an increase in child-initiated conversations, and in open and challenging questions. VERP/Active Literacy group members were also positive about the intervention; in particular, they felt they were better able to reflect on their interactions and the impact their behaviour had on children. The research suggests that staff were able to generalize their learning from VERP into literacy teaching.

The positive results seen for the VERP/Active Literacy trained staff are extremely encouraging, particularly considering the short time scale of the project. Nevertheless, the limitations of the research outlined earlier (for example, small sample size and the matching of the experimental and control groups) mean that the results should be treated with caution. Continued implementation of the programme should be monitored to ensure effects are lasting. Further evaluation over a longer period could focus on the impact of the project on the children.

Due to active support from the education officer for early years and childcare, a roll-out of VERP is underway. At the time of writing, staff from a further 12 establishments have been trained, in addition to ten educational psychologists.

CHAPTER 22

'Containing Conversations'[1]

Introducing VERP into a Secure Forensic Service for Adolescence

Helen Gibson, Martin Elliott and Emily Archer

Bluebird House is a secure forensic in-patient service for young people aged 12–19. The introduction of Video Enhanced Reflective Practice (VERP) (the shared reflection in groups on short, edited video clips of the worker's own day-to-day professional practice) to the service is the focus of this chapter. It outlines the context in which young people and staff work together, and describes how VERP was introduced. Some tentative evaluation outcomes are shared, as well as participant experience and the authors' reflections on the impact of VERP.

Author context

Helen Gibson and Martin Elliott completed their Video Interaction Guidance (VIG) training in 1996, among the first VIG guiders in

---

1   Thank you to Helen Williams, a former clinical assistant at Bluebird House, for her enthusiasm for the approach; Warren Dungar, clinical assistant, for his support with the statistics; and to all the participants who have contributed to the introduction of VERP.

England, and now practice in VIG/VERP, training and supervising others in the method. VIG is the shared review of small video clips of interaction according to a number of principles (see Kennedy, Landor and Todd 2011). Emily Archer was a participant on the VERP training and contributed significantly to the course evaluation. Helen Gibson, supported by Martin Elliott, took a lead role in introducing VERP in her capacity as a systemic psychotherapist at Bluebird House. Martin has over 25 years' experience working in Child and Adolescent Mental Health (CAMHS), both as a clinical nurse specialist and a team manager. Emily Archer worked as a healthcare support worker at Bluebird House for two and a half years after graduating in psychology.

Bluebird House model of care: A model of emotional containment

Bluebird House is one of five nationally commissioned secure forensic services in England. It has three mixed wards, with 20 beds in total. Young people are detained in England under the Mental Health Act and may be subject to Ministry of Justice restrictions. Forensic mental health services provide assessment and treatment of people with a mental disorder and a history of criminal offending, or those who are at risk of offending. To meet the criteria for admission, the referrer must provide evidence that the young person is either a significant risk to themselves or to others, and that all alternative means of support in a less restrictive environment have been considered. Each young person will be diagnosed with or undergoing assessment for a psychiatric condition such as schizophrenia, bi-polar disorder, emerging personality disorder or post-traumatic stress disorder.

The nature of the secure environment and the distress and difficulties with which the young people present is challenging for staff at Bluebird House. For this reason there is a well-resourced multidisciplinary team including art therapy, education, family therapy, nursing, occupational therapy, psychiatry and psychology. Since opening in February 2008, Bluebird House has developed its own model of care that informs practice in six key areas, illustrated below (see Figure 22.1).

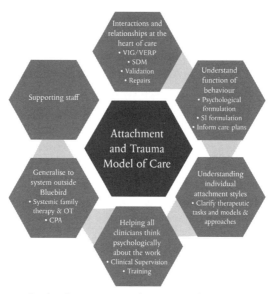

Figure 22.1 Bluebird House attachment and trauma model of care

Source: Model developed by Bluebird House

The Bluebird House attachment and trauma model of care aims to help provide consistency in staff appreciation of the presenting needs of the young people, and to provide clarity and guidance on how staff might meet these needs. It aims to provide all staff with a shared understanding of how the young person's experience of attachment and trauma have influenced their brain development, their ability to regulate emotions, their belief systems, their patterns of forming relationships, and their behaviours, and give a grounding in skills that the team can develop to most effectively work with young people. (Bluebird House 2013)

This model highlights the need for the young people to experience both emotional and environmental containment before other therapeutic interventions may proceed. 'Emotional containment' is where 'a person receives and understands the emotional communication of another without being overwhelmed by it and communicates it back to the other person. This process can restore the capacity to think in the other person' (Douglas 2007, p.33). Providing emotional containment is an important aspect of the work of staff at Bluebird

House, and is often provided within the context of conversations, hence the term 'containing conversations'.

Whether as a therapist, a doctor or a staff member on the ward, the 'bread and butter' work of Bluebird House is conversation with the young people and the systems that support them. All of those involved in the young person's care have a responsibility for creating and holding a space for a containing conversation because, 'when we touch people clumsily or harshly, even in the most fleeting of encounters, there is a potential for consequences that may extend through the years' (Reed 2013, p.428).

Introduction of VERP

The focus for VERP at Bluebird House is emotional containment. VERP was introduced to enhance the quality of these conversations, and in turn, the therapeutic relationships. The authors have hypothesized that these relationships will be enhanced if staff are able to attune themselves to young people and colleagues, give of themselves emotionally and have a sense of self-efficacy in this challenging work environment. Reviewing successful communication in VERP, it was hoped, would facilitate a richer and subtler experience of a past event than might ever have been possible during the live event. VERP was also introduced in the hope of reducing the risk of burnout, retaining staff, and increasing the consistency of therapeutic relationships. Therefore, three areas were the focus for more formal evaluation of VERP: burnout, self-efficacy and attunement.

Burnout, self-efficacy and attunement

Burnout is a well-known area of concern in settings such as Bluebird House. It is described as 'a syndrome of emotional exhaustion and cynicism that occurs frequently among individuals who do "people-work" of some kind' (Maslach et al. 1996, p.99). Once emotionally exhausted, it can become hard for staff to give of themselves emotionally, which in turn can lead to negative perceptions of clients and their difficulties. Staff may also begin to have negative feelings about themselves and experience dissatisfaction in their work. Retention of staff can become a concern.

Self-efficacy is defined here as 'the belief in one's capabilities to organize and execute the courses of action required to manage prospective situations' (Bandura 1995, p.2). In order to develop therapeutic relationships, staff need to feel able to engage and interact with young people, family members and each other. These interactions are emotionally challenging, and staff can quickly begin to feel they have insufficient skill or expertise to manage and engage in these interactions. When staff have a sense of themselves as effective clinicians and communicators, they are likely to be more ready to enter into these conversations and to manage difficult behaviour.

Developing attunement is a key aspect of VERP. Attunement can be defined as a 'kinesthetic and emotional sensing of others, knowing their rhythm, affect and experience by metaphorically being in their skin, and going beyond empathy to create a two-person experience of unbroken feeling connectedness by providing a reciprocal affect and/or resonating response' (Erskine 1998, p.236). The young people at Bluebird House engage in a lot of confusing care-eliciting behaviours in response to not feeling understood or 'held in mind' and, 'without attunement to the immediacy of the moment, the dialogical process can be inhibited' (Seikkula and Trimble 2005, p.466).

Taster sessions

Before the first course was delivered, four VERP taster sessions were offered over a three-month period to all members of staff working at Bluebird House in an attempt to encourage multidisciplinary working and to share learning throughout the unit. These taster sessions aimed to give staff an overview of the method, and to outline the course so that an informed decision could be made when signing up to the training. They lasted for one and a half hours and accommodated up to four people, comprising a short presentation to outline the aims of VERP for the service and its basic principles. In addition, one member of the group volunteered to be videoed in a role-play scenario so that a demonstration of a shared review could be modelled. Shared reviews involved participants meeting to reflect jointly on filmed examples of positive interactions.

VERP training

Two VERP courses were run between March 2011 and March 2012 and were completed by 11 participants. Both took place in five sessions over three months. They consisted of two full days' training with three two-hour sessions of shared review between them. The participants were a ward manager, three senior nurse practitioners, two healthcare support workers, two clinical psychologists, a clinical psychology assistant, an occupational therapy team leader, a deputy head teacher, a family therapist, an art therapist, a speech and language therapist, a social worker and two psychiatrists. Four participants did not complete, due to a change of job, and two chose not to continue.

Training Day 1

On the first day trainees shared their hopes for the course. These varied from 'being able to help young people and their families build better relationships through communicating effectively with them', to 'contributing to developing a culture of identifying and reinforcing positive skills and achievements of staff and young people'. The morning covered the key principles of VERP, including the theory of primary and secondary intersubjectivity (Trevarthen 1998), and the principles of attuned interactions. The afternoon was practice-based, with the participants using the video camera, being filmed and reflecting back to each other the strengths that they had observed in each other's communication. At the end of Day 1, participants decided on a relevant context in which to make their first film. Examples were 'chairing a ward round', 'engaging a young person in an activity on the ward' and 'supervising a staff member'. A date was set for the first group's shared review, approximately two weeks later.

Shared review sessions

Participants were required to film themselves in three different situations and to attend three two-hour group shared reviews. Each person brought a film for the group to review. They were encouraged to attend even if they did not have a clip, in order to be part of the reflections for their colleagues and to continue with their learning. These shared review sessions were offered fortnightly at varying times of the day to meet the needs of the staff involved, and to give staff an opportunity to book into reviews that fitted with their shift pattern. This enabled attendance at least three times over a three-month period.

Although participants left Day 1 of the training with enthusiastic plans, putting this into practice was not so easy. Some participants found it challenging to make their first film. Staff who worked within a more structured day such as occupational therapy and psychology found it easier to plan and create filming opportunities. Others cited busy schedules, lack of opportunity and not having a camera available as barriers to filming. With determination and additional support and encouragement from the guider, all participants were able to achieve the goal of making three films.

Training Day 2

On the second day of training the group members were invited to share their experiences so far, including their learning from the shared reviews, skills and strengths and working points for the future. In addition, Day 2 was intended to be an introduction to full Video Interaction Guidance (VIG) training, and so the afternoon focused on practising the editing of video clips. Time was given to decide whether members wished to end their VERP experience at this point, opt into ongoing monthly group shared review sessions or apply to complete their full VIG training. VIG differs from VERP since the focus is on a change goal of the client instead of the trainee, and the VIG guider, instead of the VERP trainee, takes the video footage and chooses the clips for the shared review. Length of engagement will depend on the situation's needs.

Evaluation of VERP at Bluebird House

The VERP course at Bluebird was evaluated using a range of data including: author reflections; participant experiences; and measures (of burnout, self-efficacy and attunement) of participants at the start and end of the VERP course.

Author reflections

The authors developed the process of training as it progressed. Due to shift patterns and the unpredictable nature of the work at Bluebird House, the authors found that clear structure and expectations needed to be put in place for the VERP trainees. Dates needed to be set for the first shared review at the end of Day 1, and members were encouraged to make a note of the situation they intended to use for their first film. However, some flexibility was necessary. For example, some shared reviews needed to be offered on an individual basis due to the confidential nature of the material. This flexibility depended on the capacity of the VERP guider. Even if participants received individual shared reviews, they were encouraged to take part in the group shared reviews to support the collaborative working and dynamics of the group.

The two VERP courses were initially planned to run over a three-month period, but both groups requested an extension. On reflection, a more realistic period would have been four to five months; any longer would risk a loss in momentum. The authors found the need for regular peer supervision, particularly to reflect on the complexity of the relationships within the unit and the role the guider played in supporting the participants between reviews. As in-house members of staff, the authors found this particularly complex; getting the right balance between supporting trainees and encouraging active learning was a challenge.

Although most participants who completed the course opted to continue regular shared reviews afterwards, this did not happen. It could be hypothesized that, without the structure and rigour of a training course, the time and space could not be found or be justified within the work schedule. It may have been more practical for the VERP guider to respond to individual requests for additional reviews following a VERP course. Two participants went on to take up full VIG training (three stages over a minimum of two years). This has allowed them to offer VIG to staff members who did not wish to or could not complete the full VERP training.

Participants' experience of VERP

Two participants were approached to give their views on the training for the purpose of this study. The dominant themes included: their motivation to attend; their experience of both being videoed and involved in shared reviews; and personal areas of development.

One of these participants was a healthcare support worker based on one of the wards:

> I applied for a place on the VERP project with the aim of becoming more aware of my own communicative style and the way that the young people with whom I worked responded to me as a result. I hoped that improving my awareness of my natural style would enable me to enhance my communication skills and my ability to interact with young people and colleagues. Fortunately the motivation to improve these skills was strong, as it had to overpower the part of me that wanted to run a mile at the prospect of watching myself on video!
>
> While I cannot say that the camera had become my friend by the end of the project, the realization that the benefits of VERP sessions outweighed the discomfort of seeing myself on film had begun to take hold. Being presented with evidence of instances where my communication style had elicited a positive response from another increased my confidence enormously and I left VERP sessions with an enhanced belief in my abilities.
>
> As the videos that I created featured interactions with colleagues as well as young people, I saw benefits in both these areas. My increased confidence in interactions with other staff members improved my ability to have clinical discussions, offer support to colleagues and utilize group supervision sessions. I also felt more able to take a lead in

interactions with young people at times when I would have avoided doing so in the past. This was particularly the case during instances of challenging behaviour, which I felt more able to address with young people as I gained belief in my communicative abilities.

The other was an occupational therapy manager:

The main thing that really struck me when I first saw VERP presented was how it can improve interactions through a positive experience. I liked having the space to look at my video and see what I was doing well and it made me more aware of what I was good at and I loved coming out of the session feeling quite good about what I saw and thinking 'I am not as bad as I thought!!'

I wanted to experience VERP and then be able to use it within my occupational therapy team both thinking about my goals around interaction and helping them with theirs or even encouraging them to go on the course themselves.

Personally I feel more confident in being able to manage difficult situations (managing violence and aggression) within the unit because I have confidence in myself at being attuned to the young people and co-regulating them more effectively. I also feel more confident in managing my team.

Impact of VERP on burnout, self-efficacy and attunement

Evaluation of the impact on workers taking the VERP course on burnout, self-efficacy and attunement used scales applied at the start (Time 1, on arrival at Training Day 1) and end of the courses (Time 2, at the start of Training Day 2). All 11 participants who completed the training engaged in the evaluation. Attribution of the impact of VERP is, of course, limited, since it was possible only to say whether changes in the measures were unlikely to have happened by chance. Causality was not attributable, due to the lack of controls, small number of participants and lack of measures taken at some future time. However, the measures taken give some indication of impact.

The *Maslach Burnout Inventory* (MBI) – Human Services and Education (3rd edition) (Maslach, Jackson and Leiter 1996) – measures 22 feelings or emotions that form three subscales. The 'Emotional Exhaustion' subscale (nine items) assesses the extent to which the participant feels emotionally drained by their work, 'Depersonalization' (five items) measures feelings of cynicism and coldness towards service users and the 'Personal Accomplishment' subscale (eight items) measures the sense of achievement and beliefs about their own competency. Related *t*-tests were carried out for each subscale in order to identify whether any changes had occurred following completion of the VERP course. A significantly decreased sense of Personal Accomplishment (t (6)=-3.708, $p<0.05$) and Emotional Exhaustion (t (6)=3.914, $p<0.05$) were reported at Time 2 compared to Time 1. There was also a trend towards reduced depersonalization at Time 2 compared to Time 1. This appears to indicate that VERP was effective in reducing the negative emotional impact on staff; however, their sense of personal accomplishment also decreased. Possible explanations for this finding are discussed at the end of this chapter.

Attunement was assessed using a questionnaire, which was developed and utilized in a study of VIG/VERP in a young person's unit (Strathie, Strathie and Kennedy 2011). It consists of seven items, each rated on a 5-point scale (shared in an email conversation with Strathie 2012). The Difficult Behaviour Self-efficacy Scale (Hastings and Brown 2002) was used to assess feelings of confidence, control and satisfaction when dealing with challenging behaviour, the belief that the participant has a positive effect on these behaviours, and how difficult they find it to work with such behaviours. It consists of five items, each of which is rated on a 7-point scale (see Figure 22.2).

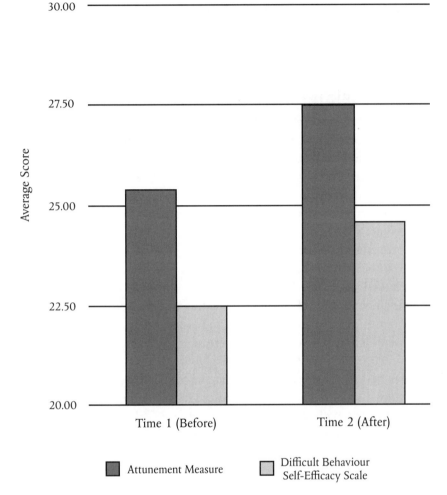

Figure 22.2 Attunement Measure and Difficult Behaviour
Self-Efficacy Scale

Source: Model developed by Bluebird House

Both the Attunement Measure and the Difficult Behaviour Self-
efficacy Scale were approaching statistical significance using a related
t-test for Time 1 to Time 2 comparisons. The descriptive statistical

analysis suggest that at Time 2 participants felt more attuned to the needs of their service users and also felt a greater sense of self-efficacy with regard to dealing with challenging behaviour.

Discussion

VERP courses of five sessions over three months were completed by 11 workers in Bluebird House, primarily to impact on burnout, self-efficacy and attunement. Overall, evaluation suggests VERP training has had a positive impact on aspects that the authors believe to be central to the development of strong therapeutic relationships and effective communication. It is curious that the sense of personal accomplishment decreased. It may be that the VERP course provided a containing space and relationships that enabled the trainees to acknowledge their own limitations and areas for growth. This acknowledgement will be significant for further skills development and important for client-led goal-setting in the future.

From participant experience and descriptive statistics, it seems that VERP may be effective in increasing staff members' perceptions of their ability to be attuned to the young people and in increasing a sense of self-efficacy for managing difficult behaviour. Further exploration into any changes reported by the young people on their interactions with staff members would enrich this conclusion. It is also likely that this increased confidence in managing challenging situations and compassion towards the young people involved has contributed to the significant reduction in emotional exhaustion.

Part Seven

CONCLUSIONS

CHAPTER 23

Reflections on the Potential of Video Enhanced Reflective Practice (VERP) to Support Agency in the Contemporary Workplace

Wilma Barrow and Liz Todd

Introduction

This chapter explores what agency means in the contemporary workplace, and how it is limited by some of the changes and uncertainties in the lives of many practitioners. We consider how agency is required for the active role of the practitioner in the process of ongoing learning and reflection, and how Video Enhanced Reflective Practice (VERP) can be used to support this active role. We recognize that the concept of agency cannot be taken for granted. The literature on agency reflects a range of theoretical approaches (see, for example, Biesta and Tedder 2007; Billett 2006; Edwards 2005; Eteläpelot *et al.* 2013; Priestley *et al.* 2012). Eteläpelot *et al.* (2013), in their review of theoretical approaches, suggest that the term 'agency' tends to be associated with 'active striving, taking initiative, or having an influence on one's own life situation' (p.46).

To address the complex challenges faced by communities in the domains (and beyond) of health, education and social care we need agentic practitioners. Uncertainty in the contemporary workplace has led to a growing interest at both an academic and policy level in agency at work (Eteläpelot *et al.* 2013). Budgetary restrictions within many settings in which VERP is used have led to change and uncertainty in the working lives of many practitioners. One study claims that a hidden cost of leaner social service organizations is the reduced opportunity to develop and transfer key practices, some of which enable social workers to keep themselves safe (Baines 2004). The pervasive nature of performativity is also felt by those working in education, social work and beyond. Beck and Giddens use the concept of the risk society to explain this cultural phenomenon, characterized by loss of public trust in institutions and increased regulation, surveillance and micro-management of professionals (Avis 2003; Ball 2003; Littlechild 2008; Stalker 2003). Ball (2003) suggests that the global cultural phenomenon of performativity is characterized by 'a mode of regulation that employs judgements, comparisons and displays as means of incentive, control, attrition and change based on rewards and sanctions' (p.216).

Trivette *et al.*'s (2009) review of the literature on adult learning argues that the most effective approaches involve the learner as an active participant within the training process. This is particularly relevant given some of the challenges within the contexts in which many currently practice. It is our contention that VERP offers an alternative to instrumentalist expert-led training in the workplace. We suggest that VERP may be used by agentic professionals to facilitate positive change in the relationships and ethos of the workplace. VERP uses short video clips in which practitioners view positive moments of their own interactions with service users or other practitioners (for example, in a team meeting or supervision context). Through the VERP process they are guided to identify strengths in their own communication that have contributed to the positive interaction demonstrated in the video. VERP emphasizes the dyadic nature of communication. Its focus, therefore, is mutuality and attuned relationships rather than building an individual's skill base. As VERP emphasizes the need to make space for the other, it is able to support more participative and democratic forms of practice, both within and beyond the training process. This chapter follows a paper (Barrow and Todd 2011) in which we argue that democratic practice involves reciprocal communication that is 'not closed down by an expert or dominant voice providing the "last word"' (p.279).

We now begin to explore in more detail how agency at work might be understood, before examining how VERP as an approach that actively involves the practitioner in their own learning and reflection might support agentic practice and facilitate positive changes within the workplace.

Conceptualizing agency from a relational perspective

As noted above, the literature on agency reflects a range of philosophical and theoretical positions (Priestley, Biesta and Robinson, 2012). A comprehensive overview of the literature on professional agency can be found in Etälapelot *et al.* (2013). We focus here on those approaches to agency that rest on philosophical assumptions similar to our own. As in our paper (Barrow and Todd 2011), we assume a relational basis to our being, thus we eschew an individualistic approach to agency (Kağitçibaşi 2005). The ways in which individuals are positioned in relation to social context is a key factor when distinguishing different approaches to agency (Etälapelot *et al.* 2013). Subject-orientated sociocultural models of agency assume that individuals exercise their agency in relation to others, and in and through the social structures they inhabit, without being reduced to these (Billett 2006). Relationships within the workplaces may provide a resource to support agency, but may also act as a constraint (Edwards 2005, 2011; Edwards and Mackenzie 2005).

Practitioners are therefore situated within the very contexts that impose themselves on their practice in the ways described above. In making this assumption we distance ourselves from those who adopt a humanistic approach. Humanistic approaches to agency consider the individual to operate with 'unencumbered autonomy and agency' (Billett 2006, p.60). We further contend that, while practitioners operate within a relational context, their work is also practical and embodied. They therefore experience the impact of the material conditions within which they work and, in exercising their agency, need to take account of the implications of these conditions for themselves, their colleagues and service users. From this perspective, agency does not imply that practitioners may practice in any way they choose. Billett and Pavlova (2005) rather suggest that 'it is more useful to view personal agency in terms of securing a "sense of self" within contested and negotiated relations of workplaces' (p.199).

The key question at this point revolves around the extent to which the practitioner can engage in transformative activities, given their position within culturally and historically situated relational structures. If VERP is to be used as a tool to transform our own communicative practices and those within the organizations within which we work, then we need to address this question. This question is important if VERP is to avoid being absorbed by the performative requirements of the contemporary workplace, where staff training can be approached as merely a list of skills to be ticked off.

While assuming individual practitioners are part of a relational context, we accept that they can select appropriately from that context (Billett 2006). They are therefore able to employ their own meanings and values as they develop in their professional identity (Casey 2003). This positions the individual as insider–outsider in relation to the social context of the workplace, enabling them to bring some critical capacity to bear on it (Wegerif 2011). Although we assume that, as relational beings, we 'co-author' our ideas with others, according to Markova, this also 'demands evaluation of the other, struggle with the other and judgement of the message of the other' (Markova 2003, p.256). Thus we can make and construct choices for ourselves (Billett and Pavlova, 2005). Within the working culture outlined at the outset of this chapter there remains some hope that we can avoid being subsumed within an ethos of performativity. Linell (2007) argues that even when certain discourses become dominant within a community, society or culture, dialogue continues within and across the boundaries of these discourses, and through this dialogue challenge and change is possible. This perspective allows us to hold on to the possibility that our work can have transformative potential. The previous chapters have illustrated this through discussion of the ways in which VERP has supported participative and democratic practice, sometimes in challenging circumstances.

Anne Edwards has developed a theory of relational agency (Edwards 2005, 2011). It is her contention that the challenges we face within our professional contexts require fresh thinking and new responses. Her theory addresses how such thinking and responses might be nurtured. She defines relational agency as 'a capacity to align one's thoughts and actions with those of others in order to interpret problems of practice and to respond to those interpretations' (2005, p.169). She draws from Engeström's notion of expansive learning across boundaries (Engeström and Sannino 2010). Boundary-crossing learning takes place within the contested site of the boundary between professionals, and between professionals and service users. It is Edwards' view that communities of practice as a model of learning are limited, as they do not help us to understand how we might develop new understandings or responses to cope with change. This resonates with others who argue that a dialogic basis to learning requires difference (Markova 2003; Matusov 2011; Wegerif 2008).

Rather than change resulting from practitioners internalizing existing expertise or interpretations within a particular workplace organization, this approach recognizes the value of working within boundary zones of sociocultural difference (Edwards 2005). These boundary-crossing experiences can provoke new understandings as they make space for hearing the perspectives of others, enabling a fresh response to new problems. Rather than change resulting from top-down learning experiences, during which we internalize the expertise that exists within our own particular professional groupings, this approach recognizes the value of working in boundary zones of sociocultural difference. Akkerman and Bakker (2011) argue that transformative learning in practice involves continuous joint work and negotiation while maintaining sociocultural difference. There are significant political implications for the ways in which workplace learning is conceptualized and organized. Such an approach to learning cannot be 'delivered' by a top-down expert or through an apprenticeship model (Matusov 2011). If we are to work in ways that use other practitioners' differences as a resource, we need to adopt a particular stance in relation to them. Matusov suggests that learning with others requires that 'the participants should not only expect to be surprised by each other (dialogic interaddressivity) but also have to share a focus on a common subject that is both interesting and problematic for all' (p.104). From this perspective, unlike an instrumental approach to learning, change is a two-way process and all can learn through the process.

Akkerman and Bakker (2011), who share Edwards' view of the transformative potential of boundary work, argue that there are a number of possible mechanisms that can lead to change in such conditions. Their discussion on boundary objects is of particular interest to us. These are artefacts that can act as a bridge between practitioners from different contexts, such as a reflective log (Star 2010). Akkerman and Bakker argue that boundary objects support but do not replace communication, as they are the 'nexus of perspectives' (p.141). Their use needs to be open to multiple perspectives. It seems reasonable to assume that video, or the particular way in which video is used in VERP, can be a boundary object supporting communication between people who hold diverse views on practice in order to support new ways of thinking about that practice. However, the video alone is not enough. There is a need to communicate about the video, which is why the role of dialogue is central.

We have so far considered some of the threats to agency in the workplace, and some of the ways in which our agency at work is most effectively exercised in relation with others. Given the approach to agency we have adopted, we now consider how VERP might be used to support agentic practice.

Practical implications and the potential of VERP as a tool to support agentic practice

Three implications for practice are considered in this final section; the potential of VERP is discussed in relation to each.

Supporting relationships through helping practitioners 'know how to know who'

Relational agency requires us to be confident in working with our own professional expertise, yet also to relate in ways that allow us to 'recognize and respond to what others might offer' (Edwards 2011, p.34). We suggest that this requires us to view agency not just as something we 'have', but also as something we 'do' (Priestley *et al.* 2012, p.3), and involves both values and skills. From a values perspective, relational agency requires us to recognize 'the other' (including service users) as a valued resource in our joint struggle to resolve challenges we meet in practice. This requires us to interact with them in ways that 'elicit their interpretations and negotiate aligned action' (Edwards 2005, p.175). Star (2010) argues that it remains possible to cooperate with others in the absence of consensus, but that this will be demanding for all involved. It requires both communicative skill and a stance that values the other. Edwards suggests that 'knowing how to know who' is a capacity that may be developed (2011, p.35).

The potential of VERP to support the reciprocal interaction and relationship has been seen throughout this book. Being able to elicit the interpretations of others and 'negotiating aligned action' requires the nurture of reciprocal relationships. VERP's theoretical underpinnings and the growing research evidence suggest that it may support communication in ways that enable sensitive and reciprocal interaction. Accepting a relational notion of agency requires practitioners to be able to draw on resources brought by other practitioners and service users in ways that support creative and participative responses to complex new problems. We contend that VERP is a tool that supports such agency by foregrounding the importance of the other through its emphasis on responding to and building on others' initiatives. Furthermore, VERP's active engagement of practitioners in the process of evaluating their own developing interactive sensitivity through use of the attunement principles can support the development of the capacity of 'knowing how to know who'. In this way, VERP may be seen to facilitate agentic practitioners to engage in participative and democratic practice.

Equipping the individual with resources

We have argued that relational agency involves working across boundaries. Akkerman and Bakker suggest that boundary work requires 'personal fortitude' (2011, p.140), and this may be a particular challenge for those working across new boundaries with others whose practice is unfamiliar. Here we consider how individuals might be equipped in order to meet this challenge.

We have argued that although individual practitioners are socially situated, their subjective experiences remain important. Etälapelot et al. (2013) suggest that the individual's self-efficacy beliefs are a subjective dimension impacting on agency. As VERP uses positive self-modelling (Dowrick 1999), individual practitioners may find their negative beliefs about their own practice being challenged. Many VERP practitioners experience that the use of positive video clips of practitioners' own interaction in their working context is a 'catalytic tool' (Baumfield et al. 2009). Baumfield et al. (2009) argue that catalytic tools enable practitioners to reframe experience through their ability to create dissonance. This can lead them to question negative meanings about their own practice, leading to the development of more positive beliefs.

Video arguably has considerable potential as a catalytic tool as it provides 'rich authentic' information (Johnson, Sullivan and Williams 2009). It is our experience that practitioners' exposure to rich yet positive images of themselves on film is often accompanied by powerful emotional reactions. These reactions may be explained through the mechanisms of perspective-taking and perspective-making (Akkerman and Bakker 2011). Perspective-making involves clarifying your own perspective, while perspective-taking involves looking at yourself through the eyes of another. Akkerman and Bakker argue that, through these processes, individuals are enabled to enrich their identity beyond its current status. They also claim that perspective-taking is supported by the use of objects. Video therefore offers possibilities as a tool to support these potential change mechanisms. VERP practitioners often find that those they work with believe that they are tapping into a qualitatively different perspective on their own practice when viewing the video clips. The following comment was made by a teacher whose initial view that a lesson had gone badly changed on viewing the video footage of the lesson: 'It just shows you how wrong you can be with a snapshot initial judgement of a lesson...when I was in it, it didn't feel that way.'

The strengths-based emphasis of VERP may help to increase perceived self-efficacy (Cross and Kennedy 2011). Further research exploring the links between VERP and perceived self-efficacy would be helpful; however, it seems reasonable to postulate that VERP may be resourcing individual practitioners in ways that support agency by enabling positive shifts at the level of beliefs about practice.

We also recognize that VERP is an approach to professional development that can be threatening to some, particularly in a context where practitioners are increasingly micro-managed. Video is widely used as a surveillance device. Its use within professional development contexts to support learning and reflection therefore requires sensitivity, transparency and trust. It also requires respect for the subjectivity and agency of the other, who may feel uncomfortable about the process (Landor 2014).

Creating a professional development culture which strengthens agency

The VERP process, as we have seen throughout this book, provides practitioners with the opportunity to engage with others as they learn about and reflect on their own practice. Following research with teachers, Priestley *et al.* (2012) conclude that, even when individuals have experience and a clear value base to their work, their agency can be 'stymied in situations where collaborative work is limited and difficult' (p.14). Edwards and Mackenzie (2005) argue that relational agency is more likely to be nurtured within contexts characterized by trusting and reciprocal relationships. They argue that there is a need to consider the 'affective and dialogic' (p.300) aspects of learning and development opportunities.

Within the professional cultures outlined in the introduction to this chapter, these aspects of learning may be ignored and yet, as we see here, they are important to agentic practice. Greenleaf and Katz (2004) suggest that 'professional development settings are most often characterized by monologic forms of discourse, participation structures that deny learners roles and valid voices in these settings' (p.174). These kinds of settings inhibit agency and lack the dialogical mechanisms required to transform understanding and practice. We consider that VERP, like Video Interaction Guidance (VIG), offers a dialogic approach to practitioner development within which space is created to hear and respond to the other (Barrow and Todd 2011). The VERP process is embedded in dialogue, often within a group context. It allows a range of perspectives to be shared, acting as a catalyst for new learning and reflection (Cooper *et al.* 2013). In contrast to using a top-down apprenticeship model that risks a totalizing, monologic or expert approach to learning (Matusov 2011), a VERP guider makes space for other voices and thereby supports fresh thinking through the group dialogue.

VERP offers practitioners the opportunity to learn and develop within a collaborative environment that can create a context for a more participative and democratic ethos within the workplace.

Conclusion

We have argued that VERP provides an alternative to expert-led instrumentalist workplace training, and that it can support professional agency to bring about positive changes in the workplace. VERP offers an approach to professional learning and development, based on the fundamental importance of relationships. As we have explored the concept of agency at work, we have argued that there are ways of relating to colleagues and service users that can resource professionals' agency and lead to more participative and democratic models of professional learning and practice. Within a wider working culture characterized by performativity, VERP presents an important means of developing these relationships and supporting relational agency.

REFERENCES

Aarts, M. (2008) *Marte Meo, Basic Manual*. Revised 2nd edn. Harderwijk, the Netherlands: Aarts Productions.

Abbott, J. (1994) *Learning Makes Sense: Recreating Education for a Changing Future*. Letchworth: Education 2000.

Achenbach, T. (1992) *Manual for Child Behaviour Checklist – 3, and 1992, Profile*. Burlington, VT: Department of Psychiatry, University of Vermont.

Ainsworth, M.D.S., Blehar, M.C., Waters, E. and Wall, S. (1978) *Patterns of Attachment: Assessed in the Strange Situation and at Home*. Hillsdale, NJ: Lawrence Erlbaum.

Akkerman, S.F. and Bakker, A. (2011) 'Boundary crossing and boundary objects.' *Review of Educational Research 81*, 2, 132–169.

Alborz, A., Pearson, D., Farrell, P. and Howes, A. (2009) 'The Impact of Adult Support Staff on Pupils and Mainstream Schools.' In *Research in Evidence in Educational Library*. London: EPPI-Centre, Social Science Research Unit, Institute of Education, University of London.

Alvero, A.M., Bucklin, B.R. and Austin, J. (2001) 'An objective review of the effectiveness and essential characteristics of performance feedback in organizational settings (1985–1998).' *Journal of Organizational Behavior Management 21*, 1, 3–29.

Antonovsky, A. (1988) *Unraveling the Mystery of Health. How People Manage Stress and Stay Well*. San Francisco, CA: Jossey-Bass Publishers.

Argyris, C. and Schön, D. (1974) *Theory in Practice*. San Francisco, CA: Jossey-Bass.

Argyris, C. and Schön, D. (1978) *Organizational Learning: A Theory of Action Perspective*. Reading, MA: Addison-Wesley Publishing Co.

Arnold, C. and Baker, T (2012) 'Transition from school to work: Applying psychology to "NEET".' *Educational and Child Psychology 29*, 3, 67–80.

Aron, A., Aron, E.N. and Smollan, D. (1992) 'Inclusion of other in the self scale and the structure of interpersonal closeness.' *Journal of Personality and Social Psychology 63*, 596–612.

Avis, J. (2003) 'Re-thinking trust in a performative culture: The case of education.' *Journal of Educational Policy 18*, 3, 315–332.

Baartman, L.K.J. and de Bruijn, E. (2011) 'Integrating knowledge, skills and attitudes: Conceptualising learning processes towards vocational competence.' *Educational Research Review 6*, 2, 125–134.

Bager-Charleson, S. (2010) *Reflective Practice in Counseling and Psychotherapy*. London: Sage.

Baines, D. (2004) 'Losing the eyes in the back of our heads: Social services skills, lean caring and violence.' *Journal of Sociology and Social Welfare 31*, 3, 31–50.

Ball, S. (2003) 'The teacher's soul and the terrors of performativity.' *Journal of Education Policy 18*, 2, 215–228.

Balshaw, M. (2010) 'Looking for some different answers about teaching assistants?' *European Journal of Special Needs Education 25*, 4, 337–338.

Bandura, A. (1977a) *Social Learning Theory.* Englewood Cliffs, NJ: Prentice Hall.

Bandura, A. (1977b) *Self-efficacy: The Exercise of Control.* New York: Freeman.

Bandura, A. (1995) 'Exercise of Personal and Collective Efficacy in Changing Situations.' In A. Bandura (ed.) *Self-efficacy in Changing Societies.* Cambridge: Cambridge University Press.

Barber, M. and Mourshed, M. (2007) *How the World's Best-performing School Systems Come out on Top.* September. New York: McKinsey & Company. Available at https://mckinseyonsociety.com/downloads/reports/Education/Worlds_School_Systems_Final.pdf

Barrow, W. and Todd. L. (2011) 'Beyond Therapy: Supporting a Culture of Relational Democracy.' In H. Kennedy, M. Landor and L. Todd (eds) *Video Interaction Guidance: A relationship-based Intervention to Promote Attunement, Empathy and Wellbeing* (pp.278–289). London: Jessica Kingsley Publishers.

Baumfield, V., Hall, E., Higgins, S. and Wall, K. (2009) 'Catalytic tools: Understanding the interaction of enquiry and feedback in teacher's learning.' *European Journal of Teacher Education 32*, 4, 423–435.

Beebe, B. (2004) 'Co-constructing mother–infant distress in face-to-face interactions: Contributions of microanalysis'. *Zero to Three May*, 40–48.

Beebe, B. and Lachmann, F.M. (2002) *Infant Research and Adult Treatment: Co-constructing Interactions.* Hillsdale, NJ: The Analytic Press.

Beebe, B. and Lachman, F.M. (2014) *The Origins of Attachment: Infant Research and Adult Treatment.* Hove: Routledge.

Begley, J. (2013) 'Trainee Educational Psychologists' Experiences of Video-enhanced Reflective Practice.' London: Institute of Education. Unpublished Year 1 Research Report.

Bennathan, M. and Boxall, M. (2000). *Effective Intervention in Primary Schools: Nurture Groups.* Abingdon: David Fulton Publishers.

Benner, P. (1984) *From Novice to Expert: Excellence and Power in Clinical Nursing Practice.* Mendo Park, CA: Addison-Wesley.

Berger, P.L. and Luckmann, T. (1966) *The Social Construction of Reality: A Treatise in the Sociology of Knowledge.* Garden City, NY: Anchor Books.

Biemans, H. (1990) 'Video Home Training: Theory, Method and Organization of SPIN.' In J. Kool (ed.) *International Seminar for Innovative Institutions.* Ryswijk: Ministry of Welfare, Health and Culture.

Biesta, G.J.J. and Tedder, M. (2007) 'Agency and learning in the lifecourse: Towards an ecological perspective.' *Studies in the Education of Adults 39*, 132–149.

Bigby, C., Clement, T., Mansell, J. and Beadle-Brown, J. (2009) '"It's pretty hard with our ones, they can't talk, the more able-bodied can participate": Staff attitudes about the applicability of disability policies to people with severe and profound intellectual disabilities.' *Journal of Intellectual Disability Research 53*, 4, 363–376.

Billett, S. (2006) 'Relational interdependence between social and individual agency in work and working life.' *Mind, Culture and Activity 13*, 1, 53–69.

Billett, S. and Pavlova, M. (2005) 'Learning through working life: Self and individuals' agentic action.' *International Journal of Lifelong Education 24*, 5, 195–211.

Billington, T. (2006) 'Psychodynamic theories and the "science of relationships" (Bion): A rich resource for professional practice in children's services.' *Educational and Child Psychology 23*, 4, 72–79.

Birbeck, J. and Williams, K. (2013) 'Video Enhanced Reflective Practice – Professional Development in the Early Years.' Presentation at the VERP International Conference, June, Newcastle-upon-Tyne.

Bittles, A.H. and Glasson, E.J. (2004) 'Clinical, social and ethical implications of changing life expectancy in Down syndrome.' *Developmental Medicine and Child Neurology 46*, 4, 282–286.

Blake, R.R. and Mouton, J.S. (1978) *The New Managerial Grid*. Houston, TX: Gulf.

Blatchford, P., Bassett, P., Brown, P., Martin, C., Russell, A. and Webster, R. (2009) *The Deployment and Impact of Support Staff Project: Research Brief (DCSF-RB148,)*. London: Department for Children, Schools and Families.

Blomberg, G., Stürmer, K. and Seidel, T. (2011) 'How pre-service teachers observe teaching on video: Effects of viewers' teaching subjects of the video.' *Teaching and Teacher Education 27*, 1131–1140.

Bloomberg, K., West, D. and Iacono, T.A. (2003) 'PICTURE IT: An evaluation of a training program for carers of adults with severe and multiple disabilities.' *Journal of Intellectual and Developmental Disability 28*, 260–282.

Bolton, G. (2014) *Reflective Practice: Writing and Professional Development*. 4th edition. London: Sage.

Bomber, L. (2011) *What About Me? Inclusive Strategies to Support Pupils with Attachment Difficulties Make it through the School Day*. King's Lynn: Worth Publishing Ltd.

Borko, H., Jacobs, J., Eiteljorg, E. and Pittman, M.E. (2008) 'Video as a tool for fostering productive discussions in mathematics professional development.' *Teaching and Teacher Education 24*, 417–436.

Bowlby, J. (1988) *A Secure Base: Parent–Child Attachment and Healthy Human Development*. New York: Basic Books.

Boyatzis, R.E. and Kolb, D.A. (2000) 'Performance, Learning and Development as Modes of Growth and Adaptation throughout our Lives and Careers.' In M. Peiperl *et al.* (eds) *Career Frontiers: New Conceptions of Working Lives* (pp.76–98). London: Oxford University Press.

Bradach, J.L. (2003) 'Going to Scale: The challenge of replicating social programmes.' *Stanford Social Innovation Review*. Spring. Available at http://tinyurl.com/meg26hl, accessed on 27 January 2014.

Braun, G. (2011) 'Organisations today: What happens to attachment?' *Psychodynamic Practice 17*, 2, 123–139.

Braun, V. and Clarke, V. (2006) 'Using thematic analysis in psychology.' *Qualitative Research in Psychology 3*, 2, 77–101.

Bridges, J., Flatley, M. and Meyer, J. (2010) 'Older people's and relatives' experiences in acute care settings: Systematic review and synthesis of qualitative studies.' *International Journal of Nursing Studies 47*, 89–107.

British Psychological Society, The (2012) *Accreditation through Partnership Handbook. Guidance for Educational Psychology Programmes in England, Northern Ireland and Wales*. Leicester: The British Psychological Society.

Brons, C. (1999) *Camera Training*. Groningen: Christine Brons.

Brophy, J. (2004) *Motivating Students to learn*. 2nd edition. Mahwah, NJ: Lawrence Erlbaum Associates.

Bruner, J. (1977) 'Early Social Interaction and Language Acquisition.' In H.R. Schaffer (ed.) *Studies in Mother–Infant Interaction* (pp.271–289). New York: Academic Press.

Bruner, J.S. (1981) 'The social context of language acquisition.' *Language and Communication 1*, 1, 1–19.

Bruner, J.S. (1996) 'Folk Pedagogy.' In *The Culture of Education.* Cambridge, MA: Harvard University Press.

Bruschweiler-Stern, N. (2004) 'A Multi-focal Neonatal Intervention.' In A. Sameroff, S. McDonough and K. Rosenblum (eds) *Treating Parent–Infant Relationship Problems* (pp.188–212). New York: Guilford Press.

Cairns, B. and Alexander, S. (2013) 'Developing a creative and effective psychological service.' *Educational Psychology in Scotland 14*, 1, 7–11.

Caldicott Guardians (1997) *Caldicott Guardians.* Available at www.ohb.scot.nhs.uk/images/pdf/NHS%20Scotland%20Caldicott%20Guardians.%20Principles%20in%20Practice.pdf

Callicott, K. and Leadbetter, J. (2013) 'An investigation of factors involved when educational psychologists supervise other professionals.' *Educational Psychology in Practice 29*, 4, 383–403.

Carpenter, J., Patsios, D., Wood, M., Shardlow, S., *et al.* (2011) *Newly Qualified Social Worker Programme: Evaluation on the Second Year (2009, to 2010,).* Leeds: Children's Workforce Development Council.

Carroll, K.E. (2009) 'Outsider, insider, alongsider: Examining reflexivity in hospital-based video research.' *International Journal of Multiple Research Approaches 3*, 3, 46–263.

Carroll, K. and Mesman, J. (2011) 'Ethnographic context meets ethnographic biography: A challenge for the mores of doing fieldwork.' *International Journal of Multiple Research Approaches 5*, 2, 155–168.

Carter, L., Ulrich, D. and Goldsmith, M. (2005) *Best Practices in Leadership Development and Organization Change: How the Best Companies Ensure Meaningful Change and Sustainable Leadership.* San Francisco, CA: Pfeiffer.

Casey, C. (2003) 'The learning worker, organizations and democracy.' *International Journal of Lifeline Education 22*, 6, 620–634.

Cave, R., Roger, A. and Young, R. (2011) 'Enhancing Teacher and Student Interactions in Higher Education through Video Enhanced Reflective Practice.' In H. Kennedy, M. Landor and L. Todd (eds) *Video Interaction Guidance. A Relationship-based Intervention to Promote Attunement, Empathy and Wellbeing.* London: Jessica Kingsley Publishers.

Celebi, M. (2013) 'Video Enhanced Reflective Practice in Children Centres.' Presentation at the VERP International Conference, June, Newcastle-upon-Tyne.

Checkland, P.B. and Scholes, J. (1990) *Soft Systems Methodology in Action.* Chichester: John Wiley.

Cheetham, G. and Chivers, G. (2005) *Professional Competence and Informal Learning.* Northampton, MA: Edward Elgar Publishing.

Clark, A. (2012) 'Visual Ethics in a Contemporary Land.' In S. Pinks (eds) *Advances in Visual Methodology.* London: Sage.

Conger, J.A. and Hunt, J.G. (1999) 'Charismatic and transformational leadership: Taking stock of the present and future.' *Leadership Quarterly 10*, 121–128.

Cooper, M., Chak, A., Cornish, F. and Gillespie, A. (2013) 'Dialogue: Bridging personal, community and social transformation.' *Journal of Humanistic Psychology 53*, 1, 70–92.

Cooperrider, D.L. and Whitney, D. (2005) *Appreciative Inquiry: A Positive Revolution in Change.* San Francisco, CA: Berrett-Koehler.

Cooperrider, D.L. Whitney, D. and Stavros, J.M. (2008) *Appreciative Inquiry Handbook.* 2nd edn. Brunswick, OH: Crown Customs Publishing Inc.

Cordingley, P., Bell, M., Thomason, S. and Firth, A. (2005) 'The Impact of Collaborative Continuing Professional Development (CPD) on Classroom Teaching and Learning.' *Review: How do Collaborative and Sustained CPD and Sustained but not Collaborative CPD Affect Teaching and Learning?* London: EPPI-Centre, Social Science Research Unit, Institute of Education, University of London.

Cross, J. and Kennedy, H. (2011) 'How and Why Does VIG Work?' In H. Kennedy, M. Landor and L. Todd (eds) *Video Interaction Guidance: A Relationship-based Intervention to Promote Attunement, Empathy and Wellbeing* (pp.58–81). London: Jessica Kingsley Publishers.

Cummings, C., Dyson, A. and Todd, L. (2011) *Beyond the School Gates: Can Full Service and Extended Schools Overcome Disadvantage?* London: Routledge.

Dalin, P. (1993) *Changing the School Culture.* London: Cassell.

Damen, S., Kef, S., Worm, M., Janssen, M.J. and Schuengel, C. (2011) 'Effects of video-feedback interaction training for professional caregivers and adults with visual and intellectual disabilities.' *Journal of Intellectual Disability Research 55*, 581–595.

Danielowich, R.M. (2013) 'Shifting the reflective focus: Encouraging student teacher learning in video-framed and peer-sharing contexts.' *Teachers and Teaching 20*, 3, 264–288.

DCSF (Department for Children, Schools and Families) (2008) *Every Child a Talker: Guidance for Early Language Lead Practitioners.* National Strategies. Nottingham: DCSF. Available at http://webarchive.nationalarchives.gov.uk/20110202093118/http://nationalstrategies.standards.dcsf.gov.uk/node/153355.

Degotardi, S. and Sweller, N. (2012) 'Mind-mindedness in the nursery: Associations with early childhood practitioner sensitivity and stimulation.' *Early Childhood Research Quarterly 27*, 253–265.

Derry, S. J., Pea, R. D., Barron, B., Engel, R. A., Erickson, F., Goldman, R., et al. (2010). 'Conducting video research in the learning sciences: Guidance on selection, analysis, technology, and ethics.' *The Journal of the Learning Sciences, 19*, 3–53.

de Groot, A.D. (1961) *Methodologie: Grondslagen van onderzoek en denken in de gedragswetenschappen.* Gravenhage: Mouton & Co.

de Shazer, S. (1988) *Clues: Investigating Solutions in Brief Therapy.* New York: Norton.

DfE (Department for Education) (2013) *School Workforce in England: November 2012,*. London: DfE.

Dickinson, D.K. and Tabors, P.O. (eds) (2001) *Beginning Literacy with Language: Young Children Learning at Home and School.* Baltimore, MD: Brookes Publishing.

DiPardo, A. and Potter, C. (2003) 'Beyond Cognition: A Vygotskian Perspective on Emotionality and Teachers' Professional Lives.' In A. Kozulin, B. Gindis, V.S. Ageyev and S.M. Miller (eds) *Vygotsky's Educational Theory in Cultural Context.* Cambridge: Cambridge University Press.

Dogget, C. and Lewis, A. (2013) 'Using Appreciative Inquiry to facilitate organisational change and develop professional practice within an EPS.' *Educational and Child Psychology 30*, 4, 124–143.

Doria, M.V., Strathie, C. and Strathie, S. (2011) 'Supporting Vulnerable Families to Change through Video Interaction Guidance.' In H. Kennedy, M. Landor and L. Todd (eds) *Video Interaction Guidance: A Relationship-based Intervention to Promote Attunement, Empathy and Wellbeing* (pp.121–133). London: Jessica Kingsley Publishers.

Douglas, H. (2007) *Containment and Reciprocity. Integrating Psychoanalytic Theory and Child Development Research with Children.* London: Routledge.

Dowrick, P.W. (1999) 'A review of self-modelling and related interventions.' *Applied Preventative Psychology 8*, 1, 23–39.

Dowrick, P.W. (2011) 'Self modeling: Expanding the theories of learning.' *Psychology in the Schools, Special Issue: Self-modeling 49*, 1, 30–41.

Dowrick, P.W. and Biggs, J. (1983). *Using Video: Psychological and Social Applications.* Chichester: Wiley.

Duffy, F., Gordon, G.H., Whelan, G., Cole-Kelley, K. and Frankel, R. (2004) 'Assessing competence in communication and interpersonal skills: The Kalamazoo II Report.' *Academic Medicine 79*, 6, 495–507.

Dunsmuir, S. and Leadbetter, J. (2010) *Professional Supervision: Guidelines for Practice for Educational Psychologists.* November. Leicester: The British Psychological Society. Available at www.ucl.ac.uk/educational-psychology/resources/ DECP%20Supervision%20report%20Nov%202010.pdf

Dunsmuir, S., Brown, E., Iyadurai, S. and Monsen, J. (2009) 'Evidence-based practice and evaluation: From insight to impact.' *Educational Psychology in Practice 25*, 1, 53–70.

Dweck, C.S. (2000) *Self-theories: Their Role in Motivation, Personality and Development (Essays in Social Psychology).* Philadelphia, PA: Psychology Press.

Dweck, C.S. (2006) *Mindset: The New Psychology of Success.* New York: Random House.

Earley, P. and Bubb, S. (2004) *Leading and Managing Continuing Professional Development.* London: Paul Chapman.

Education Endowment Foundation (2015) www.educationendowmentfoundation.org. uk, accessed on 29 January 2015.

Edwards, A. (2005) 'Relational agency: Learning to be a resourceful practitioner.' *International Journal of Educational Research 43*, 3, 168–182.

Edwards, A. (2007) 'Relational agency in professional practice: A Chat analysis.' *ACTIO. An International Journal of Human Activity 1*, 1–17.

Edwards, A. (2009) 'Relational agency in collaborations for the well-being of children and young people.' *Journal of Children's Services 4*, 1, 33–43.

Edwards, A. (2010) *Being an Expert Professional Practitioner. The Relational Turn in Expertise.* London: Springer.

Edwards, A. (2011) 'Building common knowledge at the boundaries between professional practices: Relational agency and relational expertise in systems of distributed expertise.' *International Journal of Educational Research 50*, 1, 33–39.

Edwards, A. and D'Arcy, C. (2004) 'Relational agency and disposition in sociocultural accounts of learning to teach.' *Educational Review 56*, 2, 147–155.

Edwards, A. and Mackenzie, L. (2005) 'Steps towards participation: The social support of learning trajectories.' *International Journal of Lifelong Education 24*, 4, 287–302.

Elklan (2009) *Early Language Builders: Advice and Activities to Encourage Pre-school Children's Communication Skills.* Elklan. Available at www.elklan.co.uk, accessed on 28 August.

Ellström, P.E. (1997) 'The Many Meanings of Occupational Competence and Qualification.' In W.J. Nijhof and J.N. Streumer (eds) *Key Qualifications in Work and Education* (pp.39–50). Dordrecht, Netherlands: Kluwer Academic Publishers.

Engestrom, Y. and Sannino, A. (2010) 'Studies of expansive learning: Foundations, findings and future challenges.' *Educational Research Reviews 5*, 1–14.

Eraut, M. (1994) *Developing Professional Knowledge and Competence.* London: Falmer.

Erickson, G., Minnes Brandes, G., Mitchell I. and Mitchell, J. (2005) 'Collaborative teacher learning: Findings from two professional development projects.' *Teaching and Teacher Education 21*, 7, 787–798.

Erskine, R. (1998) 'Attunement and involvement: Therapeutic responses to relational needs.' *International Journal of Psychotherapy 3*, 235–244.

Eteläpelot, A., Vähäsantanen, K., Hökka, P., and Paloniemi, S. (2013) 'What is agency? Conceptualising professional agency at work.' *Educational Research Review 10*, 45–65.

Feeney, B.C. and Collins, N.L. (2004) 'Interpersonal Safe Heaven and Secure Base Caregiving Processes in Adulthood.' In W.S. Rholes and J.A. Simpson (eds) *Adult Attachment: Theory, Research and Clinical Implications* (pp.301–338). London and New York: Guilford Press.

Feuerstein, R. and Feuerstein, S. (1991) 'Mediated Learning Experience: A Theoretical Review.' In R. Feuerstein, P.S. Klein and A.J. Tannenbaum (eds) *Mediated Learning Experience (MLE): Theoretical, Psychosocial and Learning Implications* (pp.3–51). London: Freund.

Finlay, W.M.L., Antaki, C., Walton, C. and Stribling, P. (2008) 'The dilemma for staff in "playing a game" with a person with profound intellectual disabilities: Empowerment, inclusion and competence in interactional practice.' *Sociology of Health and Illness 30*, 4, 531–549.

Fixsen, D.L., Naoom, S.F., Blase, K.A., Friedman, R.M. and Wallace, F. (2005) *Implementation Research: A Synthesis of the Literature*. FMHI Publication, University of South Florida, Louis de la Parte Florida Mental Health Institute, National Implementation Research Network.

Flin, R., Winter, J. and Sarac, C. (2009) *Human Factors in Patient Safety: Review of Topics and Tools*. Geneva: World Health Organization.

Fonagy, P. (1991) 'Thinking about thinking: some clinical and theoretical considerations in the treatment of a borderline patient.' *International Journal of Psychoanalysis 72*, 639–656.

Fonagy, P. and Target, A. (1997) 'Attachment and reflective function: Their role in self-organization.' *Development and Psychopathology 4*, 679–700.

Fonagy, P., Gyorgy, G., Jurist, E.L. and Target, M. (eds) (2004) *Affect Regulation, Mentalization and the Development of the Self.* London: Karnac.

Fook, J. (2012). *Social Work: A Critical Approach to Practice.* 2nd edn. London: Sage.

Forster, S.L. and Iacono, T. (2008) 'Disability support workers' experience of interaction with a person with profound intellectual disability.' *Journal of Intellectual and Developmental Disability 33*, 2, 137–147.

Friendly greetings (2013) 'Friendly greetings from a contented future old woman.' Hej Torbjörn [Hello Torbjörn]. *Tidningen 7*, 45.

Fukkink, R. (2008) 'Video feedback in widescreen: A meta-analysis of family programs.' *Clinical Psychology Review 28*, 6, 904–916.

Fukkink, R.G. and Helmerhorst, K. (2013) 'Video Feedback for Professionals: Design and Effects in Various Settings.' 1st International Conference on Video Enhanced Reflective Practice (VERP), June, Newcastle-upon-Tyne. Available at www.ncl.ac.uk/cflat/documents/VERPConferenceNewsletter10-11June2013.pdf

Fukkink, R.G. and Todd, L. (2011) 'What is the Evidence that VIG is Effective?' In H. Kennedy, M. Landor and L. Todd (eds) *Video Interaction Guidance. A Relationship-based Intervention to Promote Attunement, Empathy and Wellbeing.* London: Jessica Kingsley Publishers.

Fukkink, R.G., Todd, L. and Kennedy, H. (2011) 'Video Interaction Guidance: Does it Work?' In H. Kennedy, M. Landor and L. Todd (eds) *Video Interaction Guidance* (pp.82–104). London: Jessica Kingsley Publishers.

Fukkink, R.G., Trienekens, N. and Kramer, L.J.C. (2011) 'Video feedback in education and training: Putting learning in the picture.' *Educational Psychology Review 23*, 45–63.

Fullan, M. (1992) 'Causes/Processes of Implementation and Continutation.' In N. Bennett, M. Crawford and C. Riches (eds) *Managing Change in Education* (pp.109–132). London: The Open University.

Fuller, F.F. and Manning, B.A. (1973) 'Self-confrontation reviewed: A conceptualization for video playback in teacher education.' *Review of Educational Research 43*, 469–528.

Gavine, D. and Forsyth, P. (2011) 'Use of VIG in Schools.' In H. Kennedy, M. Landor and L. Todd (eds) *Video Interaction Guidance: A Relationship-based Intervention to Promote Attunement, Empathy and Wellbeing* (pp.134–143). London: Jessica Kingsley Publishers.

Gergely, G. and Watson, J. (1996) 'The social biofeedback model of parent-affect mirroring.' *International Journal of Psycho-Analysis 77*, 1181–1212.

Gerhardt, S. (2004) *Why Love Matters: How Affection Shapes a Baby's Brain.* Hove: Brunner-Routledge.

Ghaye, T. (2011) *Teaching and Learning through Reflective Practice: A Practical Guide for Positive Action.* 2nd edn. Abingdon: Routledge.

Giangreco, M.F. (2010) 'One-to-one paraprofessionals for students with disabilities in inclusive classrooms: Is conventional wisdom wrong?' *Intellectual and Developmental Disabilities 48*, 1, 1–13.

Ginsburg, H.P., Cami, A.E. and Preston, M.D. (2010) 'Beginnings: Inquiries: How Can they Be Taught Well?' In N. Lyons (ed.) *Handbook on Reflection and Inquiry* (pp.455–472). New York: Springer.

Glaser, B.G. and Strauss, A.L. (1967) *The Discovery of Grounded Theory: Strategies for Qualitative Research.* Chicago, IL: Aldine.

Glasgow City Council (2012) *Standards and Quality Report 2011,–2012,*. Available at www.Glasgow.Gov.Uk/Chttphandler.Ashx?Id=15558&P=0, accessed on 14 August 2014.

Glen Strathie Partnership (2014) 'Glen Strathie is the leading exponent in the method of Video Enhanced Reflective Practice.' Available at www.VERP.uk.com

Goldman, R. (2007) 'Video Representations and the Perspectivity Framework: Epistemology, Ethnography, Evaluation and Ethics.' In R. Goldman, P. Pea, B. Barron and S.J. Derry (eds) *Video Research in the Learning Sciences* (pp.3–37). Mahwah, NJ: Lawrence Erlbaum.

Goleman, D., Boyatzis, R. and McKee, A. (2002) *The New Leaders: Transforming the Art of Leadership into the Science of Results.* New York: Little, Brown & Co.

Granger, M. (2014) 'An educational psychologist's journey using video interaction guidance in educational psychology in Scotland.' *Special Issue: Video Interaction Guidance. Educational Psychology in Scotland 15*, 1, 56–58.

Greene, A. (2004) 'Democratic Health Care and Disciplinary Closure: Working in a Multidisciplinary Health-care Team with Adolescent Diabetes.' In N. Rapport (ed.) *Anthropological Journal on European Cultures 13*, 111–133.

Greene, A. (2009) 'What health care professionals should do: A view from young people with diabetes: A qualitative study of young people's accounts of patient-centred care for Type 1 diabetes.' *Paediatric Diabetes 10*, s13, 50–57.

Greenleaf, C.L. and Katz, M. (2004) 'Ever Newer Ways to Mean: Authoring Pedagogical Change in Secondary Subject-area Classrooms.' In A.F. Ball and S.W. Freedman (eds) *Bakhtinian Perspectives on Language, Literacy and Learning* (pp.172–202). Cambridge: Cambridge University Press.

Groeneveld, M.G., Vermeer, H.J., van IJzendoorn, M.H. and Linting, M. (2011) 'Enhancing home-based child care quality through video-feedback intervention: A randomized controlled trial.' *Journal of Family Psychology 25*, 86–96.

Groom, B. and Rose, R. (2005) 'Supporting the inclusion of pupils with social, emotional and behavioural difficulties in the primary school: The role of teaching assistants.' *Journal of Research in Special Educational Needs 5*, 20–30.

Gudex, C., Horsted, C. and Bakke, L (2008) 'Marte Meo anvendt på plejehjem' ['Marte Meo used in Nursing Homes']. *Sygeplejersken 18*, 52–57.

Hargie, O., Saunders, C. and Dickson, D. (1983) *Social Skills in Interpersonal Communication.* Hoboken, NJ: John Wiley & Sons Ltd.

Hargreaves, J. and Page, L. (2013) *Reflective Practice.* Cambridge: Polity Press.

Haringey Local Safeguarding Children Board (2009) *Serious Case Review 'Child A'.* London: Department for Education.

Harrison, R. and Kessels, J. (2004) *Human Resource Development in a Knowledge Economy.* Basingstoke: Palgrave Macmillan.

Hastings, R.P. and Brown, T. (2002) 'Behavioural knowledge, causal beliefs and self-efficacy as predictors of special educators' emotional reactions to challenging behaviours.' *Journal of Intellectual Disability Research 46*, 144–150.

Hattie, J. and Timperley, H. (2007) 'The power of feedback.' *Review of Educational Research 77*, 1, 81–112.

Hawkins, P. and Shohet, R. (2012) *Supervision in the Helping Professions.* 4th edn. Maidenhead: Open University Press.

Hawkins, P. and Smith, N. (2013) *Coaching, Mentoring and Organizational Consultancy: Supervision, Skills and Development.* 2nd edn. Maidenhead: Open University Press.

Hay, D. (2004) 'How Do We Learn?' In D. Gray, S. Cundell, D. Hay and J. O'Neill (eds) *Learning Through the Workplace.* Cheltenham: Nelson Thornes Ltd.

Hayes, B., Dewey, J. and Sancho, M. (in press). 'Using Video Interaction Guidance to develop intrapersonal and interpersonal skills in professional training for educational psychologists.' *International Journal of Teaching and Learning in Higher Education.*

Hedenbro, M. and Wirtberg, I. (2012) *Samspelets Kraft: Marte Meo – möjlighet till utveckling* [*The Power of Interaction: Marte Meo – The Possibility for Development*]. Lund: Palmkrons.

Hellier, C. (2006) 'Using a Solution Focus Approach.' Positive Psychology Resources. Available at www.centreforconfidence.co.uk/pp/techniques. php?p=c2lkPTEmdGlkPTMmaWQ9MTcy

Hellier, C. (2008) 'How can educational psychology support the emotional wellbeing strand of the curriculum for excellence? Health and Wellbeing Policies – A shared responsibility: Educational psychologists adding value.' *Professional Development Programme* (pp.3–9). Available at www.educationscotland.gov.uk/Images/ PDPSummary2010_tcm4-629069.pdf, accessed on 30 August 2014.

Hellier, C. (2009) 'Developing post-school psychological services in Scotland – Fit for purpose.' *Educational and Child Psychology 26*, 1, 22–31.

Hellier, C. (2010) 'Summary of professional development projects for educational psychologists. Health and Wellbeing policies – a shared responsability. Educational psychologists adding value.' PDF 3–9. Available at: www.educationscotland.gov. uk/Images/PDPSummary2010_tcm4-629069.pdf

Helmerhorst, K.O.W., Riksen-Walraven, J.M., Fukkink, R.G., Gevers Deynoot-Schaub, M.J.J.M and Tavecchio, L.W.C. (submitted) *Effects of the Caregiver Interaction Profile Training on Caregiver-Child Interactions in Child Care Centers.*

Hewitt, J. (2009) 'Video Interaction Guidance: A Training Tool for Classroom Assistants Working in Mainstream Classrooms.' Submitted in part-fulfilment of the Doctorate in Educational, Child and Adolescent Psychology. Belfast: Queen's University. Unpublished manuscript.

Higgins, M.C. and Kram, K.E. (2001) 'Reconceptualizing mentoring at work: a developmental network perspective.' *The Academy of Management Review 26*, 2, 264–288.

Higgins, S., Katsipataki, M., Kokotsaki, D., Coleman, R., Major, L. and Coe, R. (2014) *The Sutton Trust – Education Endowment Foundation Teaching and Learning Toolkit.* London: Education Endowment Foundation. Available at http://educationendowmentfoundation.org.uk/toolkit

Hill, C.E. and Lent, R.W. (2006) 'A narrative and meta-analytic review of helping skills training: Time to review a dormant area of inquiry.' *Psychotherapy: Theory, Research, Practice, Training 43*, 154–172.

Holden, G., Meenaghan, T., Anastas, J. and Metrey, G. (2002) 'Outcomes of social work education: The case for social work self-efficacy.' *Journal of Social Work Education 38*, 115–133.

Hosford, R.E. (1980) 'Self-as-a-model: A cognitive, social-learning technique.' *Counseling Psychology 9*, 1, 45–62.

Hosford, R.E. and Mills, M.E. (1983) 'Video in Social Skills Training.' In P.W. Dowrick and S.J. Biggs (eds) *Using Video: Psychological and Social Applications* (pp.125–149). Hoboken, NJ: Wiley.

Hostyn, I. and Maes, B. (2009) 'Interaction between persons with profound intellectual and multiple disabilities and their partners: A literature review.' *Journal of Intellectual and Developmental Disability 34*, 4, 296–312.

Howatson-Jones, L. and Standing, M. (2013) *Reflective Practice in Nursing.* 2nd edn. London: Sage.

Howe, C. (1981) *Acquiring Language in a Conversational Context.* New York: Academic Press.

Huhra, R.L., Yamokoski-Maynhart, C.A. and Prieto, L.R. (2008) 'Reviewing videotape in supervision: A developmental approach.' *Journal of Counseling and Development 86*, 412–418.

Humphreys, D., Sebba, J., Gallannaugh, F. and Mujis, D. (2007) *Effective Teaching and Learning for Pupils in Low Attaining Groups.* London: Department for Children, Schools and Families.

Hung, J.H.F. and Rosenthal, T.L. (1981) 'Therapeutic Videotaped Playback.' In J.L. Fryrear and B. Fleshman (eds) *Videotherapy in Mental Health* (pp.5–46). Springfield, IL: Charles C. Thomas.

Hulsman, R.L., Ros, W.J.G., Winnubst, J.A.M. and Bensing, J.M. (1999) 'Teaching clinically experienced physicians' communication skills. A review of evaluation studies.' *Medical Education 33*, 655–668.

I CAN (no date) 'How Many Children have SCLN?' Rainworth: I CAN. Available at www.ican.org.uk/What_is_the_issue/About%20SLCN/How%20many%20children%20have%20SLCN.aspx, accessed on 28 August.

Illick, I. (1973) *Tools for Conviviality.* New York: Harper and Row.

Isaacs, W. (1999) *Dialogue and the Art of Thinking Together: A Pioneering Approach to Communicating in Business and in Life.* New York: Doubleday.

Janicki, M. (2011) 'Quality outcomes in group home dementia care for adults with intellectual disabilities.' *Journal of Intellectual Disability Research 55*, 8, 763–776.

Jarvis, J. (2011) 'How and Why Does VIG Work?' In H. Kennedy, M. Landor and L. Todd (eds) *Video Interaction Guidance: A Relationship-based Intervention to Promote Attunement, Empathy and Wellbeing* (pp.58–81). London: Jessica Kingsley Publishers.

Johnson, B., Sullivan, A.M. and Williams, D. (2009) 'A one-eyed look at classroom life: Using new technologies to enrich classroom based activities.' *Issues in Educational Research 19*, 1, 34–47.

Juffer, F., van Ijzendoorn, M.H. and Bakermans-Kranenburg, M. (1997) 'Intervention in transmission of insecure attachment: A case study.' *Psychological Reports 80*, 531–543.

Kabat-Zinn, J. (1990/2013) *Full Catastrophe Living: How to Cope with Stress, Pain and Illness Using Mindfulness Meditation.* London: Piatkus.

Kağitçibaşi, C. (2005) *Family, Self and Human Development Across Cultures: Theory and applications*, 2nd edn. Mahwah, NJ: Lawrence Erlbaum.

Kelly, B. and Perkins, D.F. (2012) *Handbook of Implementation Science for Psychology in Education.* Cambridge: Cambridge University Press.

Kennedy, H. (2011) 'What is Video Interaction Guidance (VIG)?' In H. Kennedy, M. Landor and L. Todd (eds) *Video Interaction Guidance: A Relationship-based Intervention to Promote Attunement, Empathy and Wellbeing* (pp.20–43). London: Jessica Kingsley Publishers.

Kennedy, H. and Sked, H. (2008) 'Video Interaction Guidance: A Bridge to Better Interactions for Individuals with Communication Impairments.' In S. Zeedyk (ed.) *Promoting Social Interaction for Individuals with Communication Impairments: Making Contact.* London: Jessica Kingsley Publishers.

Kennedy, H., Landor, M. and Todd, L. (eds) (2011) *Video Interaction Guidance: A Relationship-based Intervention to Promote Attunement, Empathy and Wellbeing.* London: Jessica Kingsley Publishers.

Kerr, D., Cunningham, C. and Wilkinson, H. (2006) *Responding to the Pain Experiences of People with a Learning Difficulty and Dementia.* York: Joseph Rowntree Foundation.

Kluger, A.N. and DeNisi, A. (1996) 'The effects of feedback interventions on performance: A historical review, a meta-analysis, and a preliminary feedback intervention theory.' *Psychological Bulletin 119*, 2, 254–284.

Kobak, R. and Madsen, S. (2008) 'Disruptions in Attachment Bonds: Implications for Theory Research and Clinical Intervention.' In J. Cassidy and P. Shaver (eds) *Handbook of Attachment: Theory Research and Clinical Application.* New York: Guilford Press.

Kolb, D.A. (1983) *Experiential Learning: Experience as the Source of Learning and Development.* Englewood Cliffs, NJ: Prentice-Hall Inc.

Kolb, D.A. (1987) *Experiential Learning.* 2nd edn. Englewood Cliffs, NJ: Prentice-Hall.

Koski, K., Martikainen, K., Burakoff, K. and Launonen, K. (2010) 'Staff members' understandings about communication with individuals who have multiple learning disabilities: A case of Finnish OIVA communication training.' *Journal of Intellectual and Developmental Disability 35*, 279–289.

Koski, K., Martikainen, K., Burakoff, K., Vesala, H. and Launonen, K. (2014) 'Evaluation of the impact of supervisory support on staff experiences of training.' *Tizard Learning Disability Review 19*, 2, 77–84.

Lakey, B. and Orehek, E. (2011) 'Relational regulation theory: A new approach to explain the link between perceived social support and mental health.' *Psychological Review 118*, 3, 482–495.

Lamb, P., Lane, K. and Aldous, D. (2013) 'Enhancing the spaces of reflection; A buddy peer-review process within physical education initial teacher education.' *European Physical Education Review 19*, 1, 21–38.

Landor, M. (2014) 'Video Enhanced Reflective Practice (VERP): Lessons from Sweden.' *Educational Psychology in Scotland, Special Issue: Video Interaction Guidance 15*, 1, 33–36.

Landor, M. (2014) 'Theories and contexts of reflective practice' In G. Bolton (ed.) *Reflective Practice: Writing and Professional Development.* 4th edn. London: Sage.

Lawson, I. and Cox, B. (2010) 'Exceeding expectation: The principles of outstanding leadership.' *International Journal of Leadership in Public Services 6*, 1, 4–13.

Leat, D. and Higgins, S. (2002) 'The role of powerful pedagogical strategies in curriculum development.' *The Curriculum Journal 13*, 1, 71–85.

Lin, A. (2007) '"What's the use of triadic dialogue?" Activity theory conversational analysis of pedagogical practices.' *Pedagogies: An International Journal 2*, 2, 77–94.

Linell, P. (2007) 'Essentials of dialogism' Aspects and Elements of a Dialogical Approach to Language, Communication and Cognition.' Available at https://isis.ku.dk/kurser/blob.aspx?feltid=180233, accessed on 4 Febraury 2015.

Lingard, B. (2007) 'Pedagogies of indifference.' *International Journal of Inclusive Education 11*, 245–266.

Lishman, J. (1994) *Communication in Social Work.* Basingstoke: Palgrave Macmillan.

Littlechild, B. (2008) 'Child protection social work: Risks of fears and fears of risks–impossible tasks from impossible goals?' *Social Policy & Administration 42*, 6, 662–675.

Lofthouse, R. and Birmingham, P. (2010) 'The camera in the classroom: Video-recording as a tool for professional development of student teachers.' *Teacher Advancement Network Journal 1*, 2.

Lowe, K.B., Kroeck, K.G. and Sivasubramaniam, N. (1996) 'Effectiveness correlates of transformational and transactional leadership: A meta-analytic review of the MLQ literature.' *Leadership Quarterly 7*, 385–426.

Lunde, L.-H. and Munch, M. (2012) 'Marte Meo.praktikerutdanning i omsorgen for personer med demens – presentasjon av et evalueringsprosjekt ['Marte Meo practioner-training in caring for people with dementia – Presentation of an evaluation project']. *Demens & Alderspaykiatri 16*, 3, 20–24.

McArdle, K. and Coutts, N. (2003) 'A strong core of qualities – A model of the professional educator that moves beyond reflection.' *Studies in Continuing Education 25*, 2, 225–237.

McCluskey, U. (2005) *To be Met as a Person: The Dynamics of Attachment in Professional Encounters.* London: Karnac.

McCarron, M. and McCallion, P. (2005) 'A revised stress and coping framework for staff carers of persons with intellectual disabilities and dementia.' *Journal of Policy and Practice in Intellectual Disabilities 2*, 2, 139–148.

McCarron, M., McCallion, P., Fahey-McCarthy, E. and Connaire, K. (2010) 'Staff perceptions of essential prerequisites underpinning end-of-life care for persons with intellectual disability and advanced dementia.' *Journal of Policy and Practice in Intellectual Disabilities 7*, 2, 143–152.

McCartan, D. and Todd, L. (2011) 'Narrative Therapy and VIG: Windows into Preferred Identities'. In H. Kennedy. M. Landor and L. Todd (eds) *Video Interaction Guidance. A Relationship-based Intervention to Promote Attunement, Empathy and Wellbeing* (pp.255–266). London: Jessica Kingsley Publishers.

McLeod, G. (1987) 'Microteaching: End of research era.' *International Journal of Educational Research 11*, 5, 531–541.

MacIntyre, G., Green Lister, P., Orme, J., Crisp, B.R., Manthorpe, J., Hussein, S. and Sharpe, E. (2011) 'Using vignettes to evaluate the outcomes of student learning: Data from the evaluation of the new social work degree in England.' *Social Work Education 30*, 2, 207–222.

Mackay, T. and Hellier, C. (2009) 'Editorial. Post-school psychological services.' *Educational and Child Psychology 26*, 1, 5–7.

Maddux, J. (2005) 'Self-efficacy: The Power of Believing You Can.' In C.R. Snyder and S. Lopez (eds) *Handbook of Positive Psychology* (pp.277–287). New York: Oxford University Press.

Maslach, C., Jackson, S.E. and Leiter, M.P. (1996) *Maslach Burnout Inventory* (3rd edn). Palo Alto, CA: Consulting Psychologists Press.

Maslow, A. (1954). *Motivation and Personality.* New York: Harper.

Mason, J. (2002) *Qualitative Researching.* London: Sage.

Matusov, E. (2011) 'Irreconcilable differences in Vygotsky's and Bakhtin's approaches to the social and the individual: An educational perspective.' *Culture and Psychology* 17, 99–119.

Markova, I. (2003) 'Constitution of the self: Intersubjectivity and dialogicality.' *Culture and Psychology 9,* 3, 249–259.

Mauss, M. (1993) *The Gift, the Form and Reason for Exchange in Archaic Societies.* London: Routledge.

Meharg, S.S. and Lipsker, L.E. (1991) 'Parent training using video-tape self-modeling.' *Child and Family Behavior Therapy 13,* 4, 1–27.

Meins, E. (1997) *Security of Attachment and the Social Development of Cognition.* Hove: Psychology Press.

Meins, E. and Fernyhough, C. (2010) 'Mind-mindedness Coding Manual. Version 2.0.' Unpublished manuscript. Durham University, Durham, UK.

Meins, E. and Fernyhough, C. (2013) 'Children's Understanding of Emotion Mediates the Relation between Mind-mindedness and Theory of Mind.' Paper presented at the Society for Research in Child Development Biennial Conference, April, Seattle.

Meins, E., Muñoz-Centifanti, L.C., Fernyhough, C. and Fishburn, S. (2013b) 'Maternal mind-mindedness and children's behavioral difficulties: Mitigating the impact of low socioeconomic status.' *Journal of Abnormal Child Psychology 41,* 543–553.

Meins, E., Fernyhough, C., Arnott, B., Leekam, S.R. and Turner, M. (2011) 'Mother-versus infant-centered correlates of maternal mind-mindedness in the first year of life.' *Infancy 16,* 137–165.

Meins, E., Fernyhough, C., Arnott, B., Leekam, S.R. and de Rosnay, M. (2013a) 'Mind-mindedness and theory of mind: Mediating roles of language and perspectival symbolic play.' *Child Development 84,* 1777–1790.

Meirink, J.A., Meijer, P.C. and Verloop, N. (2007) 'A closer look at teachers' individual learning in collaborative settings.' *Teachers and Teaching 13,* 2, 145–164.

Meirink, J.A, Imants, J., Meijer, P.C. and Verloop, N. (2010) 'Teacher learning and collaboration in innovative teams.' *Cambridge Journal of Education 40,* 2, 161–181.

Mezirow, J., Taylor, E.J. and associates (2009) *Transformative Learning in Practice: Insights from Community, Workplace and Higher Education.* San Francisco, CA: Jossey-Bass.

Moon, J. (2005) *Learning Through Reflection: Guide for Busy Academics No. 4,.* York: The Higher Education Academy.

Moran, A. and Abbott, L. (2006) *The Development of Inclusive Schools in Northern Ireland: A Model of Best Practice.* London: Department for Education.

Morrison, T. and Wonnacott, J. (2010) *Supervision: Now or Never. Reclaiming Reflective Supervision in Social Work.* Available at www.in-trac.co.uk/supervision-now-or-never/

Munro, E. (2011) *The Munro Review of Child Protection: Final Report, a Child-Centred System.* Cm 8062. London: The Stationery Office.

Murphy, J.J. (2008) *Solution-focused Counseling in Schools.* 2nd edn. Alexandria, VA: American Counseling Association.

Murray, S. and Noland, B. (2013) *Video Modelling for Young Children with Autistic Spectrum Disorders: A Practical Guide for Parents and Professionals.* London: Jessica Kingsley Publishers.

Music, G. (2011) *Nurturing Natures. Attachment and Children's Sociocultural and Brain Development.* Hove: Psychology Press.

Myers, S. (2007) *Solution-focused Approaches.* Lyme Regis: Russell House Publishing.

Nafstad, A. and Rødbroe, I. (1999) *Co-creating Communication. Perspectives on Diagnostic Education for Individuals Who Are Congenitally Deafblind and Individuals Whose Impairments May Have Similar Effects.* Dronninglund: Nord-Press.

National Early Literacy Panel (2008) *Developing Early Literacy: Report of the National Early Literacy Panel.* Washington, DC: National Institute for Literacy.

NFER (National Foundation for Educational Research) (2014) *A Randomised Trial of Catch-up: Numeracy Evaluation Report and Executive Summary November 2013,.* London: Education Endowment Foundation.

Nikopoulos, C. and Keenan, M. (2006) *Video Modelling and Behaviour Analysis: A Guide to Teaching Social Skills to Children with Autism.* London: Jessica Kingsley Publishers.

Nind, M. and Hewett, D. (2005) *Access to Communication: Developing Basic Communication with People with Severe Learning Difficulties.* 2nd edn. London: David Fulton.

Nummijoki, J. and Engestrom, Y. (2010) 'Towards Co-configuration in Home Care of the Elderly.' In H. Daniels, A. Edwards, Y. Engestrom, T. Gallagher and S. Ludvigsen (eds) *Activity Theory in Practice. Promoting Learning across Boundaries and Agencies.* Abingdon: Routledge.

Ofsted (Office for Standards in Education, Children's Services and Skills) (2004) *Special Educational Needs and disability: Towards Inclusive Schools.* London: Ofsted.

Ofsted (2010) *Workforce Reform in Schools: Has it Made a Difference? An Evaluation of Changes Made to the School Workforce 2003,–2009,.* Manchester: Ofsted.

Oliveira, A.W. (2010) 'Improving teacher questioning in science inquiry discussions through professional development.' *Journal of Research in Science Teaching 47,* 4, 422–453.

Panksepp, J. (1998) *Affective Neuroscience. The Foundations of Human and Animal Emotions.* Oxford: Oxford University Press.

Pattoni, L. (2012) 'Strengths-based Approaches for Working with Individuals.' IRISS Insights, no. 16. Available at www.iriss.org.uk/resources/strengths-based-approaches-working-individuals, accessed on 25 July 2014.

Pendleton, D., Schofield, T., Tate, P. and Havelock, P. (1984) *The Consultation: An Approach to Learning and Teaching.* Oxford: Oxford University Press.

Phillips, D. and Williams, K. (2013) 'Connect, Reflect and Grow.' Presentation at the VIG Conference, February, Basingstoke.

Pianta, R.C. (2001) *STRS: Student–Teacher Relationship Scale: Professional Manual.* Odessa, FL: Psychological Assessment Resources.

Pink, S. (2013) *Doing Visual Ethnography.* London: Sage.

Polderman, N. (2007) 'Attachment and Video Interaction Guidance: Basic Trust.' Cited in H. Kennedy, M. Landor and L. Todd (eds) *Video Interaction Guidance. A Relationship-based Intervention to Promote Attunement, Empathy and Wellbeing.* London: Jessica Kingsley Publishers.

Pollard, A. (2008) *Reflective Teaching.* London: Continuum.

Prest, L.A., Darden, E.C. and Keller, J.F. (1990) '"The fly on the wall" reflecting team supervision.' *Journal of Marital and Family Therapy 16,* 3, 265–273.

Priestley, M., Biesta, G., and Robinson, S. (2012) 'Understanding Teacher Agency: The Importance of Relationships.' Paper presented at the Annual Meeting of the American Research Association, Vancouver, 13–17 April.

Priestly, M., Biesta, G. and Robinson, S. (2013) 'Teachers as Agents of Change: Teacher Agency and Emerging Models of Curriculum.' In M. Priestly and G. Biesta (eds) *Reinventing the Curriculum: New Trends in Curriculum Policy and Practice*. London: Bloomsbury.

Priestley, M., Edwards, R., Priestley, A. and Miller, K. (2012) 'Teacher agency in curriculum making: Agents of change and spaces for manoeuvre.' *Curriculum Inquiry 42*, 2, 191–214.

Prizant, B., Wetherby, A., Rubin, E., Laurent, A. and Rydell, P. (2006) *The SCERTS Model: A Comprehensive Educational Approach for Children with Autism Spectrum Disorders.* Baltimore, MD: Paul H. Brookes Publishing.

Proctor, B. (2008) *Group Supervision: A Guide to Creative Practice.* 2nd edn. London: Sage.

Raffo, C. and Dyson, A. (2008) 'Full service extended schools and educational inequality in urban contexts – new opportunities for progress?' *Journal of Educational Policy 22*, 3, 263–282.

Raffo, C., Dyson, A. Gunter, H., Hall, D., Jones, L. and Kalambouka, A. (2007) *Education and Poverty: A Critical Review of Theory, Policy and Practice.* York: Joseph Rowntree Foundation.

Raffo, C., Dyson, A., Gunter, H., Hall, D., Jones, L. and Kalambouka, A. (2009) 'Education and poverty: Mapping the terrain and making the links to educational policy.' *International Journal of Inclusive Education 13*, 4, 41–58.

Ragins, B.R. and Kram, K.E. (2007) *The Handbook of Mentoring at Work: Theory, Research and Practice.* Thousand Oaks, CA: Sage.

Reed, A. (2013) 'Therapist attentiveness and negative capability in dialogical family meetings for psychosis.' *Journal of Family Therapy 35*, 427–440.

Regnard, C., Reynolds, J., Watson, B., Matthews, D., Gibson, L. and Clarke, C. (2007) 'Understanding distress in people with severe communication difficulties: Developing and assessing the Disability Distress Assessment Tool (DisDAT).' *Journal of Intellectual Disability Research 51*, 4, 277–292.

Rich, P.J. and Hannafin, M. (2009) 'Video annotation tools: Technologies to scaffold, structure, and transform teacher reflection.' *Journal of Teacher Education 60*, 1, 52–67.

Rick, I. and Long, D. (2006) 'Visibilising clinical work: Video ethnography in the contemporary hospital.' *Health Sociology Review 15*, 2, 156–168.

Robinson, S.E. (2011) 'Teaching paraprofessionals of students with autism to implement pivotal response treatment in inclusive school settings using a brief video feedback training package.' *Focus on Autism and Other Developmental Disabilities 26*, 2, 105–118.

Rock, D. (2009) 'Managing with the brain in mind.' *Strategy + Business 56*, 58–57.

Rosenblum, K.L., McDonough, S.C., Sameroff, A.J. and Muzik, M. (2008). 'Reflection in thought and action: Maternal parenting reflectivity predicts mind-minded comments and interactive behavior'. *Infant Mental Health Journal 29*, 362–376.

Sarin, S. and McDermott, C. (2003) 'The effect of team leader characteristics on learning, knowledge application and performance of cross-functional new product development teams.' *Decision Sciences 34*, 4, 707–739.

Savin-Baden, M. (2003) *Facilitating Problem-based Learning: Illuminating Perspectives.* Buckingham: Open University Press/SHRE.

Scaife, J. (2010) *Supervising the Reflective Practitioner: An Essential Guide to Theory and Practice.* Abingdon: Routledge.

Schein, E.H. (1999) *Process Consultation Revisited: Building the Helping Relationship.* Boston, MA: Addison-Wesley Publishing.

Schön, D.A. (1983) *The Reflective Practitioner: How Professionals Think in Action.* New York: Basic Books.

Schore, A. (1994) *Affect Regulation and the Origin of the Self: The Neurobiology of Emotional Development.* Mahwah, NJ: Lawrence Erlbaum.

Scottish Government (2002) *A Curriculum for Excellence 3,–18,*. Available at www.scotland.gov.uk/Publications/2004/11/20178/45862, accessed on 25 July 2014.

Scottish Government (2009) *Getting It Right for Every Child.* Available at www.scotland.gov.uk/Resource/Doc/1141/0065063.pdf, accessed on 25 July 2014.

Scottish Government (2010) *Index of Multiple Deprivation.* Available at www.scotland.gov.uk/Topics/Statistics/SIMD, accessed on 30 August 2014.

Scourfield, J., Tolman, R., Maxwell, N., Holland, S., Bullock, A. and Sloan, L. (2012) 'Results of a training course for social workers on engaging fathers in child protection.' *Children and Youth Services Review 34,* 8, 1425–1432.

Seidel, T., Stürmer, K., Blomberg, G., Kobarg, M. and Schwindt, K. (2011) 'Teacher learning from analysis of videotaped classroom situations: Does it make a difference whether teachers observe their own teaching or that of others?' *Teaching and Teacher Education 27,* 2, 259–267.

Seikkula, J. and Trimble, D. (2005) 'Healing elements of therapeutic conversations: Dialogue as an embodiment of love.' *Family Process 44,* 461–475.

Senge, P.M. (2000) *Schools That Learn: A Fifth Discipline Fieldbook for Educators, Parents, and Everyone who Cares about Education.* New York: Doubleday.

Senge, P.M. (2003) 'Taking personal change seriously: The impact of organizational learning on management practice.' *Academy of Management Executive 17,* 2, 47–51.

Senge, P.M. (2006) *The Fifth Discipline: The Art and Practice of the Learning Organisation.* London: Random House.

Sharp, C. and Fonagy, P. (2008) 'The parent's capacity to treat the child as a psychological agent: Constructs, measures and implications for developmental psychopathology.' *Social development 17,* 3, 737–754.

Shields, A.M. and Cicchetti, D. (2001) 'Narrative representations of children's emotion dysregulation as predictors of maltreated children's rejection by peers.' *Developmental Psychology 37,* 3, 321–337.

Shute, V.J. (2008) 'Focus on formative feedback.' *Review of Educational Research 78,* 153–189.

Šilhánová, K. and Sancho, M. (2011) 'VIG and the Supervision Process.' In H. Kennedy, M. Landor and L. Todd (eds) *Video Interaction Guidance: A Relationship-based Intervention to Promote Attunement, Empathy and Wellbeing.* London: Jessica Kingsley Publishers.

Silverman, J., Kurtz, S. and Draper, J. (2013) *Skills for Communicating with Patients.* London: Radcliffe Publishing.

Simpson. G.R. and Henderson, M. (1995) Illustrations in Marianne Henderson's translation of Lia van Rosmalen's manual for Video Interaction Guidance for group workers and parents, unpublished.

Snow, C., Burns, M. and Griffin, P. (1998) *Preventing Reading Difficulties in Young Children.* Washington, DC: National Academy Press.

Stalker, K. (2003) 'Managing risk and uncertainty in social work: A literature review.' *Journal of Social Work 3,* 2, 311–323.

Star, S.L. (2010) 'This is not a boundary object: Reflections on the origin of a concept.' *Science, Technology and Human Value 35,* 601–617.

Stenwall, E., Jönhagen, M.E., Sandberg, J. and Fagerberg, I. (2008) 'The older patient's experience of encountering professional care givers and close relatives during an acute confusional state: An interview study.' *International Journal of Nursing Studies* 45, 1577–1585.

Stenwall, E., Sandberg, J., Jönhagen, M.E. and Fagerberg, I. (2007) 'Encountering the older confused patient: Professional care givers' experiences.' *Scandinavian Journal of Caring Science 21*, 4, 515–522.

Stern, D.N. (1985) *The Interpersonal World of the Infant.* London: Karnac Books.

Stern, D.N. (2004) *The Present Moment in Psychotherapy and Everyday Life.* New York: W.W. Norton & Company.

Stern, D.N. (2010) *Forms of Vitality: Exploring Dynamic Experience in Psychology, the Arts, Psychotherapy and Development.* Oxford: Oxford University Press.

Stewart, N. (2011) *How Children Learn – The Characteristics of Effective Early Learning.* London: The British Association for Early Childhood Education.

Stoll, L., Bolam, R., McMahon, A., Wallace, M. and Thomas, S. (2006) 'Professional learning communities: A review of the literature.' *Journal of Educational Change 7*, 4, 221–258.

Stone, D., Patton, B. and Heen, S. (1999) *Difficult Conversations: How to Discuss What Matters Most.* London: Penguin.

Stone, D., Patton, B. and Heen, S. (2000) *Difficult Conversations.* London: Penguin.

Strathearn, L., Li, J., Fonagy, P. and Montague, R. (2008) 'What's in a smile? Maternal brain responses to infant facial cues.' *Paediatrics 122*, 1, 40–51.

Strathie, S., Strathie, C. and Kennedy, H. (2011) 'Video Enhanced Reflective Practice.' In H. Kennedy, M. Landor and L. Todd (eds) *Video Interaction Guidance: A Relationship-based Intervention to Promote Attunement, Empathy and Wellbeing* (pp.170–180). London: Jessica Kingsley Publishers.

Strydom, A., Shooshtari, S., Lee, L., Raykar, V., Torr, J., Tsiouris, J. *et al.* (2010) 'Dementia in older adults with intellectual disabilities – Epidemiology, presentation and diagnosis.' *Journal of Policy and Practice in Intellectual Disabilities 7*, 2, 96–110.

Swann, W. and Loxley, A. (1998) 'The impact of school-based training on classroom assistants in primary schools.' *Research Papers in Education 13*, 2, 141–160.

Taplin, D.H. and Clarke, H. (2012) *Theory of Change Basics: A Primer on Theory of Change.* New York: ActKnowledge. Available at www.theoryofchange.org, accessed on 27 November 2014.

Tarrant, P. (2013) *Reflective Practice and Professional Development.* London: Sage.

Thomas, G. (2010) 'Can reflective practice be taught?' *Educational Studies 36*, 4, 403–414.

Thompson, S. and Thompson, N. (2008) *The Critically Reflective Practitioner.* Basingstoke: Palgrave Macmillan.

Thurlings, M., Vermeulen, M., Bastiaens, T. and Stijnen, S. (2013) 'Understanding feedback: A learning theory perspective.' *Educational Research Review 9*, 1–15.

Thurman, S., Jones, J. and Tarleton, B. (2005) 'Without words – meaningful information for people with high individual communication needs.' *British Journal of Learning Disabilities 33*, 2, 83–89.

Tickell, C. (2011) *The Early Years: Foundations for Life, Health and Learning – An Independent Report for the Early Years Foundation Stage (EYFS).* London: Department for Education.

Timperley, H., Wilson, A., Barrar, H. and Fung, I. (2007) *Teacher Professional Learning and Development: Best Evidence Synthesis Iteration.* Wellington: Ministry of Education.

Topping, K.J. and Ferguson, N. (2005) 'Effective literacy teaching behaviours.' *Journal of Research in Reading 28*, 2, 125–143.

Trevarthen, C. (1980) 'The Foundations of Intersubjectivity: Development of Interpersonal and Cooperative Understanding of Infants.' In D. Olsen (ed.) *The Social Foundations of Language and Thought: Essays in Honor of J.S. Bruner* (pp.316–342). New York: Norton.

Trevarthen, C. (1998) 'The Concept and Foundations of Infant Intersubjectivity.' In S. Braten (ed.) *Intersubjective Communication and Emotion in Early Ontogeny.* Cambridge, MA: Cambridge University Press.

Trevarthen, C. (2011a) 'What is it like to be a person who knows nothing? Defining the active intersubjective mind of a newborn human being.' *Infant and Child Development, Special Issue: The Intersubjective Newborn 20*, 1, 119–135.

Trevarthen, C. (2011b) 'Confirming Companionship in Interests, Intentions and Emotions: How VIG Works.' In H. Kennedy, M. Landor and L. Todd (eds) *Video Interaction Guidance: A Relationship-based Intervention to Promote Attunement, Empathy and Wellbeing.* London. Jessica Kingsley Publishers.

Trevarthen, C. (2014). 'Sensitive guidance to encourage "zest for learning".' *Educational Psychology in Scotland, Special issue: Video Interaction Guidance 15*, 1, 10–3.

Trevarthen, C. and Aitken, K.J. (2001) 'Infant intersubjectivity: Research, theory and clinical application.' *Journal of Child Psychology and Psychiatry 42*, 1.

Tripp, T.R. and Rich, P.J. (2012) 'The influence of video analysis on the process of teacher change.' *Teaching and Teacher Education 28*, 728–739.

Trivette, C., Dunst, C., Hamby, D. and O'Herin, C. (2009) 'Characteristics and consequences of adult learning methods.' *Research Brief 3*, 1, 1–28.

Turnell, A and Edwards, S. (1999) *Signs of Safety: A Solution and Safety Orientated Approach to Child Protection Casework.* London: Norton.

Underdown, A. (2013) 'Parent–infant relationships: Supporting parents to take a reflective stance.' *Journal of Health Visiting 1*, 2, 76–79.

Underdown, A. and Barlow, J. (2012) *Maternal Emotional Wellbeing and Infant Development. A Good Practice Guide for Midwives.* London: RCM. Available at www.rcm.org.uk/college/your-career/information-services/resources/, accessed on 27 November 2014.

University of London, IOE (Institute of Education) (2004) *The Effective Provision of Pre-School Education (EPPE) Project.* London: Department for Education and Skills/IOE.

Uvnas Moberg, K. (2013) *The Hormone of Closeness: The Role of Oxytocin in Relationships.* London: Pinter and Martin Ltd.

van Berckelaer-Onnes, I.A. and Hoekman, J. (1991) *AUTI-R: Schaal voor Vroegkinderlijk Autisme.* Amsterdam: Pearson.

van den Heijkant, C., Quak, G., van Swet, J., Vloet, K., de Vos, M. and van der Wegen, R. (2004) *School Video Interactie Begeleiding.* Antwerpen-Apeldoorn: Garant.

van der Sande, J. (1995) 'Project Video Interaction Guidance – Working with Professionals and Parents in a Special Education Setting.' Paper presented at the Association of Child Psychology and Psychiatry Conference, 15 September, Edinburgh.

van Geert, P. and Steenbeek, H. (2005) 'The dynamics of scaffolding.' *New Ideas in Psychology 23*, 3, 115–128.

van Manen, M. (1991) *The Tact of Teaching: The Meaning of Pedagogical Thoughtfulness.* London, Ontario: The Althouse Press.

van Nuys, D. (2009) 'An interview with David Wallin, Ph.D. on the implications of attachment theory for psychotherapy.' 13 July. Available at www.mentalhelp.net/poc/view_doc.php?type=doc&id=29433, accessed on 27 November 2014.

Vermeulen, H., Bristow, J. and Landor, M. (2011) 'Mindfulness, Attunement and VIG: Being Fully Present while Communicating.' In H. Kennedy, M. Landor and L. Todd (eds) *Video Interaction Guidance: A Relationship-based Intervention to Promote Attunement, Empathy and Wellbeing.* London: Jessica Kingsley Publishers.

Vygotsky, L.S. (1978) 'Interaction between Learning and Development.' In M. Cole, V. John-Steiner and E. Souberman (eds) *Mind in Society: The Development of Higher Psychological Processes* (pp.79–91). Cambridge, MA: Harvard University Press. [Cited in H. Daniels, M. Cole and J.W. Wertsch (2007) *The Cambridge Companion to Vygotsky.* Cambridge: Cambridge University Press.]

Wagner, P. (2008) 'Consultation as a Framework for Practice.' In B. Kelly, L. Woolfson and J. Boyle (eds) *Frameworks for Practice in Educational Psychology: A Textbook for Trainees and Practitioners.* London: Jessica Kingsley Publishers.

Wasik, B. (2008) 'When fewer is more: Small groups in early childhood classrooms.' *Early Childhood Education Journal 35,* 6, 515–521.

Watkins, C. (2002) *Effective Learning.* Research Matters No. 17. London: Institute of Education National School Improvement Network.

Watson, C. (2014) 'Effective professional learning communities? The possibilities for teachers as agents of change in schools.' *British Educational Research Journal 40,* 1, 18–29.

Watson, I., Buchanan, J., Campbell, I. and Briggs, C. (2003) *Fragmented Futures: New Challenges in Working Life.* Sydney: Federation Press.

Webster, R., Blatchford, P. and Russell, A. (2012) *The Guide on the Side: Realizing the Value of Teaching Assistants.* London: Institute of Education (IOE) London Blog. Available at http://ioelondonblog.wordpress.com/category/peter-blatchford/

Webster, C., Greene, A. and Greene, S. (in press) 'Development of novel video-based behavioural intervention to optimize self-management in children with poorly-controlled Type 1 diabetes ("VIG-Diabetes").' *Journal of Diabetes Nursing/Diabetes Care for Children and Young People.*

Wegerif, R. (2008) 'Dialogic or dialectic: The significance of ontological assumptions in research on educational dialogue.' *British Educational Research Journal 34,* 3, 347–361.

Wegerif, R. (2011) 'Towards a dialogic theory of how children learn to think.' *Thinking Skills and Creativity 6,* 3,179–190.

Weiner, B.J. (2009) A theory of organizational readiness for change. *Implementation Science 4,* 67.

Weinert, F.E. (2001) 'Concept of Competence: A Conceptual Definition.' In D.S. Rychen and L.H. Salganik (eds) *Defining and Selecting Key Competencies* (pp.45–64) Seattle, WA: Hogrefe and Huber Publishers.

Weitzman, E. and Greenberg, J. (2010) *ABC and Beyond: Building Emergent Literacy in Early Childhood Settings.* Toronto: The Hanen Centre.

Wels, P.M.A. (2002) *Helping with a Camera: The Use of Video for Family Intervention.* Nijmegen: Nijmegen University Press.

Wels, P.M.A. (2004) *Helping with a Camera: The Use of Video for Family Intervention.* 2nd edition. Nijmegen: Nijmegen University Press.

Wels, P. and Robbroeckx, L.M.H. (1996) *Manual of Nijmegen Child Rearing Situation Questionnaire.* Lisse: Swets & Zeitlinger.

Wetzels, A.F.M., Steenbeek, H.W. and Fraiquin, M. (2011) 'TalentenKracht in de Klas: Een Coachingsprogramma voor Leerkrachten van Groep 1-4.' Department of Developmental Psychology, University of Groningen, The Netherlands. Unpublished manuscript. Wetzels, A.F.M., Steenbeek, H.W. and van Geert, P. (2013) 'Video Feedback Coaching for Teachers (VFC-T): How to Teach Science to the Earliest Grades.' Presentation at the VERP International Conference, June, Newcastle-upon-Tyne.

WHO (World Health Organization) (2009) *Patient Safety Curriculum Guide for Medical Schools.* World Alliance for Patient Safety. Available at www.who.int/patientsafety/ education/curriculum/EN_PSP_Education_Medical_Curriculum/en/, accessed on 12 January 2014.

Wilkinson, H., Kerr, D. and Cunningham, C. (2005) 'Equipping staff to support people with an intellectual disability and dementia in care home settings.' *Dementia: The International Journal of Social Research and Practice 4,* 3, 387–400.

Williams, F. (2014) 'Getting started with vig in an educational psychology service in educational psychology in Scotland.' *Special Issue: Video Interaction Guidance. Educational Psychology in Scotland 15,* 1, 64–66.

Williams, W.L. and Gallinat, J. (2011) 'The effects of evaluating video examples of staff's own versus others' performance on discrete-trial training skills in a human service setting.' *Journal of Organizational Behavior Management 31,* 2, 97–116.

Wlodkowski, R.J. (1999) *Enhancing Adult Motivation to Learn: A Comprehensive Guide for Teaching all adults.* San Francisco, CA: Jossey-Bass,.

Wood, D., Bruner, J.S. and Ross, G. (1976) 'The role of tutoring in problem solving.' *Journal of Child Psychology and Psychiatry 17,* 2, 89–100.

Yin, R. (2003) *Case Study Research: Design and Methods.* Thousand Oaks, CA: Sage.

Zeedyk, M.S. (ed.) (2008) *Promoting Social Interaction for Individuals with Communicative Impairments: Making Contact.* London: Jessica Kingsley Publishers.

Zwozdiak-Myers, P. (2012) *The Teacher's Reflective Practice Handbook.* Abingdon: Routledge.

GLOSSARY FOR VIDEO ENHANCED REFLECTIVE PRACTICE (VERP)

Accreditation An assessment of a *trainee VIG guider's* competencies at the end of each stage of training by an accrediting *supervisor*.

Activation Process by which the VERP *guider/supervisor* encourages *initiatives* from and active participation by the client/*trainee guider* using open-ended questions, open body language and friendly expectant facial expressions in order to elicit what they already know.

Attuned naming A type of *reception/receiving* where the VERP *guider* describes in a friendly tone what the trainee may be doing, thinking or feeling (or VERP trainee and client).

Attuned response A response to an *initiative* showing sensitivity and positive acceptance, which keeps the interaction moving in or towards the *'yes' cycle.*

Attuned/attunement A harmonious and responsive interaction where both partners share positive emotion within a *communicative dance.*

AVIGuk Association for Video Interaction Guidance UK. Organization that promotes and develops *VIG* in the UK and beyond, and provides quality assurance for the method. See www.videointeractionguidance.net

Co-construction of meanings The means by which the *VERP guider* and the trainee (or trainee and client) offer, receive, exchange and develop their ideas and opinions and enlarge their shared understanding within an *attuned* relationship.

Communicative dance Reciprocal and positive interaction between individuals that shares the features of music and dance in the timing and rhythm.

Compensation Process by which the *guider/supervisor* guides, leads or offers opinions and suggestions to the client/*trainee guider* in order to provide information they are currently missing.

Follow *VERP guider* responds to the trainee's *initiative* and concerns (or *VERP* trainee and client), allowing them to lead the interaction, and supporting it. This often leads to *attunement*.

Guider Person *accredited* according to *AVIGuk* standards and criteria to deliver *VIG* and *VERP*.

Helping question Focuses on and is owned by the VERP trainee. It is about increasing effective ways of interacting with others, in terms of the *attunement principles*, in order to reach their goal, the overall outcome (e.g. 'to improve collaborative working during team meetings'). Starting with 'What am I doing to…' or 'How am I…', it presupposes that there are times when it is already happening, for example, 'What am I doing that is supporting short turn-taking?' or 'How am I inviting the others to initiate more?'

Initiative A communication (non-verbal and/or verbal) that begins an interaction or introduces a new 'topic' into the interaction.

Mediated learning Feuerstein's concept of the person's learning being facilitated by a more experienced other who is *attuned* to their level of understanding and who can judge the amount and kind of help that they need to be successful.

Mentalization The ability to understand the mental states of oneself and others that underlie behaviour.

Microanalysis of interaction Breaking down sequences of interaction into very small elements, lasting only seconds, in order to understand their impact on the communication.

Mindfulness Originating from Buddhist traditions, mindfulness refers to paying attention in the here-and-now to experience, thoughts and feelings in a non-judgemental and curious way.

Mind-mindedness The ability to accurately infer others' mental states.

'No' cycle Pattern of interaction where negative/discordant communications and emotions are initiated, exchanged and perpetuated.

Primary intersubjectivity Basic face-to-face *attuned* communication between two people where emotions are expressed and perceived in a two-way dialogue. It can be seen in non-verbal communication when body language, hand movements, eyes, voice tones and facial expressions all combine in a synchronized communicative 'dance' (Trevarthen).

Principles of attuned interactions and guidance Core elements of communication on which *VIG* is based, comprising: being attentive; encouraging initiatives; receiving initiatives; developing *attuned* interactions; guiding; and deepening the discussion.

Reception/receiving A communication (non-verbal and/or verbal) that acknowledges and positively accepts an *initiative*, showing it has been understood.

Scaffolding Bruner's concept of how skilled individuals provide structure and assistance to 'scaffold' or assist novices' learning, through sensitive moment-by-moment adjustments.

Secondary intersubjectivity More sophisticated than *primary intersubjectivity*, communication between two people where they share their attention to each other with a third subject such as an object or task.

Self-modelling Learning from observing oneself demonstrating on video the desirable behaviour.

Sensitivity Ability to perceive the other's signals accurately, and to respond to them promptly and appropriately.

Seven steps (to attuned interactions and guidance in the shared review) A seven-step cyclical model describing how a *guider* might flexibly use *activation* and *compensation* and the video clips during a *shared review*; a framework to guide deep reflection.

Shared review A session where the VERP *guider* and trainee (or trainee and client) watch and discuss the *video clips*, reflecting together on their significance (previously called 'feedback').

Social constructionism Approach which challenges the notion of one 'objective reality', showing how individuals in conversation with others co-construct and re-construct past, present and future events through ongoing reflection and dialogue.

Space in one's mind Being able to hold in mind an awareness of how the other might be thinking and feeling. In earliest form, for example, in a premature infant, this refers to the innate ability to communicate with another through a natural turn-taking pattern of *initiatives* and pauses (Trevarthen).

Still/freeze frame A static or still shot from the video to emphasize a salient positive moment of interaction.

Trainee guider Person who can deliver *VIG* and *VERP* under *AVIGuk* supervision.

Turning points/moment of change A moment at which an interaction shifts into a new dynamic, for example, when a teacher makes a longer pause and the pupil responds with more information.

Video Short (unedited) video that is taken of the *VERP* trainee and their client interacting. Video is taken to have both people in frame simultaneously.

Video clips Video clips micro-edited by the VERP guider trainee to demonstrate *interaction* that is 'better than usual' for *shared review*, usually lasting anything from a few seconds to under a minute.

Video Enhanced Reflective Practice (VERP) A variation of *VIG* to support individuals or groups to reflect on and develop their communication skills with their clients, through reflection and *shared review* of edited *video clips* of their day-to-day practice. *VERP* is often delivered in a short course format comprising a day of initial training followed by three or four half-day *shared review* sessions.

Video Feedforward (VFF) An intervention that promotes behavioural change, as clients are shown skilfully edited video images of themselves succeeding in tasks or situations they find difficult, thus providing the opportunity to *self-model*. It is called 'Feedforward' because it involves showing the client 'created' future images of themselves achieving, to differentiate it from the 'feedback' of images of their past achievement, as in *VIG* and *VERP*.

Video Interaction Guidance (VIG) An intervention to help clients move from discordant to attuned communication by supporting them to reflect through dialogue on the microanalysis of *video clips* of their own successful *attuned* interactions.

VIG supervisor Accredited according to *AVIGuk* standards and criteria to train, supervise and accredit *VIG* trainees.

Working points Areas identified by *VERP* trainee during the initial training or *shared review* as ones that they would like to work on improving.

'Yes' cycle Pattern of interaction where *attuned* communications and emotions are initiated, exchanged and maintained.

Zone of proximal development (ZPD) The level at which the learner is currently functioning and from where they can have their learning supported and extended slightly by the right kind of help; the zone between what a learner can achieve given maximum support, and what they can achieve independently (Vygotsky).

AUTHOR INFORMATION

Emily Archer is a psychological practitioner within primary care. She completed VERP training while working with adolescents as a health care support worker. Emily is interested in VERP's effect on staff confidence and morale, and the impact that this could have on practice.

Wilma Barrow, DEdPsy, is an educational psychologist at Scottish Borders Council and academic and professional tutor on the Doctor of Applied Educational Psychology programme at Newcastle University. She is interested in the role of dialogue within educational psychology practice and its transformative potential for teaching, learning and participative practices.

Joanna Begley is a trainee educational psychologist at the Institute of Education, London. She is involved in an ongoing programme of VERP as part of her doctorate, and has conducted research exploring trainee experiences of VERP. She is interested in personal and professional self-development, particularly regarding interactions with others.

Jo Birbeck is a senior educational psychologist in Hampshire. An AVIGuk-accredited practitioner, national supervisor and VERP trainer, she has developed practice in understanding and change in family situations, including adoption and fostering, and in staff development in early years and school settings.

Lucy Browne, DEdCHPsy, is an educational psychologist who works for Kent Educational Psychology Service. She is interested in interventions to support children at risk of social and school exclusion. She is a VIG Guider (Stage 4) and regularly includes the use of VIG to work with parents, carers and professionals via VERP.

Katja Burakoff, MA, a speech and language therapist, works as a planning officer at the Communication and Technology Centre Tikoteekki of the Finnish Association on Intellectual and Developmental Disabilities. She is a certified VIG supervisor. Together with Kaisa Martikainen she has developed the OIVA Interaction Model® and the training model for OIVA guiders.

Emma Cartwright is a postgraduate student studying health psychology, with a particular interest in diabetes as she has the condition. She was introduced to VIG as a participant to a study through the diabetes clinic, and is now keen to use VIG to encourage youth engagement within the clinical setting.

Monika Celebi is a parent–infant psychotherapist and movement therapist who has pioneered VERP to train early years professionals and VIG for parent–infant groups. She is an accredited VIG guider, advanced supervisor and trainer. Monika is currently developing VIG projects in Tower Hamlets, the Home Counties and Oxfordshire, and with the Mental Health Foundation.

Carole Chasle, PhD, is a senior educational psychologist for Derbyshire County Council. Carole's interest and training in VIG began in 2007, and she is now a qualified guider, supervisor and trainer. Carole has contributed to a VIG international conference in Dundee (2009), and was a contributor to the book, *Video Interaction Guidance* (2011).

Maria V. Doria, PhD, MBA, is a chartered psychologist and a certified VIG/VERP guider who works in psychotherapy, training and research in interpersonal relationships. She is currently a research manager in mental health and care practices of the non-governmental organization Action Against Hunger, a psychologist consultant for UNESCO, and has been an honorary research fellow at the University of East Anglia (UK) since 2007.

Martin Elliott has worked in child and adolescent mental health as a clinical nurse specialist and clinical team manager in Wiltshire. He became a VIG supervisor in 2000, and currently uses VIG clinically in a safeguarding and assessment service, together with offering freelance VIG training and supervision.

Nancy Ferguson is a deputy principal educational psychologist in North Lanarkshire Council, Scotland. She is a VIG supervisor and has been using the approach in schools and with families for 14 years. Nancy has a longstanding research interest in the area of literacy development and effective teaching and learning.

Sheridan Forster, PhD, is a speech pathologist and researcher who has been using and promoting VIG in Australia since 2009. Her PhD (2011) focused on interaction between adults with profound intellectual and multiple disabilities and support workers. She has seen VIG and VERP be powerful supports, enhancing the confidence and skills of support workers.

Ruben Fukkink is a professor (lector) at the University of Applied Sciences of Amsterdam and professor of early childhood education and care at the University of Amsterdam. His research area is urban education and childcare. Video feedback is a prominent theme in his work on professional development and parenting support.

Helen Gibson is a freelance systemic psychotherapist and supervisor. She is also an AVIGuk practitioner, trainer and supervisor. She was introduced to VIG in 1998 and has remained committed to the method ever since. She is particularly excited by the potential for VERP and VIG to promote systemic change within organizations, classrooms and families.

Alex Greene is a medical anthropologist at Dundee University. Her research interests are patient safety, multidisciplinarity and person-centred approaches to care for young people, in particular the social and cultural interplay between policy, care delivery and patient satisfaction. She uses VIG methods to support youth advocacy and to influence policy and health service development.

Ben Hayes, DEdPsy AFBPsS, is a senior educational psychologist with Kent Educational Psychology Service and a professional and academic tutor at University College London. He is an AVIGuk trainer and supervisor, and his publications relating to children and schools include research into the impact of video interventions.

Cyril Hellier, PhD, is a Health Profession Council-registered psychologist and a fellow of The British Psychological Society, having extensive experience in applying psychology to human and organisational development, and adapting video feedback for multiple training purposes. He is a VIG superviser, one of the original VIG practitioners in Scotland.

Jo Hewitt, DECAP, works as an educational psychologist in Belfast. She was introduced to VIG while completing a doctorate in educational, adolescent and child psychology at Queen's University Belfast. In 2009 her doctoral research on using a VERP approach to support classroom assistants was awarded the PRAXIS prize.

Bev Jowett is a university teacher in the Department of Sociological Studies at the University of Sheffield, teaching on qualifying and post-qualifying social work courses. Prior to moving to the university she had over 20 years' experience as a local authority social worker, the majority of this being in children and families services.

Sanne Huijbregts is a teacher and researcher at the Department of Education at the University of Applied Sciences of Amsterdam. Her teaching and research interests are early childhood education, centre-based childcare, urban education and the professional development of educators working with young children.

Jenny Jarvis is a counselling psychologist and national VIG supervisor. She worked in child and adolescent mental health before going freelance. She initiated many VIG projects in East Anglia, including parent–infant mental health services. Jenny is now intensively supervising JUCONI professionals in VIG in Ecuador, where extreme deprivation and violence puts 40 per cent of children at risk of their lives.

Hilary Kennedy, AFBPsS, is an educational psychologist and a leading developer of VIG within AVIGuk. She is currently a freelance VIG trainer, working on projects around the world and focusing increasingly on VIG's applicability in pregnancy and the first two years of life, neglect, safeguarding and domestic violence.

Miriam Landor, MEdPsy, AFBPsS, is a freelance AVIGuk national supervisor and trainer in VIG, VERP and Video Feedforward. She previously worked as a preschool home visiting support teacher, an educational psychologist and a university lecturer. She is interested in continuing to network through writing and editing on VIG matters.

Anna-Greta Ledin is a freelance senior psychologist and specialist in clinical psychology. As practitioner, trainer and licensed supervisor, Anna-Greta has experience of providing Marte Meo support to people of all ages, from infants to the elderly. Her passion is creating opportunities for people to connect and to live their daily life to the full.

Susan Lyon is a speech and language therapist using VIG with young non-verbal children and their families. More recently she has developed the use of VERP for staff working with children who have speech, language and communication needs in early years settings and schools.

Kaisa Martikainen, MA, a speech and language therapist, works as a development coordinator at the Communication and Technology Centre, Tikoteekki, at the Finnish Association on Intellectual and Developmental Disabilities. She is a certified VIG supervisor. Together with Katja Burakoff she has developed the OIVA Interaction Model® and the training model for OIVA guides.

Jane P. Nestel-Patt is founder, director, certified master trainer for SPIN®USA: National Training Institute for VIG in the USA. For more than 18 years she has been applying the model to a broad range of disciplines and settings in each of the Institute's four VIG branches: parent coaching/family therapy; teacher training; staff development; and leadership.

Terri E. Pease, PhD, is director of research and a master trainer at SPIN®USA, the National Training Institute for VIG in the USA. She was certified in VIG in 1999. She also consults to professionals across the USA on child welfare, parent education, domestic violence and sexual violence.

Kirsty Quinn is an educational psychologist in the UK. Kirsty became interested in VERP during initial training where her dissertation focused on building on children's participation in classroom dialogue. Her interest in classroom interactions has continued with a focus on emotional engagement and interaction leading to her recent doctoral thesis, using VERP to explore teacher mind-mindedness.

Lia van Rosmalen is manager of human resource and development at Combinatie Jeugdzorg, Eindhoven. She started as a social worker in child protection, and from 1990 became first a practitioner, trainer and then supervisor in VHT and VIG. She has been involved in several projects using VIG/VHT for children and families and also for professionals. Her drive now is to increase the development of professionals.

Michelle Sancho, DEdPsy, is an assistant principal educational psychologist working in West Berkshire. She is an honorary lecturer at University College, London, as well as a research adviser on the doctoral level initial educational psychology training course. Her work involves regular use of VIG with a variety of clients, and includes VIG supervision of a range of professionals.

Stephanie Satariano, DEdPsy, is a chartered educational and child psychologist. She is an accredited VIG/VERP practitioner and a trainee supervisor. She has a strong interest in using VIG/VERP throughout her work to promote positive and attuned communication styles, and to increase confidence in parents, professionals and young people.

Robin Sen is lecturer in social work at the University of Sheffield, and previously worked as a child and family social worker. He commissioned the VERP project described in this book, took part in it himself as a VERP learner, and is currently undertaking Level 2 VIG training.

Sandra Strathie is a national VIG supervisor with many years' experience of training VIG supervisors and guiders and delivering VIG and VERP training. Sandra is a registered social worker and practice educator who is currently working with a number of partners to develop VERP-based modules and courses.

Liz Todd is professor of educational inclusion at Newcastle University. She is interested in VIG and narrative as democratic approaches to change for individuals and communities. Her other books are: *Partnerships for Inclusive Education: A Critical Approach to*

Collaborative Working; and *Beyond the School Gates: Can Full-service and Extended Schools Overcome Disadvantage?*.

Angela Underdown, PhD, works as a VIG and VERP supervisor and is deputy director of Warwick Infant and Family Wellbeing Unit, where she is involved in infant mental health education and research. She is an infant mental health advisor to the Institute of Health Visiting and an AIMH committee member.

Helen Upton is a senior educational psychologist with Wandsworth Schools and Community Psychology Service, and a professional and academic tutor at the University of London Institute of Education, where she is involved in the initial training of educational psychologists. An accredited VIG/VERP guider, Helen uses VIG to support families and VERP to develop the consultation skills of trainee educational psychologists.

Clare Webster is a paediatric registrar with a special interest in diabetes and endocrinology, working in NHS Tayside. Since being introduced to VIG in 2010 she has been enthusiastic about the application of VIG within health, in particular as a tool to support young people with diabetes in their self-management.

Annemie Wetzels studied Developmental Psychology at the University of Groningen, where she is now a PhD student. She has developed a video feedback coaching programme for lower-grade teachers. This aims to improve teachers' skill in stimulating talented children's science learning, as part of the Dutch Curious Minds programme.

Fiona Williams is a senior educational psychologist working for Glasgow City Council. She is an advanced AVIGuk supervisor and enjoys training, coaching and mentoring others in the development of individual VIG skills, and is interested in supporting the development of larger-scale projects.

Karen Williams is an inclusion team leader working for Services for Young Children in Hampshire, and supports a portage team working with children with special educational needs. As a VIG supervisor she is keen to promote trusting relationships and extend learning for all children, their parents and early years practitioners.

SUBJECT INDEX

AUTHOR INDEX